Y0-BSM-143

New Parade 1

Senior Authors

Mario Herrera

Theresa Zanatta

Consulting Authors

Alma Flor Ada

Christine Ewy

Anna Uhl Chamot

Carolyn Kessler

Jim Cummins

J. Michael O'Malley

Writer

Christine Kay Williams

Longman

Acknowledgments

Consulting Reviewers

Brigite Fonseca, Colegio Bom Jesus de Joinville, Joinville, Brazil • **Cleide da Silva**, Openhouse Ensino de Inglés, Santos, Brazil • **Luz Marina Franco**, Colegio El Carmelo, Santafé de Bogotá, Colombia • **Irene Gómez de Reina and Mariela Quintero**, Liceo Patria, Santafé de Bogotá, Colombia • **Magdalena Moreno**, Liceo Naval, Santafé de Bogotá, Colombia • **Maribel Muñoz**, Escuela Holanda, Ministerio de Educación Pública, San Jose, Costa Rica • **Cynthia de Cano**, Instituto Guatemalteco Americano, Guatemala City, Guatemala • **Keiko Abé-Ford**, Communication and Language Associates, Tokyo, Japan • **Francis Acosta López Serdán, Vanessa Olvera Vega, and Maria del Pilar Paez Laguna**, Colegio Guadalupe, Mexico City, Mexico • **Maricela Camino**, Centro Escolar Yaocalli, Mexico City, Mexico • **Jean Pierre Brossard**, Proulex, Guadalajara, Mexico • **Maggie Fabrian del Conde**, Instituto Felix de Jesus Rougier, Mexico City, Mexico • **Elsa Jiménez**, SEPC Primary English Program, Saltillo, Mexico • **Ruth Jossa Valtierra and Myriam Romero Muñoz**, Colegio Tepeyac, Mexico City, Mexico • **Raquel Loaiza**, Escuela Loaiza de Inglés, Reynosa, Mexico • **Mary Margaret Rose**, Sultanate Private School, Madinal Qaboos, Oman • **Angie Alcocer**, Colegio Maria Alvarada, Lima, Peru • **Walter Alvarez**, Colegio Santa Teresita, Lima, Peru • **Silvia Osores**, Colegio Immaculada, Lima, Peru • **Anna Marie Amudi**, Dhahran Ahliyya School, Dammam, Saudi Arabia • **Denise Özdeniz**, Teacher Trainer, Istanbul, Turkey • **Youssef Arifi**, Al Ghazali School, Abu Dhabi, United Arab Emirates • **Lupita Arraga**, Colegio Bellas Artes, Maracaibo, Venezuela • **María Gabriela de Pressutto**, Colegio IDEA, Valencia, Venezuela • **María Elena Izaguirre**, Colegio Canigua, Caracas, Venezuela • **Silvia Landa**, Secretaría de Educación, Carabobo, Venezuela • **Carmen Mendoza**, Colegio Emil Friedman, Caracas, Venezuela

New Parade Level 1 Teacher's Edition

Editorial director: Louise Jennewine
Publisher: Anne Stribling
Director of design and production: Rhea Banker
Development editor: Lucille M. Kennedy
Production manager: Alana Zdinak
Managing editor: Linda Moser
Senior production editor: Mike Kemper
Manufacturing supervisor: Dave Dickey
Cover design: Pearson Education Development Group
Art direction and production: Pearson Education Development Group

Songs and Chants Unit 7, page 62: "Happy Birthday to You!" by Mildred J. Hill and Patty S. Hill. Copyright © 1935, renewed 1962, Summy-Birchard Music, a Division of Summy-Birchard, Inc. All rights reserved. Used by permission.

Illustrations Page abbreviations are as follows: (T) top, (B) bottom, (L) left, (R), right, (C) center.

Paige Billin-Frye 25(B), 26(B); Nan Brooks 3(B), 15(B), 21(B), 26(T), 32, 34(T), 46(B), 61(B), 65(B); Rick Brown 4(T), 35(B), 41(B), 53(B), 64(B), 75(T), 81(T), 82(B), 84(B), 85(T), 91(B); Randy Chewning 29(T), 33(T), 40, 43, 49(T); Alex Pardo DeLange 53(T), 61(T), 64(T), 71(T), 74(B), 79(T), 81(B), 85(T), 90; Tony DeLuna 11, 35(T); Chris Demarest 93; Eldon Doty 6, 12(T), 16(B), 20, 25(B), 49(B), 80; Tim Haggerty 31(B), 52(T), 54, 60; Steve Henry xxxi, xxxv, xxxviii, 11(T), 23(B), 42, 73, 99, 109; Jared Lee 5, 12(B); Steve McInturff 21(T), 23(T), 25(C); Cora Nicholas 76(T); Laura Ovresat 3(T), 13, 33(B), 62, 63(T), 83(T); Tomoyo Pitcher 4(B), 30, 39(T), 51(T), 55(T), 56(B), 71(B), 76(B), 82(T), 84(T), 91(T), 95, 97, 103, 105, 107; Joe Rogers 80; Fred Schrier 16(T), 45, 51(B), 65, 66(B), 86(B); Dorothy Stott 34(B), 63(B), 70; Debbie Tilley xxxiii, xxxvi, xxxvii; Randy Verougstraete 10, 24(B), 31(T), 44(B), 50, 73(B), 75(B), 101; Marsha Winborn xxxii, xxxiv, xxxix.

Little Book Art Unit 1, Marsha Winborn; Unit 2, Patrick Girouard; Unit 3, Liisa Chauncy Guida; Unit 4, Debbie Tilley; Unit 5, Rusty Fletcher; Unit 6, Sally Jo Vitsky; Unit 7, Ruth Flanigan; Unit 8, Ben Mahan; Unit 9, Sheila Bailey.

Picture Dictionary Art Nan Brooks 42-51; Tim Haggerty 2-11; Tomoyo Pitcher 52-61, 72-81; Fred Schrier 12-21, 62-71, 82-91; Dorothy Stott 32-41.

Mascot Art Chris Demarest 2-91.

Photographs Unless otherwise acknowledged, all photographs are the property of Addison Wesley Longman, Inc. Page abbreviations are as follows: (T) top, (B) bottom, (L) left, (R) right, (C) center.

56: Animals Animals: Ruth Cole (TCR), Gerard Lacz (TCL), Robert Maier (BR), Colin Milkins/Oxford Scientific Films (TR), Ben Osborne/Oxford Scientific Films (BCL), Leonard Lee Rue III (BCR); Jeff Foott/Bruce Coleman Inc. (BL); Dave B. Fleetham/Tom Stack & Associates (TL).

Cover and Title Page Art Tracy M. Lee

Pearson Education, 10 Bank Street, White Plains, NY 10606

ISBN: 0-201-60434-5

7 8 9 10 11 12 13 14 15 — POH — 10 09 08 07 06

Contents

Senior Authors

Mario Herrera has been an English teacher for 25 years, from elementary to post-graduate programs. He has a bachelor's degree in Education and a Master's degree in TEFL (Teaching English as a Foreign Language). He does research and experimentation on how to teach English overseas more effectively. He is co-author of the first edition of *Parade*, as well as of the EFL series *Balloons* for pre-school, and the EFL series for high-elementary and junior high school students *My Friends* (all published by Longman/Pearson Education). He has also written for specific junior high school markets in Mexico. As an international academic consultant, Mr. Herrera has traveled the world for the past twelve years on behalf of Pearson Education, directing seminars and in-service training sessions throughout the Americas, Europe, the Middle East, and Asia. He has won several academic awards for his presentations.

Theresa Zanatta is an author, teacher, teacher trainer, and education consultant. She has been writing, teaching, and training teachers and trainers for more than 15 years. She is based in Barcelona, Spain, but has worked in more than 20 countries around the world—in Europe, the Middle East, Africa, Asia, Canada, and the United States. During this time she has also held the positions of Director, North American Institute in Badalona, Spain, and Director, Adult English Program of the North American Institute in Barcelona. In addition, she regularly teaches at the University of Barcelona, Valle D'Hebron, in their postgraduate program for elementary teachers. Ms. Zanatta has a B.S. degree from St. Michael's College, University of Toronto, a teaching Certificate in TEFL from the Royal Society of Arts, London, and a Master's degree in TEFL in curriculum design and development from the Universitat de Barcelona. Ms. Zanatta is co-author of the first edition of *Parade* (Longman/Pearson Education, 1996).

Consulting Authors

Alma Flor Ada holds a Ph.D. from the Pontificia Universidad Católica del Perú and was for two years a scholar at the Mary Bunting Institute, Harvard University, doing post-doctoral research. A life-long advocate of children's and parents' rights, she has been a pioneer and constant supporter of bilingualism and bilingual education in the United States. She directs a doctoral studies program in international multicultural education and second language acquisition and has guided numerous research projects in these areas as a professor at the University of San Francisco. A specialist in children's literature, her books include: *The Gold Coin* (Christopher Award-winner); *Encaje de Piedra* (Martha Jalotti Gold Medal); *Dear Peter Rabbit; My Name Is María Isabel;* and *Where the Flame Trees Bloom.* Ms. Ada is also co-editor of *A Chorus of Cultures,* as well as author of *The Magical Encounter.*

Anna Uhl Chamot is currently an Associate Professor in the Department of Teacher Preparation at George Washington University. In addition to research, she also manages two Title VII Special Alternative Instructional Programs in Arlington, Virginia, Public Schools. Her publications include articles in *TESOL Quarterly, Language Learning,* and *Applied Linguistics;* her ESL (English as a Second Language) instructional materials include content-ESL books in history and mathematics, and a textbook series based on the CALLA model, *Building Bridges: Content and Learning Strategies for ESL.* She has co-authored two books with J. Michael O'Malley, *Learning Strategies in Second Language Acquisition* and *The CALLA Handbook: Implementing the Cognitive Academic Language Learning Approach.* Dr. Chamot holds a Ph.D. in ESL and applied linguistics from the University of Texas at Austin, and a Master's degree in foreign language education from Teachers College, Columbia University.

Jim Cummins (Ph.D. University of Alberta, 1974) has been a professor in the Modern Language Centre and Curriculum Department of the Ontario Institute for Studies in Education. He has published several books related to bilingual education and ESL student achievement including: *Bilingualism and Special Education: Issues in Assessment and Pedagogy* (Multilingual Matters, 1984); *Bilingualism in Education: Aspects of Theory, Research and Policy* (Longman, 1986, with Merrill Swain); *Minority education: From shame to struggle* (Multilingual Matters, 1988, with Tove Skutnabb-Kangas); and *Empowering Minority Students* (California Association for Bilingual Education, 1989). His research focuses on the challenges educators face in adjusting to classrooms where cultural and linguistic diversity is the norm.

Christine Ewy has an education consulting business based in Illinois. She is also adjunct faculty for Northern Illinois and National-Louis Universities where she teaches graduate classes that lead to ESL and bilingual certification. Her K–12 experience includes teaching elementary, middle school and high school levels. Christine is author of *Teaching the Teacher Within: Long-Term Success for Bilingual and Monolingual Students,* and co-author of *Literacy Development Strategies for Teachers* *and Students.* Ms. Ewy's expertise evolved from her formal degrees, her interactions with students and teachers, her work in developing and leading others to develop curriculum, and her freelance writing for publishers of education materials.

Carolyn Kessler is Professor of English as a Second Language/Applied Linguistics at the University of Texas at San Antonio where she teaches graduate courses in second/foreign language acquisition theory and practice. Additionally, she is director of Texas Education Agency special projects, providing professional development for instructional personnel, teachers and administrators, in ESL adult and family literacy programs throughout Texas. Dr. Kessler has worked extensively in staff development for school districts and other agencies throughout Texas and many parts of the U.S. in programs for non-native speakers of English. Among recent books and monographs authored or co-authored are: *Cooperative Language Learning: A Teacher's Resource Book; Making Connections: An Integrated Approach to ESL* (an ESL series for middle school and high school students); *Literacy con Cariño: A Story of Migrant Children's Success;* and *Teaching Science to English Learners: Grades 4–8.*

J. Michael O'Malley was Supervisor of Assessment and Evaluation in Prince William County Public Schools in Virginia, where he established a performance assessment program in grades K–12. He was previously Senior Researcher in the National Foreign Language Resource Center at Georgetown University and for six years was Director of the Evaluation Assistance Center at Georgetown University. He received his Ph.D. in psychology from George Peabody College in 1969. Dr. O'Malley was co-developer of the Cognitive Academic Language Learning Approach (CALLA). CALLA was introduced in 1986 and was the subject of his 1994 work *The CALLA Handbook* with Anna Uhl Chamot, as well as their earlier book on the research and theory underlying the approach. The late Dr. O'Malley was noted for his research on learning strategies in second language acquisition and for his work on assessment of language minority students.

Writer

Christine Kay Williams has been involved in ESL/EFL education for many years. She helped develop and produce *Hooray for English!* (ScottForesman, 1995, 1989) and the beginning levels of the *ScottForesman English* series (ScottForesman, 1991). She also wrote the Teacher's Edition of *In Charge, Level 1* (ScottForesman, 1993), an advanced level of the *ScottForesman English* series. She has taught ESL in a variety of settings and currently teaches at the English Language Center at Towson State University in Baltimore, Maryland. She holds an M.A. degree in linguistics with a certificate in TESOL from Ohio University.

Each level of *New Parade* contains the following components: the Student Book, the Workbook, the Teacher's Edition, the Audio Program, and the Picture Cards, the Posters, and the Video and Video Guide.

Student Book

The Student Book contains nine units, each of which is centered around a theme of high interest to students. Each unit provides a wide variety of pictures, stories, poems, chants, songs, articles, exercises, games, and projects which stimulate communication, keep motivation high, and provide structure and vocabulary practice. In addition, each unit contains a Little Book. Each unit ends with an activity for oral assessment and a page of written assessment. The self-assessment feature (*I can do this* in Books 1–3 and *My Journal* in Books 4–6) provides the students with an opportunity for self-evaluation as well. Additional pages include an introduction to the Student Book mascots at the beginning of the book and a farewell at the end of the book. Cutout pages for many different projects and games are also included.

Workbook

The Workbook includes activities designed to reinforce each unit section in the Student Book. Both structured practice and less-controlled activities are represented, along with puzzles, projects, and assessment activities. There are three sets of assessment pages, covering Units 1–3, 4–6, and 7–9, to measure accumulated knowledge and evaluate progress. Each Workbook page contains the Picture Dictionary that corresponds to the Student Book. This way, the students have the necessary vocabulary accessible. In the back are the Language Activities Section and Little Book Comprehension pages. There is also "My Page," where the students list *My Favorite Words* and *Words That Are Hard for Me.*

Teacher's Edition

The Teacher's Edition contains full-size reproductions of the Student Book pages placed opposite the corresponding pages of complete teaching objectives and a lesson plan for both the Student Book and the Workbook. Instructions and answers for the activities are included. The unit opener pages for each unit list communication and language objectives, learning strategies and thinking skills, content connections, materials (required and optional), the key vocabulary, and Picture Dictionary for the unit. Within the Optional Materials list for a unit, titles of *Little Celebrations* story books related to the unit theme can often be found. Additional material in this front section includes

information on reaching all students, songs and rhymes, crafts, pair and group work, games, assessment charts, and so on. The Teacher's Edition also contains a Placement Test, a Unit Test after each unit, and three Mastery Tests covering Units 1–3, 4–6, and 7–9. A chart of the International Phonetic Alphabet, a vocabulary list, an index, a complete Scope and Sequence of the *New Parade* series, and Time Guidelines are also included.

Video and Video Guide

The *New Parade Video,* one per level, sets the stage for each unit and surrounds the students with natural language. The video units are real-life extensions of the Student Book themes. The vocabulary and language structures are carefully limited to those introduced up to and included in the unit. The students are encouraged to interact with the video. The Video Guide suggests places to pause the video and offers additional teaching tips.

Audio Program

The audio tapes/CDs contain models for conversation, materials for the Listening sections in both the Student Book and the Workbook, and a variety of lively songs and chants that the students will enjoy. Chants and songs which do not appear in the Student Book, but are in the Teacher's Edition, are also on the audio.

Picture Cards

The *New Parade* series includes a variety of attractive real-life Picture Cards designed to stimulate both communication and vocabulary development. The cards can be used by the teacher to present or review structures and vocabulary and also by the students to tell or write stories, generate word maps, play games, and so on.

The Lesson Plan

The lesson plan for each unit consists of five parts: Warm Up, Presentation, Practice, Application, and Assessment.

Warm Up The Warm Up is an effective way to help the students begin to think in English and to review previously introduced material. Warm Ups of different types help provide variety and interest in the lesson. If the students have been seated for a relatively long while, a Warm Up that involves physical movement will refresh them. A Warm Up involving physical movement can be very simple. For example, if the objective is to review colors, write the names of the colors on different parts of the board and have the students wearing those colors line up in front of the appropriate word. If the objective is to review weather vocabulary, post pictures of different weather conditions around the classroom and have the students go touch the picture illustrating the word you give them. If the objective is to distinguish singular from plural nouns, have the students remain seated when they hear a singular noun and jump up when they hear a plural one.

A Warm Up to prepare the students for a period of concentration may involve matching, drawing, or writing. The students can work in groups to match pictures with the corresponding words on slips of paper. The students draw pictures according to the words or descriptions you give them. Give them words on slips of paper or pictures to use in an oral or written story. Give each student an object or picture and have the students ask and answer questions such as, "What's this?" and "What color is this?" Familiar songs and chants are also enjoyable and motivating Warm Ups.

Presentation The first part of the presentation often involves preteaching. Preteaching some key vocabulary items or structures ensures the students' understanding and helps to build their confidence before using the Student Book pages. In most cases, showing a picture, object, or demonstrating an action will clarify meaning. Whenever possible, elicit the information from the students first; provide it yourself only as a last resort.

It is important to provide a context for the situations in the Student Book before using the Student Book pages. If the unit focuses on animals, for example, you will want to provide pictures, posters, stuffed animals, and so on to familiarize the students with the names of the animals and to elicit what they already know about animals. Another important part of the presentation involves the clarification of the lesson goals for the students. A clear understanding of the purpose of an activity helps the students learn more effectively and the lesson unfold more smoothly. You may state the goals of the lesson directly or elicit from the students what purposes they can identify. Begin any presentation of a unit in the Student Book by focusing the students' attention on the unit title and/or a picture. Have the students predict from the title what the unit will be about and have them say all they can about the picture. Encourage the flow of information; do not worry about specific error correction at this point. The students will then be ready to do initial activities presenting the new language such as matching up words and pictures, singing a song, chanting, or listening and repeating.

Practice A wide variety of meaningful tasks to cover the four skills and additional thinking skills and strategies in the Student Book and Workbook ensures practice of target language. These activities range from controlled to less-controlled to free expression. Some of the practice activities provide opportunities to work on a particular skill such as listening or reading; others are integrated skill exercises in which a combination of language skills are used. Some activities are designed to be done individually, others in pairs or small groups, and others as a whole class. The students are encouraged to consult with their peers to gather information, interpret results, and solve problems. Many of the activities provide the students with the opportunity to draw on their own life experiences. For example, the students interview each other to find out about their families, favorite foods, likes and dislikes, and so on. Other activities take full advantage of the students' love of color, drawing, fantasy, and creativity. Still others provide connections to the content areas the students are learning about in their other classes. For example, the students conduct an experiment and report on the results *(science)*.

Application The application provides the students with hands-on opportunities to use what they have learned. At this point, the students are ready to undertake a project or game that will require use of the target structures and vocabulary. The students may put together a class book about animals, design a weather wheel, make a card game, or follow a simple recipe. The majority of application tasks also require cooperative group activity, thereby providing the students with opportunities to practice social skills and to take responsibility for the successful completion of their tasks.

Assessment Assessment activities are provided in the Student Book, the Workbook, and the Teacher's Edition. In the Student Book, the last two pages of each unit contain materials for evaluation. The first of the assessment activities is a game, task, or project that can be used for oral assessment. The students carry out the activity, unaware that the teacher is circulating around the classroom monitoring their use of structure and vocabulary. The second of the evaluation activities is a written assessment in which the students fill in blanks, match pictures to words, and write out answers to specific questions. This is followed by the self-evaluation section, which allows the students to think about their own strengths and weaknesses in relation to the material covered in the unit. In the Workbook, the last page of each unit includes a written assessment of the target structures and vocabulary. In addition, there are three sets of cumulative evaluations, covering Units 1–3, 4–6, and 7–9. In the Teacher's Edition, there are nine individual Unit Tests and three sets of tests, also covering Units 1–3, 4–6, and 7–9. Also, a Student Oral Assessment Checklist and an Assessment Chart, along with explanations on how to use them, are provided on pages xx–xxiii.

Total Physical Response

New Parade provides many opportunities for using physical movement to develop language skills in activities adapted from Total Physical Response (TPR), as developed by James J. Asher. This technique is ideal for students at the early stages of learning, when their capabilities for verbal response are as yet undeveloped. TPR provides both intense listening practice and repeated exposure to basic vocabulary items.

To begin, give a command such as, "Open your book, close it, and open it again" while performing the action. Repeat, and then model the action with the whole class, individual rows, or groups of students. Give the command to the whole class, checking to see if they can perform it successfully. Next, give the command without modeling the action. Vary the order of the actions to make sure that the students are actually listening and understanding rather than doing a series of memorized actions. As the students' vocabulary builds, review by giving unusual or unexpected commands to test comprehension. You may, for example, tell the students to hop on one foot to the window.

When the students can carry out your commands very easily, have individual students give your commands and then their own variations of the commands. After the students are accustomed to the TPR technique, gradually introduce new vocabulary and structures. Introduce action verbs such as *walk, hop, run, point, touch, tiptoe, wave,* and so on. To clarify the differences between present and past time, for instance, give the following sequence: "Ana, go to the window." As the student does so, model, "Ana is going to the window. What is she doing? She is going to the window."

Encourage the students to work up TPR routines to review key vocabulary and structures from units studied earlier in the course. Have them work in teams or groups and give each other commands to carry out regularly throughout the term.

Songs and chants can be accompanied by the acting out of actions described in the verses as well. Every opportunity for physical movement provides release of the students' pent-up energies. The students will return to their tasks refreshed and more likely to remember the material they have practiced.

Audio Program

The audio that accompanies *New Parade* can be used in a number of ways. When the audio is used as part of the Presentation, make sure the students look over any text and pictures provided before playing the audio. You may want to read the text aloud once or twice before the students listen to the audio. Play the dialogue, poem, chant, or song on the audio several times until the students can join in easily. Repeat the audio on different days so that they can enjoy the material again. When the audio is used for listening activities, have the students look over the directions, text, questions, or charts they will fill in before they listen. Encourage them to predict what they will hear and to identify what main ideas or details they will listen for. Remind the students that they do not have to understand *every* word they hear in order to do the task successfully.

Content Connections

Not only do math, art, science, music, literature, and social studies expand the students' knowledge, but they also provide valuable opportunities to draw on the students' knowledge acquired across the curriculum.

In the unit opener pages, the connections to the different content areas are listed. You may want to elicit from the students what they have studied in their other classes and use it as an entry point for introducing an activity. You may conduct this part of the lesson in the students' first language or you may want to provide them with the vocabulary in English.

You can then use content connections for developing expanded vocabulary lists, doing small research projects, and so on. When necessary, consult with other teachers at your school to find out what the students have studied concerning the content areas they are about to do in *New Parade*. In this way, you will be able to guide the discussion more effectively.

Learning Strategies and Thinking Skills

Recently, researchers have given more and more attention to how successful language learners achieve their objectives. Much of this attention has focused on the kinds of strategies and thinking skills that learners use and the process by which learning or acquisition occurs.

New Parade has been developed with the belief that learning strategies and thinking skills provide tools for greater student autonomy and more meaningful learning. In addition, learning strategies are particularly important for the development of improved language proficiency and greater self-confidence. These same benefits come into play when learning strategies and thinking skills are systematically applied across the curriculum.

Each unit in *New Parade* includes the use of a variety of strategies and thinking skills, such as applying prior knowledge, skimming for specific information, problem-solving, inferring meaning from context, developing personalized lists, classifying vocabulary, organizing information in charts and graphs, and so on. Specific strategies and skills are found on the unit opener page of each unit.

Mini-Assessments

Ongoing mini-assessments provide an opportunity for quick evaluation of student comprehension of the material under study. In this way, the awareness of early problems leads to clarification and reteaching as needed.

At the lower elementary levels, an easy and quick mini-assessment activity at the beginning of a class is "Show Me." Have the students take out their books, flashcards, or crafts that they have prepared. For example, if you are assessing their understanding of clothing vocabulary, say, "Show me a sweater. Show me a skirt," and so on. Another quick check of comprehension involves taking items ("realia") out of a bag so that the students can name them. To assess the students' abilities to use proper word order in questions and statements, put the individual words from the questions and statements on flashcards or slips of paper, one word per card. Have the students arrange them in order to create properly sequenced sentences.

At the higher elementary levels, short dictations provide quick and easy mini-assessments. Dictations can be used to assess vocabulary, grammar structures, question-answer sequences, and so on. For example, to assess the students' understanding of questions and responses, first dictate five questions. (Tell the students to skip a line after each question.) Then have the students answer each of the dictated questions. Next, have them exchange papers for correction. With this technique, the students have immediate feedback on their performances. Another dictation method involves dictating scrambled letters or words, which the students later must put in order and then must illustrate the meaning with a picture or a sentence.

If you observe that the students are having difficulty with the mini-assessment tasks, you will want to review or reteach the appropriate vocabulary or structure until the students demonstrate understanding. Then you may want to try another mini-assessment to check their progress.

Reaching All Students

Each student in a class has a different personality, different interests, and a different learning style or combination of styles. Often, two different classes react in very different ways to the same lesson materials, delivery style, and teacher. In each situation, the materials have to be adjusted or modified to accommodate the different abilities of the students.

New Parade helps the teacher manage these differences through the provision of Reaching All Students options for follow-up activities. These have been designed in two ways: single ability level within an option at one level, and multiple ability levels within an option. On a typical Teacher's Edition page you will find two to four options. One may be for students at one level of ability to carry out at the same time other students of a differing ability carry out another option on the page. For example, the students at a lower level of development may be working in pairs to spell out words for pictures while students of higher ability may be writing a story. The mixed ability levels within one option involve students of differing abilities working towards a common goal. For instance, in making a class book together, the students of lower abilities may work on copying a title page neatly while other students draw and still other students write the text.

These options are for enrichment when time limitations are not a problem. Keep in mind that the students are provided with many other opportunities to express themselves and achieve success in using the core activities in the Student Book when extra time is not available.

Songs and Rhymes

Every culture has developed some form of music and poetry due to their power as devices for cultural identity and cohesion. Just as music unites culturally, it serves as a means for teachers to increase rapport in the classroom. Songs generate students' positive feelings and strengthen motivation as they create a state of relaxed receptivity. The students hear the music and words as well as feel the rhythm.

To set the context and clarify meaning, direct the students' attention to any illustrations surrounding the words to the songs and rhymes. Many of the verses can be accompanied by gestures and movement for added enjoyment. Use the songs and rhymes as both teaching elements and as a change of pace when the students' energy levels are low. They are a pleasurable way to focus on specific vocabulary, structure, pronunciation, rhythm, and intonation, as well as a welcome break from exercises.

Many of the songs and rhymes in *New Parade* are traditional English verses that reinforce the authenticity of the cultural experience. Many are interactive; the students are invited to make up additional verses of their own. These songs with new verses can be illustrated by the students, collected, and assembled into a class song book for use all year long.

Pronunciation Practice

Pronunciation skills are acquired through practice over a long period of time. Complete native-like accuracy in pronunciation is not a goal many students can or need to achieve. However, all learners can work to improve their pronunciation and to reduce those aspects that interfere with the ability to be understood clearly.

New Parade views errors as a natural part of the learning process. It is to be expected that students might only roughly approximate pronunciation features and patterns before they can produce them clearly and integrate them into spontaneous communication. To this end, the correction of pronunciation errors is not emphasized. Rather, the students are provided with many models of speech to follow and many opportunities to practice such items as sound/spelling correspondences, syllables, word endings, stress, rhythm, and intonation.

Use the language, songs, rhymes, and chants on the audio as models for speech. Play the audio or read the examples several times while the students listen. Be patient; the students must be able to perceive the sounds and features before they can produce them. Each unit in a *New Parade* Teacher's Edition has a pronunciation focus drawn from the language presented. Have the whole class, then groups, and finally individuals repeat the words under study.

Focus attention on those sounds the students find difficult and practice them systematically in short, game-like activities. Three suggestions for practice follow. To practice distinguishing /b/ and /p/ in the initial position, for example, label two empty containers with the letters *b* and *p* respectively. Divide the class into two teams, and provide each team with a selection of objects or pictures of objects that begin with /b/ and /p/ (book, banana, ball, pen, paper, pencil, and so on). Have one member from each team bring an object, pronounce its name, and drop it into the correct container.

To practice distinguishing /l/ and /r/ in the medial or final position, write words such as *po_ice* and *pa_ent* on the board. Provide each student with two cards, one with the letter *l* and one with the letter *r*. Have the students hold up the appropriate card for each word on the board and then pronounce each word in turn.

To practice vowel sounds, have the students make word trees. Put the students in groups. For each sound under study, provide a cutout of a large tree. Write or paint the sound/letter on the trunk of the tree. Have the students "hang" words on slips of paper containing that sound from the branches of the tree. Display the accumulated trees on the classroom wall as the term progresses. Use them for periodic pronunciation review.

The Teacher's Edition contains a chart of the International Phonetic Alphabet (IPA) with examples of vowel and consonant sounds in the initial, medial, and final positions.

Crafts

The use of art and craft projects in the language classroom ensures a student-centered, hands-on activity-based lesson. In addition to this, it provides an opportunity for parents to see and for students to show and discuss with their parents what they are learning in English class. To this end, *New Parade* includes a wide variety of fun craft activities designed to stimulate creative play and develop the students' imaginations. Art and craft projects capture the students' interest and increase their involvement with the target language, functions, and structures, thereby expanding the language-learning experience.

Craft activities aid in the promotion of language acquisition through the exploration and development of the primary senses: sight, sound, touch, and movement. At the lower elementary grade levels, this work assists students in the development of small muscle and hand-to-eye coordination, sensory discrimination, and concentration. At the higher elementary grade levels, opportunities for artistic self-expression in the language-learning process involve the "whole" student. At all grade levels, the activities afford opportunities to recycle and reuse the language in an authentic and meaningful way, as the students present their crafts for display and explain how the projects were completed.

The craft projects in *New Parade* provide avenues through which the students expand their communication and social skills by means of cooperative pair and group work. Each student is involved and contributes to the best of his or her ability level to the final result of the project and shares in the satisfaction of creation and completion. What the students have shared in learning is now visible, tangible, and evident for all to see. This feeling of accomplishment and success is highly motivating and significantly contributes to the building of the students' self-esteem.

Finally, craft activities provide an enjoyable vehicle for learning by doing. The students are engaged in hands-on activities that reinforce the different learning styles they may have. The visual learners will relate to the design, shape, and color elements of the projects; the auditory learners will concern themselves with instructions, explanations, and presentation; and the tactile/kinesthetic learners will involve themselves with cutting, pasting, and coloring.

To ensure the success of any project, establish clear rules and procedures. Begin the activity by showing a finished product so that the students can see their goal.

Make sure that the students know the purpose behind carrying out the project. Have all materials and tools at hand and in working order. Be sure to model each step in the procedure at least once, and more if necessary for understanding. Establish a buddy system in which a stronger student can guide a weaker student. Set up rules and responsibilities for clean-up. Be generous with your praise, and finally, display the finished projects in class.

Craft projects can be used for evaluation. The grade given after every craft activity should take into consideration the ability of the student to follow instructions and complete the project on time, to generate the appropriate target vocabulary and structures, and to work creatively.

Planning the Classes

New Parade is designed so that one level can be completed in one school year, provided that a minimum of two Student Book pages are completed per week. Time Guidelines are provided in the back of the Teacher's Edition, on pages 130 and 131. If you have more than enough time to complete two pages a week, you will want to use as many Reaching All Students activities as possible. Only you can judge which of these will work best in your class situation.

Each class period should consist of the following: a quick Warm Up (see page vii), activities from the lesson, Mini-Assessments whenever they seem appropriate (see page x), and a Closing. The Closing can be a fun activity that reinforces what has been taught, such as a game, a song, or a chant, or a quick, three-minute free-writing journal activity where students can make a list of three new words from the lesson or describe the part of the lesson they liked best.

When planning the activities for a lesson, it is important to do the activities in a sequence that indicates a gradual progression from simple to more complex tasks. It is also important to be aware of how to pace the class so that the students can learn in the most effective way possible.

Pacing the Classes

Pacing involves the rhythm of the lesson or how much time is allocated to each activity. You will want to keep your explanations as brief as possible and use a variety of activities to keep participation and interest high. You will also want to set goals and time limits for activities and monitor your students' performances to ensure sufficient (but not too much) time on a task. Most teachers feel comfortable with moving on when it is evident that two-thirds to three-fourths of the students have a good grasp of the activity.

Small Group and Pair Work

Learners may favor one type of classroom interaction over another, but it is usually the teacher who structures classroom activities. Effective teachers strive for a balance among whole-class work, group work, pair work, and individual work.

New Parade provides many opportunities for individual and small group work in order to maximize student use of the language. Because language is a creative and communicative process, the activities have been designed to foster interaction and the negotiation of meaning through cooperative learning, collaborative learning, and communicative language teaching. By sharing ideas and information in pairs or groups, the students are given the opportunity to use their knowledge of the language in a non-threatening environment.

To ensure effective pair work, several factors should be considered. First, there should be a real purpose for the exchange of information; each of the student partners should require information the other partner has in order to complete the activity. Second, tasks will motivate the students more if there is an end product: a completed chart, a time line, a survey, and so on. Third, the abilities and language backgrounds of the students should be considered when forming the pairs. For some activities, stronger students may be paired with weaker students; for others, students of like ability may be paired.

Group work is another way in which the students maximize their use of the language. For effective group activities, group size, student roles, and task goals should be considered. *Group size* is generally determined by each task. Remember, however, that the larger the group, the less time there is for individual member participation. *Student roles* may vary within a group according to the activity. For some tasks, a group may have a leader who makes sure that everyone has a chance to participate, a secretary who copies or writes down the answers or results, a student in charge of materials needed, and so on. In other tasks, the students may have the same roles. *Task goals* must be made clear to the students, as well as procedures and time frames.

When the students are working in pairs or small groups, it is important that the teacher circulate and monitor the students' progress. Check that the students are using English and are on task. Regarding error correction, it is best to take note of major mistakes heard and reteach or review them after the activity has finished. Interruptions for correction impede the communicative flow and draw attention away from the message. It is important to realize that errors are a natural part of the learning process and that the students may recognize errors while studying the rules but still produce them while attempting communication.

Forming the groups need not take up much class time. Have the students "count off" and then have all the "ones" work together, the "twos" work together, and so on. Later, have the groups recombine with one of each number in the group. For younger students, have them select pieces of colored yarn or strips of paper; the "reds" then work together, the "greens," and so on. A variation is to have the students select pictures from a bag and combine according to those pictures (the "cats" work together, the "dogs" work together, and so on).

Take full advantage of the pair and group work activities found in *New Parade*. These activities allow the students to extend and personalize what they have learned in each unit.

Games: Meaningful Play

Language learning is hard work. The students must make an effort to understand, to imitate, and to manipulate newly learned language. Games help many learners sustain interest and motivation in their work through meaningful play in the language learning classroom.

These enjoyable contexts for language use provide the same density of practice as more conventional drills or exercises do in many cases, and they motivate the students to use their language capabilities to the fullest. When the students are amused, challenged, intrigued, or surprised as they play a game, then the content is clearly meaningful to them, and as a result, the language will be more vividly experienced and retained.

In addition to this, good, meaningful games will involve the four language skills: reading, writing, listening, and speaking. They are true integrated skills. For these reasons, *New Parade* is filled with a wide variety of fun and challenging games. Many form an integral part of the units, and others are provided as Reaching All Students for those students who have different skill levels.

Before playing any game with the students, it is important that you practice it in order to understand the procedures clearly. The game can then be demonstrated in front of the class so that everyone understands how to play. Establish rules for playing the games. Let your students brainstorm the rules. Elicit them and put them on the board. Keep the rules simple. Then invite the class to choose six to eight rules they feel comfortable with such as, "Speak in English," "Don't cheat," "Follow the rules," "Don't shout," and "Stay in your seats."

Examples of games found in *New Parade* include Spelling Bees, Simon Says, Twenty Questions, Concentration®, Picasso Bingo, and so on. Each of these provides an opportunity for recycling and reviewing material taught earlier in the course, promotes a collaborative spirit, encourages student interaction, and fosters the use of the target language.

Spelling Bees require no previous preparation and are therefore easy to set up. Begin by dividing the class into two teams. Have each group of students think of a name for their team. Then, give a member of the first team the first word to spell. If it is spelled correctly, that team gets a point. The other team then gets the next word. For every word spelled correctly, a point is awarded. The first team to reach a certain number of points wins. A variation is to set up the Spelling Bee so that all the students participate simultaneously. Begin by having all the students stand up. Each student is given a word to spell. If it is spelled correctly, the student remains standing. If not, the student sits down. Continue giving out words to those students still standing until all but one are eliminated. To involve the students in the Bee even more, you may want them to write up the spelling list to be used and to call out the words. (The caller could be the winner from the last Spelling Bee.)

Simon Says is a game involving physical movement, and thus is appropriate for the lower elementary levels. Begin by asking all the students to stand up. Tell them that they are to act out everything that Simon says to do. They are not to act out any command given that is not preceded by "Simon Says." Simon, the person giving the commands, will say such things as, "Simon says, 'Take two steps forward,'" "Simon says, 'Clap your hands three times,'" "Simon says, 'Act like a cat,'" "Simon says, 'Wave to a friend,'" and so on. Whenever a student carries out a command that is not preceded by "Simon says," that student is eliminated and must sit down. The remaining students continue until only one, the winner, is left standing.

Twenty Questions is one example of the many guessing games in the series. Begin by choosing a topic. Identify a person or thing associated with that topic (for example, basketball and Michael Jordan). The students then try to guess who or what you have chosen by asking *yes/no* questions to which you may only answer "yes" or "no." The student who guesses the answer is then the next person to think of a topic and associated person or thing. This game can also be played in teams. In this version, every correct answer to a *yes/no* question is worth one point. The first team to reach a certain number of points wins.

Concentration® is a memory game played with flashcards. It may be played in small groups or pairs. To play, there must be duplicate sets of flashcards (two cars, two trees, and so on). Begin by placing all the cards facedown. The students take turns turning over two cards at a time. If the two cards are a match, the student keeps them. If not, they are turned over facedown again and the next student begins to play. The student with the most accumulated pairs wins. At the end of each game, it is very important that students name their pairs.

Picasso Bingo is another versatile game used throughout the series. Hand out blank pieces of paper. Have the students draw two vertical lines and two horizontal lines spaced equally apart in such a way that they have nine squares. Next, call out nine items for the students to draw or write in the squares in any order that they choose. These may be individual vocabulary words, questions, or sentences. As you name the items, write them down on nine small slips of paper. Place them in a box, bag, can, or some other container to draw from when you play the game. Before beginning, make sure that each student has nine game pieces to put on the spaces and that each space has something drawn or written in it. To play Bingo, pick a slip of paper from the bag and call out the word, question, or sentence on it. The students put a game piece on top of the corresponding square. The first student to have three squares filled either vertically, horizontally, or diagonally wins by calling out, "Bingo." The winner can be the caller the next time Bingo is played.

Before playing any game with the students, make sure that they have the language they need. Teach phrases such as, "It's your turn," "It's a match," "You miss a turn," "Oh, no," "I lost," "I won," and "I have a Bingo."

Vocabulary

Vocabulary plays a key role in the learning of any language. Without vocabulary, communication is impossible. Words, however, can be difficult to remember unless the students develop a real need for them. The activities in *New Parade* help the students develop vocabulary through a variety of tasks that stimulate a desire to communicate. The vocabulary central to each unit is presented in context and then recycled several times through different activities. Many of the activities provide lists of words as answer choices. These lists of words are called "Word Banks."

New Parade includes both active vocabulary, selected for its usefulness and frequency of occurrence in real communication, and receptive vocabulary, non-target language that enriches the different thematic contexts in the lessons. A list of the active vocabulary for each unit is included on the unit opener pages for each unit and in a comprehensive list at the back of the Teacher's Edition.

Every opportunity should be taken to involve the students in the vocabulary learning process through a variety of techniques and activities. Use realia (real items used in real life), pictures (including the illustrations in the Picture Dictionary at the top of Student Book pages), TPR (Total Physical Response), games, and craft activities. Have the students make their own sets of flashcards, class dictionary, picture dictionaries, word mobiles, posters, and so on. Display their work and change the displays periodically. Have teams of students make vocabulary quizzes for each other to take; award team points and tally them up at the end of the term.

Encourage the students to develop personal dictionaries. For the younger grades, this may involve cutting pictures out of magazines or drawing pictures and pasting them into a notebook. A blank address book is very useful as a personal Picture Dictionary, as it comes divided alphabetically. The students then write the corresponding word in English next to each picture in the section of the address book. For the upper elementary grades, the students can write the word in English, name the part of speech, write out a synonym, and use the word in an original sentence to illustrate its meaning. Have the students copy target language into their notebooks, but also allow for words that they are simply interested in—words they have heard in songs or jokes, words that relate to their interests, words that simply look strange or have an interesting sound, and so on.

Promote awareness of language learning strategies in the students by demonstrating techniques such as paraphrase and circumlocution; for example, "the thing you make a pencil point with" for *pencil sharpener,* and "to go behind someone" for *follow.*

When applicable, show the students that English words are often similar in form and meaning to words in other languages. Help them recognize these cognates, but caution them about the dangers of false cognates. Point out the value of word associations and collocations to clarify meaning. For example, *run out of time, run out of milk, run out of money, run out of chalk.* At the higher levels, show the students the value of building word family charts listing the different parts of speech and the forms a word may take, such as *photograph, photographer, photography* (nouns), *to photograph* (verb), *photographic* (adjective), and *photographically* (adverb). Finally, encourage the students to take advantage of resources such as any radio stations that play songs in English, TV programs that may be subtitled, comic books, magazines, and newspapers in English.

Language Structure

The practice activities in *New Parade* have been designed to involve the students in the discovery of the language as they work through the various tasks. By doing so, they become active participants in the learning process.

One important feature of this language practice is the Language Notes in the Student Book. These notes are meant to highlight the various teaching points of the unit and to draw the students' attention to some of the language features they are working with in the tasks. Some of these give a brief grammatical description of the target language. The students are then asked to apply these rules in accompanying exercises. In other words, the students use the deductive reasoning process. In other tasks, the students are given a number of examples and asked to discover the rules for themselves. In these, the students use the inductive reasoning process.

On the opening page of every unit in the Teacher's Edition, there is a list of the language skills and grammar points practiced in the unit. In addition, there is a list of objectives on each page of a lesson. When knowledge of a grammar rule is essential for the success of an activity, explanations and models of the structures are provided.

At the higher elementary levels, where the processing of the language is more explicit, you may want your students to prepare personal grammar reference notebooks. These notebooks, which could be titled "Grammar Rules and Structures I Have Learned," should contain an explanation of each rule or structure and an original example illustrating the concept studied. Encourage the students to show their work to their classmates so that they may learn from each other. As an additional challenge, you may want the students to try to write some of the grammar rules themselves, rather than copy them from a book. In this way, they will find they need to choose and work with English words in a context meaningful for them. This rule writing then becomes yet another opportunity for meaningful use of and experimentation with the language. If the grammar rules and structures are consistently recorded in these notebooks created and compiled by the students, they will have an invaluable study tool and a personalized reminder of what they have learned during their English course. This provides the students with a feeling of satisfaction and a sense of accomplishment.

Another way to encourage the students to further process the language is to have them reflect on the language errors they frequently make. Encourage them to keep a list of their errors and have them write out a self-corrected version for each one. A variation of this kind of correction involves peer correction. Have the students exchange their lists of errors (or homework) and correct their classmates' mistakes.

There is a whole-class correction activity that the students and teacher can do together. In this activity, called "I Bet," the teacher selects ten items, a few correct and the rest incorrect. The class is divided into two teams, each of which begins with 100 points. As the teacher shows one of the items, the first team "bets" a certain number of its total points that the item is correct (or incorrect). If the team correctly identifies the sentence as correct (or incorrect), it receives that number of points. If the team's answer is wrong, it must subtract

that number of points from its total. The team with the highest number of accumulated points is the winner. The items in this error correction activity may come from errors noticed in class, from homework, or from tests.

The language practice in *New Parade* is contextualized, meaningful, and communicative. Both the activities outlined above and others throughout the series provide the students with many opportunities to become aware of the language as they interact with it on a more individual level.

Reading

Reading is an enjoyable and invaluable way to expand vocabulary, to increase content knowledge, and to improve critical thinking skills. *New Parade* provides opportunities to develop both top-down and bottom-up processing through many different types of texts: poems, chants, songs, stories, jokes, dialogues, letters, reviews, and factual pieces. Many of the texts are from authentic, traditional sources, and all of them have been carefully chosen to be age-appropriate, informative, and motivating. In addition, the Optional Materials list found on the unit opener pages often provides titles of suggested story books that relate to each unit theme. The high-interest topics are designed to encourage the students to verbalize their own ideas in response to the text, thus providing more oral practice as well.

The stories, poems, and chants have been selected with the belief that learners need to read both texts that they can relate to in an enjoyable way and texts that develop their criteria for understanding, judging, and defining their opinions, as well as texts that promote the use of strategies and thinking skills, such as figuring out meaning from context and relating charts to a text.

New Parade provides opportunities for both reading aloud and silent reading. Poems, chants, songs, and dialogues particularly lend themselves to reading aloud. They encourage the students to recognize and practice rhythm and intonation patterns in English and to simply enjoy what they are reading through active oral participation. Reading aloud also helps listeners build visual images of the text they are hearing. Longer texts, such as stories and articles, are better processed through silent reading. The students can greatly benefit from silent readings, as it provides many opportunities to practice efficient reading strategies.

Prereading activities help prepare the students to interact intellectually with the reading text. They also encourage good reading habits such as looking at the

Teaching Techniques

title of the selection and at any pictures, captions, charts, or graphs. Previewing a text is important, as it allows the students to access what they already know about the topic, predict what the reading will be about, and create a mental framework into which they can fit the information they are about to read.

Prereading Before reading a text, encourage the students to look at the title, any headings, and any questions before or after the reading. You may want them to predict what the text will be about from these items or from five or six key vocabulary words that have been pulled out of the text and written on the board. When applicable, have them read the first sentence of each paragraph to find the main idea.

Reading During the act of reading, encourage the students to become actively involved in the text by looking for specific information. Have them ask themselves questions about the text as they read, using "Who? What? When? Where? Why? How?" Help them underline or highlight key words or ideas, and to mark key vocabulary words for later study. For the higher elementary grades, you may want to have the students take notes, make a simple outline, or diagram the most important information as they read the passage. Early

exposure to these important skills will help them be better prepared for academic reading in later courses.

Postreading Have the students answer questions about the text, making sure they can justify their answers. Help them to process the material through filling out charts, drawing diagrams, or writing reports. Have them summarize the text in their own words or act out events from the story or poem. Encourage them to illustrate their favorite part of a story and summarize that scene in a few sentences next to their drawings; then, display the pictures on the wall. As a challenge, have the students retell a story but with a different ending or with their classmates as characters in the story. When applicable, have the students tell why they liked or disliked a text, and what they would do to change the text.

Diagrams Two kinds of diagrams that the students might use are word maps and Venn diagrams. Word maps are clearly understandable visual representations of relationships among words or ideas. Because they show at a glance the associations and meanings the words have for the students, they are useful tools in understanding reading texts and developing vocabulary. The students can make a word map as a prereading activity and then expand on it after reading.

Word Map

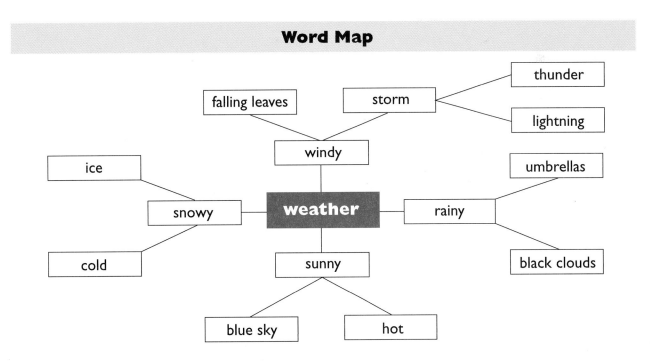

Venn diagrams also show a type of relationship. Items are compared and contrasted in a visual representation that shows how they are alike and how they are different. Applied to reading texts, Venn diagrams depict two items or story characters, or even two separate texts on the same subject, in such a way that the characteristics they share and do not share can readily be seen.

Venn Diagram

dogs
some characteristics of only dogs written here

cats
some characteristics of only cats written here

both dogs and cats
characteristics of both dogs and cats written where circles overlap

Encouragement To encourage the students to read, provide praise and rewards. You may want to keep a large chart in which each student's progress is recorded according to how many articles or books he or she has read. Paste colored stars or stickers by their names as they finish their readings, or allow them to decorate bookmarks to keep as prizes after doing the required number of readings or finishing a book. If possible, keep a supply of comic books, cartoon strips, and short articles of interest to the students in the classroom. Allow them to look through the materials in occasional, short "free" reading periods.

Writing

In the lower elementary levels, care has been taken to systematically introduce the written word and build upon it until the students are capable of writing short, two- or three-sentence paragraphs in Student Book 3. Production of the written word, though somewhat

limited at these lower levels, forms a clearly significant part of the language learning process. Typical introductory writing exercises at these levels include unscrambling words, putting sentences into logical order, completing puzzles, short dictations, and so on. In addition, the physicality of transferring information from one place to another through writing is important for long-term memory retention of new consonant combinations, words, and structures.

In the higher elementary levels, *New Parade* builds upon the skills and understanding of the writing process acquired at the lower levels, culminating in tasks that require several well-developed paragraphs. The students are led through the different stages of the writing process, from prewriting activities such as brainstorming all the way to the editing of the final draft and presentation of the written work.

Prewriting The students are provided with many opportunities throughout the series to practice planning strategies such as brainstorming, word maps, Venn diagrams, and outlines. These activities may be done individually in some cases and in pairs or small groups in others.

Writing Several types of first draft writing activities are included. The students are encouraged to focus on content and successful communication of the message over grammatical and mechanical perfection. While these latter two are worthy goals, the first draft activities are designed first to help the students get down words on paper in an organized fashion. They learn the importance of an introductory statement that identifies the main idea of the passage (the topic sentence), how to support that sentence with examples or details (the body), and how to write a concluding statement that sums up the main idea in different words (the conclusion). The reading passages in the units serve as additional models from which the students can identify introductory and concluding statements.

Editing/Rewriting First drafts, of course, imply that there will be a second and perhaps a third draft. Remind the students at this point that even famous writers do many drafts before they consider their work ready for presentation. No one produces his or her best work in just one try. This realization may help students who want their writing to be perfect the first time, and therefore experience difficulty in putting anything at all down on the page. It is very important at this stage for the students to realize that they will have several opportunities to make adjustments and changes without penalties. At this time it is appropriate to focus on accuracy and interest of content, clarity of organization, and finally on the mechanics (spelling, paragraph conventions, capitalization, and so on). Word choice may be discussed, as well as the addition, deletion, or rearrangement of information in order to produce a coherent, unified passage.

It is at this stage of the writing process that you may want to introduce the concept of peer editing, in which the students comment on each other's work and give useful feedback. Peer editing is extremely valuable because it builds students' awareness of what is relevant, accurate, and appropriate when writing. This feedback on the content and organization of their drafts not only provides additional opportunities for meaningful use of English, but also enables the students to begin to see how others (the audience) see their writing. After peer editing has taken place, have each pair of student writers and student editors confer to explain their reactions to the written piece. At this stage, make sure that the editors tell what they liked about the piece, what they wanted to know more about, and what confused them. Positive suggestions for improvement may then follow. Allow the students adequate time to work on the suggested changes after the writer/editor consultations. Once the students are satisfied that they have done their best, collect the work for evaluation and presentation.

Evaluation/Presentation At this stage of the writing process, evaluation and presentation is appropriate. Separate pieces of writing may receive a number or letter grade, but the most effective tool in helping writers measure and understand their progress is the writing portfolio, a folder of each student's written work over a period of time. When applicable, the students should be allowed some input as to which pieces remain in their portfolios for assessment. Portfolios contain more than final drafts; there may be outlines, word maps, journal entries, rough drafts, paragraphs, letters, poems, copies of group-produced work, and whatever else the students have been assigned as tasks. The teacher and the student together review the work and track the student's development, difficulties, and improvement in all parts of the writing process.

Presentation consists of the "publication" of the written product. This may be the handing in of the work to the teacher, the reading of the material to the class, the sharing of the material in small groups, the display of the work on the classroom wall, or the inclusion of the writing in a class newspaper or class-produced book. It is at this point that the students will feel the excitement and personal satisfaction of communicating through writing.

In the majority of writing tasks throughout *New Parade,* the students are given the opportunity to personalize the language they learn and to write about their world and their daily realities. In completing these writing activities, the students are often called upon to make use of their own knowledge, as well as to express their ideas and opinions in a logical way.

The Student Oral Assessment Checklist

It is important to evaluate the students' oral proficiencies in settings that are relaxed and tension-free. In the assessment of students, this means that the students will remain unaware that they are being evaluated on their oral performances. This can be achieved by involving the students in the communicative project-oriented activities or the games found before the written assessment page at the end of each Student Book unit. The activities completely involve the students in tasks that are at once entertaining and performance-based. These tasks are designed to elicit the target language and structures the students need in order to complete them successfully. The students, for example, play card games that require the production of certain question and answer sequences as well as specialized vocabulary. They may make a moving picture show and tell the story as the pictures move; also, they may follow a recipe or conduct an experiment. These activities are rich in opportunities for assessment of vocabulary and structure. Of course, oral performance can be judged in other ways as well, as the students question each other in order to fill out a chart or questionnaire, or act out dialogue sequences based on models provided in the text.

To monitor the students' performances in such a way that they remain unaware of assessment, circulate slowly around the classroom as the students work on the communicative tasks designed for this purpose. You may have a pencil and notebook with you, but it must not be too obvious that you are either taking notes or assigning a grade based on what you are hearing. Pause, standing to the side of the student or pair of students you are evaluating. You may even want to turn your back on the student you are actually listening to so that the student remains involved in the task and does not focus attention on you.

To use the Student Oral Assessment Checklist, first duplicate the number of sheets needed. Write the unit number on the appropriate line and fill in the names of the students. Then give careful attention to the questions or tasks you mean to use for evaluation. Write them in the spaces provided and then record your assessment of each student's proficiency in them. Use the key provided on the sheet: m = mastery (the student has used the target language proficiently); x = nonmastery (the student has been completely nonproficient in using the target language); w = working on (the student is somewhat proficient, but needs more work in certain areas). You may want to include additional marks or terms; modify the form as necessary so that it best fulfills your needs. Your accumulated checklists will give you an overview of your students' progress during the course.

New Parade Copyright © 2000 by Addison Wesley Longman, Inc.

Student Oral Assessment Checklist

Unit _____

m = mastery
x = nonmastery
w = working on

Students' Names

Questions/Tasks

The Assessment Chart

Just as the Student Oral Assessment Checklist provides the teacher with an overview of the students' oral proficiencies, so does the Assessment Chart provide an overview of the students' unit assessment scores and cumulative test scores regarding written production of structure and vocabulary. Unit assessment scores are assigned to the students' work done on the last page of the Student Book and on the individual Unit Test. Cumulative test scores are assigned to the students' work done on the three tests provided in the Teacher's Edition (see pages xl–xlv). These tests cover Units 1–3, 4–6, and 7–9.

To use the Assessment Chart, first fill in the students' names on the lines provided. Record either a numerical or letter grade in the unit evaluation column. This grade may reflect your assessment of the students' completion of the unit activities and/or the students' written production on the last page of each Student Book unit, Workbook unit, or individual Unit Test scores. You will also want to record the Cumulative Test scores in the columns provided.

For a complete evaluative overview of the students' progress in English, take into consideration the following: scores from the Tests, the scores in the Student Oral Assessment Checklist, the written work collected in the students' portfolios, and their participation and behavior in the classroom.

Assessment Chart

Name	Unit 1	Unit 2	Unit 3	Units 1–3 Test	Unit 4	Unit 5	Unit 6	Units 4–6 Test	Unit 7	Unit 8	Unit 9	Units 7–9 Test

Placement Test

You may be unsure of some of your students' levels of English. The guidelines that follow on this page and the Placement Test on pages xxviii-xxix will help you place your students in the appropriate level of *New Parade*.

Guidelines for Placement

Before making a decision about a student's placement, you might talk with your school's administrators, the student's other teachers, and perhaps his or her parents. Try to avoid pressure to place an older student in a level that is too advanced for him or her. Language facility is not completely age-related. If at first a student must be put into a class with younger students, you might want to make an extra effort to move the student forward in his or her development of the language so that he or she can move forward into a class with students who are the same age.

If a new student's knowledge of English is greater than that of the other students, you might want to have him or her stay in the class (with the students in his or her age group); however, you can use that student as a "resource person" in the classroom. For example, you can ask that student to help you demonstrate dialogues and games or be a small group leader. You can also encourage the student to do extra activities that are more advanced than the activities of the other students in the class.

Guidelines for Testing

Try to make the testing conditions as relaxed as possible. Remember that this may be viewed by the student as a threatening experience. You will want to do everything you can to lessen the tension. Smile, sit down at the student's level, and use a conversational approach.

If you and the student speak the same language, converse for a short time in the student's native language. Then switch to English. For example, greet the student in the native language, ask his or her name and what his or her favorite subject is. Then ask in English, "Do you speak English?" If the student answers "yes," ask questions such as these:

How old are you?
Where do you live?
How many brothers do you have?
How many sisters do you have?
What day is it today?

If the student cannot answer these basic questions, he or she should begin Book 1 of *New Parade*. If the student answers your questions correctly and with very little difficulty, go on to the Placement Test on pages xxviii-xxix.

While the student is taking the Placement Test, you should observe his or her behavior. If you see that the student is experiencing frustration, you may want to have him or her stop taking the test.

A student who answers ten of the twenty-three items correctly can begin *New Parade*, Book 2. A student who answers eighteen of the items correctly can begin *New Parade*, Book 3. A student who easily and correctly completes this test might need to be placed in a higher level of *New Parade*. You will want to continue by giving that student the Placement Test found in the Teacher's Edition of Book 4.

Procedures for Testing

The test on pages xxviii-xxix can be administered to one student or to a group of students. Duplicate a copy of the test for each student and make sure each student has a pencil or a crayon.

Begin by pointing to individual pictures on page xxviii and asking students to identify them. If a student cannot name any of the items, he or she should not continue the test and should be placed in *New Parade*, Book 1.

Page xxviii, Activity 1: Read. Draw lines to match.
Read the instructions aloud. Make sure that the students understand that they are to read silently and draw lines to match each sentence to its corresponding picture. You may wish to stop for a few minutes to glance over the students' responses. If a student marked all of the items incorrectly, have that student stop taking the test. ANSWERS: 1. b 2. d 3. a 4. c

Page xxviii, Activity 2: Listen. Circle. Read the instructions aloud. For each item, the students should circle the number in the sentence they hear. Play the audio or read the audioscript aloud two or more times for the students to complete the activity.
AUDIOSCRIPT: 1. There are twenty-four children in my class. 2. There are twelve children at the birthday party. 3. There are thirteen candles on the cake. 4. There are twenty-six presents on the table!
ANSWERS: 1. 24 2. 12 3. 13 4. 26

Page xxviii, Activity 3: Read. Number in order:
1, 2, 3, 4, 5. Read the instructions aloud. Make sure that the students understand that the sentences are not in the correct order; the students should read the sentences and decide which sentence should be first, second, third, and so on, before they write the corresponding numbers.
ANSWERS: 3. We eat sandwiches at 1:00 in the afternoon. 1. We get up at 7:00 in the morning. 2. We go to school at 9:00 in the morning. 5. We go to bed at 9:00 at night. 4. We watch TV at 4:00 in the afternoon.

Page xxix, Activity 4: Look. Listen. Circle.
Read the instructions aloud. Explain to the students that they should look at the picture, listen to the question, and circle the answer *yes* or *no.* Then play the audio or read the audioscript aloud two or more times.
AUDIOSCRIPT: 1. Is the mail carrier behind the jeep? 2. Is the mail carrier in the jeep? 3. Is the jeep in front of the post office? 4. Is the bank next to the video shop?
ANSWERS: 1. no 2. yes 3. yes 4. no

Page xxix, Activity 5: Look. Read. Write. Read the instructions aloud. Explain to the students that they should look at the picture, read the question, look for the answer in the Word Bank, and write the answer on the line after the question.
ANSWERS: 1. Yes, there are. 2. No, there isn't. 3. Yes, there is. 4. No, they aren't. 5. Yes, it is. 6. Yes, they do.

Unit Tests

The tests on pages xxxi–xxxix are individual Unit Tests for the students to take after they finish each of the nine *New Parade* Units.

Unit 1 Test

Page xxxi: Fill the book bag. Draw lines. Focus attention on the book bag and the items surrounding it. Make sure that the students understand that they are to decide which items could go into the bag. They then draw lines from their choices to the book bag.
ANSWERS: 3 pencils 2 books 5 markers

Unit 2 Test

Page xxxii: Find the family. Draw lines. Read instructions aloud. Point to words in the left column. Then instruct the students to draw lines to the appropriate pictures of family members in the right column.

ANSWERS: 1. *Baby* is drawn to second picture. 2. *Father* is drawn to sixth picture. 3. *Mother* is drawn to fourth picture. 4. *Brother* is drawn to first picture. 5. *Sister* is drawn to fifth picture. 6. *Angie* is drawn to third picture.

Unit 3 Test

Page xxxiii: Circle the word. Point out the doll in the middle of the page. Make sure the students understand that in each item they are to underline which phrase is correct and then draw a line to that feature on the doll.
ANSWERS: 1. her face 2. her hair 3. her shoulder 4. her arm 5. her knee 6. her foot

Unit 4 Test

Page xxxiv: Color their clothes. Make sure that each student has crayons or markers of the following colors: *blue, yellow, pink, orange, red, black.* Explain to the students that they will color the clothing according to the descriptions in the sentences. Read the sentences aloud to complete the activity. Check each student's answers by comparing the colors they used to the descriptions.

Unit 5 Test

Page xxxv: Find the rooms. Draw lines. Focus the students' attention on the picture of the inside of a house. Make sure they notice all the rooms that are shown. Then ask them to read the six questions below it. Instruct the students to draw lines from the questions to the rooms, as you read them aloud.

Unit 6 Test

Page xxxvi: Find the animal. Circle it. Read the instructions aloud. Make sure the students understand that they are to look at each word and then circle the appropriate pictures.
ANSWERS: 1. *Dog* is circled. 2. *Cow* is circled. 3. *Fish* is circled. 4. *Horse* is circled. 5. *Frog* is circled. 6. *Cat* is circled.

Unit 7 Test

Page xxxvii: It's Teresa's birthday. Circle the food. Focus attention on the picture of Teresa. Point out the food words on the list that she is holding. Then instruct the students to circle the food in the picture that matches the food words on Teresa's list.
ANSWERS: Food items *pizza, milk, cake, hot dog, ice cream*

Unit 8 Test

Page xxxviii: Help Marti. Draw lines. Focus attention on Marti's messy room Then ask the students to read the five instructions. Make sure they understand that they are to draw lines from the items to the appropriate areas. ANSWERS: 1. *Marbles* are drawn to in the toy box. 2. *Skate* is drawn to in the closet. 3. The *boat* is drawn to on the table. 4. *Ball* is drawn to under the table. 5. *Doll* is drawn to on the chair.

Unit 9 Test

Page xxxix: Circle the answer. Focus attention to the swimming-pool scene. Then ask the students to read the instructions. Make sure they understand that they are to circle the correct answer in each pair of sentences below the illustration. ANSWERS: 1. Lucy is swimming. 2. The woman is reading. 3. Josh is swimming. 4. The little girl is flying the kite. 5. Kim is throwing a ball. 6. Pedro is catching the ball.

Mastery Tests

The tests on pages xl–xlv are mastery tests for the students to take after completing Units 3, 6, and 9 (see also the instructions below). Before administering any of these tests, have the students complete the practice tests, which are found after Units 3, 6, and 9 in the Workbook.

Book 1, Units 1–3 Test

Page xl, Activity 1: Listen. Count. Circle. Make sure that the students understand that they are to look at the picture, listen to the question, and circle the number that answers the question. Then play the audio or read the audioscript several times for the students to complete the activity. AUDIOSCRIPT: 1. How many girls do you see? 2. How many boys do you see? 3. How many tables do you see? 4. How many books do you see? 5. How many book bags do you see? 6. How many pencils do you see? 7. How many babies do you see? 8. How many fathers do you see? ANSWERS: 1. The *two* is circled. 2. The *two* is circled. 3. The *one* is circled. 4. The *five* is circled. 5. The *three*

is circled. 6. The *three* is circled. 7. The *one* is circled. 8. The *one* is circled.

Page xli, Activity 2: Listen and color. Make sure that each student has crayons or markers of the following colors: *blue, brown, green, orange, purple, red,* and *yellow.* Explain to the students that they will color the monster according to the instructions they hear. Then play the audio or read the audioscript several times for the students to complete the activity. Check each student's answers by comparing the colors they used to the colors of the body parts in the audioscript. AUDIOSCRIPT: 1. Color his hair brown. 2. Color his hands yellow. 3. Color his feet brown. 4. Color his eyes green. 5. Color his ears orange. 6. Color his mouth red. 7. Color his legs blue. 8. Color his arms purple.

Book 1, Units 4–6 Test

Page xlii, Activity 1: Listen and color. Make sure that each student has crayons or markers of the following colors: *black, blue, brown, green, orange, pink, purple, red,* and *yellow.* Explain to the students that they will color the items in the picture according to the instructions they hear. Then play the audio or read the audioscript aloud several times for the students to complete the activity. Check each student's answers by comparing the colors they used to the colors of the items in the audioscript. AUDIOSCRIPT: 1. Color her dress pink. 2. Color her shoes black. 3. Color his shirt red. 4. Color his pants blue. 5. Color his shoes brown. 6. Color the table yellow. 7. Color the circle orange. 8. Color the triangles red. 9. Color the rectangle purple. 10. Color the squares green.

Page xliii, Activity 2: Listen and circle. Explain to the students that they should look at the pictures and circle the one they hear described. Then play the audio or read the audioscript aloud several times for the students to complete the activity. AUDIOSCRIPT: 1. It's a big dog. 2. It's a little cat. 3. The bug is crawling. 4. The horse is jumping. 5. The duck is flying. 6. The boy is watching TV. ANSWERS: 1. The *big dog* is circled. 2. The *little cat* is circled. 3. The *bug* is circled. 4. The *horse that is jumping* is circled. 5. The *duck that is flying* is circled. 6. The *boy who is watching TV* is circled.

Book 1, Units 7–9 Test

Page xliv, Activity 1: Listen and circle.
Explain to the students that they should look at the pictures and circle the word or picture for the word they hear in the sentence. Then play the audio or read the audioscript aloud several times for the students to complete the activity.
AUDIOSCRIPT: 1. Today is Sunday. 2. I see the number sixteen. 3. The car is under the table. 4. I want a bike. 5. I want marbles. 6. I have a boat. 7. I have ice cream.

ANSWERS: 1. *Sunday* is circled. 2. The number *sixteen* is circled. 3. The car that is *under* the table is circled. 4. The *bike* is circled. 5. The *marbles* are circled. 6. The *boat* is circled. 7. The *ice cream* is circled.

Page xlv, Activity 2: Read and match. Have the students draw a line from each word to the correct corresponding picture.
ANSWERS: 1. girl eating 2. boy throwing a ball 3. boy skating 4. boy swimming 5. girl running 6. girl riding a bike 7. girl flying a kite 8. boy kicking a ball

Placement Test

1. Read. Draw lines to match.

1. He's reading.

2. She's coloring.

3. They're eating.

4. It's climbing a tree.

a.

b.

c.

d.

2. Listen. Circle.

1. **21   24   29**   2. **10   12   20**

3. **13   30   50**   4. **26   60   16**

3. Read. Number in order: 1, 2, 3, 4, 5.

_____   We eat sandwiches at 1:00 in the afternoon.

_____   We get up at 7:00 in the morning.

_____   We go to school at 9:00 in the morning.

_____   We go to bed at 9:00 at night.

_____   We watch TV at 4:00 in the afternoon.

New Parade Copyright © 2000 by Addison Wesley Lorgman, Inc.

4. Look. Listen. Circle.

1. Yes   No   2. Yes   No
3. Yes   No   4. Yes   No

5. Look. Read. Write.

1. Are there monkeys in the zoo? _____.

2. Is there a cat in the zoo? _____.

3. Is there a bird in the zoo? _____.

4. Are the monkeys eating ice cream? _____.

5. Is the bird flying? _____.

6. Do the monkeys have long tails? _____.

Unit 1 Test

Fill the book bag. Draw lines.

2 desks

3 pencils

5 markers

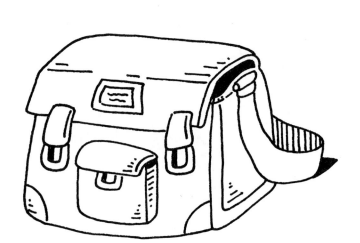

1 chair

1 table

2 books

Unit 2 Test

1. baby

2. father

3. mother

4. brother

5. sister

6. Angie

✔ Unit 3 Test

Circle the word.

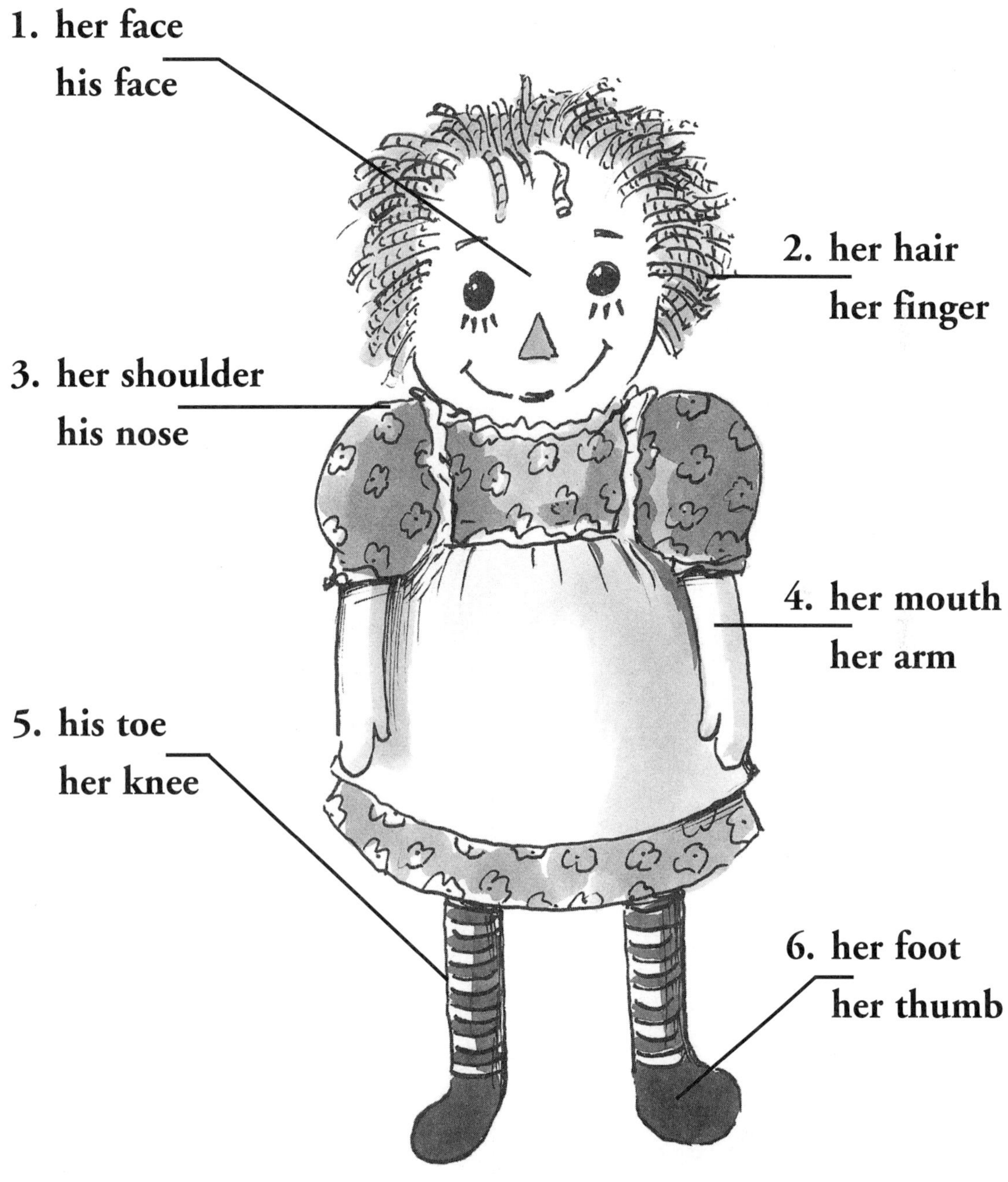

1. her face
   his face

2. her hair
   her finger

3. her shoulder
   his nose

4. her mouth
   her arm

5. his toe
   her knee

6. her foot
   her thumb

Unit 4 Test

Color their clothes.

1. Her dress is blue.

2. She has yellow socks.

3. Her shoes are pink.

4. His sweater is orange.

5. He has a red hat.

6. His pants are black.

Unit 5 Test

Find the rooms. Draw lines.

1. Where is the bedroom?   2. Where is the closet?

3. Where is the kitchen?   4. Where is the living room?

5. Where is the bathroom?   6. Where is the dining room?

Unit 6 Test

Find the animal. Circle it.

1. dog

2. cow

3. fish

4. horse

5. frog

6. cat

Unit 7 Test

It's Teresa's birthday. Circle the food.

Unit 8 Test

1. Put the marbles in the toy box.

2. Put the skate in the closet.

3. Put the boat on the table.

4. Put the ball under the table.

5. Put the doll on the chair.

✔ Unit 9 Test

Circle the answer.

1. Lucy is swimming.
   Lucy is dancing.

2. The woman is reading.
   The woman is swimming.

3. Josh is jumping rope.
   Josh is swimming.

4. The little girl is reading.
   The little girl is flying a kite.

5. Kim is running.
   Kim is throwing a ball.

6. Pedro is catching the ball.
   Pedro is jumping rope.

✔ Units 1–3 Test

1. Listen. Count. Circle.

1. **1** **2** **3**   2. **2** **4** **7**

3. **1** **2** **3**   4. **3** **5** **8**

5. **3** **6** **10**   6. **3** **6** **7**

7. **1** **4** **5**   8. **1** **2** **8**

2. Listen and color.

✔ Units 4–6 Test

1. Listen and color.

New Parade Copyright © 2000 by Addison Wesley Longman, Inc.

1.

2.

3.

4.

5.

6.

Units 7-9 Test

1. Listen and circle.

1. Today is   Sunday   Saturday   Tuesday

2. I see

3. The car is

4. I want a

5. I want

6. I have a

7. I have

2. Read and match.

Draw a line from the word to the picture.

1. eating

2. throwing

3. skating

4. swimming

5. running

6. riding

7. flying a kite

8. kicking

Introducing the Mascots

Each Student Book in the *New Parade* series has its own male and female mascots (see their pictures on page 1 of the Student Book). These mascots serve different purposes throughout the units. The students may see the mascots model target language such as, "What did you eat for lunch yesterday?" or ask questions such as, "Do you like the city or the country?" The mascots also provide information about language, such as "didn't = did not." They may also give additional directions to the students such as, "Write the secret word on the line."

In addition to their informative function, the mascots are meant to foster a sense of class identity and to provide a fun way of interacting in English in the classroom. Use enlarged illustrations of the mascots to create puppets or characters to "stick" to the board. Take a class photo in front of the board upon which are pictures of the mascots; when the photo is ready, decorate a frame for it and display it. Have the students design a class emblem with the mascot in it and display it on the door. Make bookmarks with pictures of the mascots to award as prizes. Trace the mascot design on T-shirts or handkerchiefs to give to the students. Use the names of the mascots to identify teams during group activities and games. Encourage the students to make up rhymes and songs with the mascots as the characters. Create a class cheer about the mascots. The possibilities are endless!

For the first day of class, have models of the mascots large enough for the students to see in front of the classroom. Use them to introduce or review language such as, "Hi, I'm Homer. Nice to meet you!" or "What's your name? Where are you from?" or "This is the teacher. Her name is Ms. Martin." Use them to assess the range of the students' knowledge as well. Ask the students to describe the mascots or do "interviews" with them to assess their vocabulary and knowledge of question formation and other structures. Have them write a few sentences about the mascots. Have blank name tags with the mascot logo in one corner ready for the students to fill in with their names on the first day. The students get to write something in English in their very first class period ("My name is _____."), and the teacher has a good way to identify new students.

Get-Acquainted Activities

It is very important to put the students at ease as soon as possible and to have them know that their English classroom is a fun, comfortable, and exciting place to be. Be as patient, friendly, and supportive as possible the first day of class. Encourage the students to interact in English by using any of the following activities.

The Ball Game Have ready a soft ball made of sponge or other material. Have the students stand in a circle. Say, "Hello. I'm _____." Then throw the ball to a student. Help the student say the same, using his or her own name. After the student has finished, he or she throws the ball to another student. When it is clear that the students are beginning to remember most of the names, stop throwing the ball. To check, simply point to different students in the circle and ask for their names from the other students.

The Alphabet and Name Game Have ready large cards, each one showing a letter of the alphabet. Make sure that you have as many repetitions of the same letters as needed. Begin by teaching or reviewing the pronunciation of the English letters. When the students can say them without much difficulty, model the following. Say, "S is for Sara" (if Sara is your name) or "B is for Mr. Brown" (if you prefer to be called by your last name). As you say this, hold up your letter card. Have all the students do the same with their own letters and names.

The Rhyme Game Teach the students how to shake hands or how to "high five" (two students raise their arms high and then slap their upraised hands together). Then teach this rhyme:

> I am (María).
> I'm not shy.
> Give me your hand.
> Hello there, Hi!

Begin the game by saying the rhyme with your name and then shaking hands or giving the high five to a student. That student repeats the rhyme with his or her own name and then shakes hands or high fives the teacher. When the students understand what to do, have them circulate around the room, find partners, say the rhyme, and continue circulating. Stop the activity when all the students have practiced several exchanges.

1 My Class

Communication Objectives

to introduce oneself
to exchange greetings and introductions
to identify *red, green,* and *blue*
to identify the numbers *1–10*
to identify classroom objects
to identify circles
to exchange leave-takings
to understand simple classroom commands

Language Objectives

to use the simple present tense of *be* first and third persons singular
to answer questions with *yes/no*
to answer questions with *what* plus *is*
to answer questions with *what color* plus *is*
to pronounce /k/

Learning Strategies and Thinking Skills

to classify
to understand sequence
to make associations

Content Connections

Art: to make puppets; to make name tags; to draw pictures of classroom objects
Mathematics: to count; to sequence numbers
Music: to sing a song

Materials

New Parade 1 Student Book, pages 2–11
New Parade 1 Workbook, pages 1–8; 81–83
New Parade 1 Audio: Tape/CD
New Parade 1 Video and Video Guide
New Parade 1 Posters
Classroom objects; craft sticks; glue; crayons or markers; ball; blue, green, or red pieces of paper; string; scissors; paper bags or boxes; game pieces; coins

Optional Materials: New Parade Picture Cards—playground, swing, slide, apple, bananas, ball; paper; name tags; safety pins or tape; cardboard; red, green, or blue cutouts; folders; colored objects; *Little Celebrations—Mrs. Sato's Hens* by Laura Min

Key Vocabulary

- book, book bag, chair, desk, marker, pencil, table, teacher
- circle, color, name
- one, two, three, four, five, six, seven, eight, nine, ten
- a, the
- good-bye, good morning, hello
- no, yes
- what, what color
- am, is
- I'm, it's, what's
- Get the book.; Open/Close your book.; Raise your hand.; Sit down.; Stand up.
- it
- your, this
- blue, green, red

Picture Dictionary

book pencil desk marker chair table book bag

Setting Up the Classroom

Before class, read through and familiarize yourself with Unit 1. Make sure you gather together the materials and supplies you will need. For the TPR warm-up routines on page T2, you might want to write a list of simple commands in advance. Prepare sign cards for common expressions to hang on the walls. See Warm Up, page T5. Read the Little Book, *Ready for School!* to familiarize yourself with the story.

Using the Video and the Video Guide

Begin by showing the video to set the stage for the unit. The students will get a preview of the language they will be learning in context, even if they don't understand everything at first. Repeat the video segment often, especially at the beginning of each week. As the students become familiar with the vocabulary and structures in this unit, they will understand more and more of it. Use the Video Guide to find where to stop and start the video. Encourage the students to interact with the video by answering questions, singing, and doing the actions along with the children in the video.

The video segment for Unit 1 takes place at school. The children say "Good morning," and then check to see that they have all the supplies they need for school, holding up each item as they name them. Then, in the classroom, Bobby and Ana greet their teacher. In the last scene, the children ask questions about Bobby's book bag, "What's in the bag? What's this?" Bobby writes an essay naming and counting the things in his class. He counts to ten.

Family Connections

Encourage the students to look around a room in their homes and to see how many objects they can name there. Suggest that the students teach the English names for these objects to their families. Ask the students to draw some of the blue, red, and green objects in their rooms at home. Then have them bring their pictures to class, show them to classmates and say the names of the objects they know.

Bulletin Board Ideas

Put the words *red, blue,* and *green,* along with cut-out squares of those colors across the top of the bulletin board. As the students work through the unit, encourage them to put under the correct colors, pictures of red, blue, or green objects that they cut out of magazines or draw. Use the bulletin board to review and expand the language in Unit 1. For example, "What's this?" (*It's a chair.*) "What color is it? How do you say _____ in English?"

Little Book: Ready for School!

Summary: A mother helps a boy pack his book bag to get ready for a busy day at school.

1 My Class

1. Look. Listen. Sing.

Hello. What's your name?

I'm Homer.

Good morning to you,
Good morning to you,
Good morning, dear teacher,
Good morning to you.

Objectives

to exchange greetings and introductions
to identify classroom objects
to understand simple classroom commands
to sing a song
to make puppets and name tags

Key Vocabulary

- name
- book, book bag, chair, desk, marker, pencil, table
- good morning, hello
- teacher
- I'm, what's
- your

WARM UP

1. 🧍 Use TPR to introduce or review classroom commands that the students would follow in school, such as *stand up, sit down, raise your hand, open/close your book,* and *get (the book)*. You may wish to begin each class with a short TPR activity. See page ix for more information.

2. Display real objects such as books, markers, book bags, and pencils, and check if any students know such words as *chair*.

3. Display the Poster for Unit 1.

PRESENTATION

Using the Page

ACTIVITY 1

Look. Listen. Sing.

1. Touch objects or furnishings in the classroom and introduce or review each name: *chair, desk, table,* and so on. Encourage the students to repeat the name orally.

2. 🎧 Play the audio or sing the song several times until the students can sing along.

Language Note: When referring to paper, tell students to say, "It's paper." The mass/count noun distinction will be taught later.

3. 🎧 Focus attention on Hanna and Homer. Write their names on the board. Play the audio or read their conversation several times for the students to repeat.

4. ⇄ The students cut out Homer and Hanna on page 93 and copy their names from the board. Help the students make stick puppets.

5. Have pairs of students use their Homer and Hanna puppets to act out the conversation. The students can take turns asking, "Hello. What's your name?" and saying, "I'm _____."

Reaching All Students

⇄ **Name Tags** Help the students make name tags and write their names on them. Help them tape or pin their name tags to their clothes. Have pairs of students use the name tags to practice introductions and greetings. You may want to have the students also work in groups of three. One student introduces a second student to the third by reading the name tag. Model the necessary language, "Bob, this is María."

Vocabulary Expansion Focus attention on the Picture Dictionary on pages 2–3. Have the students point to each picture and repeat the words (*book, pencil, desk, marker, chair, table, book bag, pencil*).

Workbook

Page 1, Activity 1: Draw and color. Draw a picture of yourself on the board. Say "This is me." Have the students draw and color a picture of themselves on the page. Ask individuals, "Who is this?" Help them say, "This is me."

Page 1, Activity 2: Write your name. Read the question. Point to several students and ask, "What's your name?" Help the students write their names on the line provided.

UNIT 1 • My Class

Objectives

to introduce oneself
to identify *red, green,* and *blue*
to identify classroom objects
to sing a song
to pronounce /k/

Key Vocabulary

• color, marker, name
• it
• am, is
• I'm, it's, what's
• what
• blue, green, red
• your

PRESENTATION

Using the Page
ACTIVITY 2
Play the game.

1. Have the students look at the picture, naming anything they can say in English.

2. Read the conversation two or three times for the students to repeat.

3. Have the students form a circle. Throw a ball or any other soft object to a student. Ask, "What's your name?" Have the student answer, "I'm (Teresa)." Have that student toss the ball to another student and ask, "What's your name?" and so on.

ACTIVITY 3
Look and say.

1. Give each student a piece of paper that is blue, green, or red. Introduce or review the name of each color and encourage the students to say the words. Ask the students with a certain color to follow commands such as "Blues, sit down."

2. Point to one of the pictured markers and identify its color, "It's (red)." Do this for the three markers. Repeat several times for the students to repeat.

Note: Throughout this book, you will find words in parentheses ( ): for example, "It's (red)." The parentheses indicate that other vocabulary items may be substituted.

3. Point to each marker and ask the students to identify the color. Ask, "What color is it?" *(It's blue.)*

ACTIVITY 4
Look. Listen. Sing.

1. Focus attention on the picture of the red marker. Then play the audio or sing the song. To practice pronunciation, focus on /k/ in *color.*

2. Repeat the song for the other two colors.

3. Hold up classroom objects that are red, green, or blue. Substitute the new object and color for those in the song.

Reaching All Students

Introductions Divide the class into two equal groups. Have the groups form circles, one inside the other. Make sure the students are facing each other. Begin clapping your hands. As you clap, have the circles move in opposite directions. When you stop clapping, have the two circles stop moving. Ask the students to introduce themselves to the person in front of them.

Workbook

Page 2, Activity 3: Listen and color. Have the students identify the three classroom objects. Play the audio or read the directions aloud several times. Check to see that the students have colored the objects correctly. AUDIOSCRIPT: Color the marker red. Color the pencil blue. Color the book green.

Page 2, Activity 4: Find the objects and color. Have the students use the small pictures in Activity 3 as clues to find and color the objects in the big picture. They should color all the markers red, all the pencils blue, and all the books green.

T3

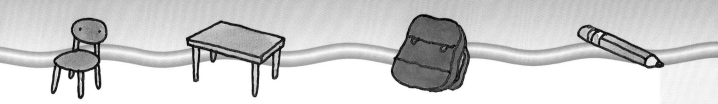

2. Play the game.

What's your name?

I'm Teresa.

3. Look and say.

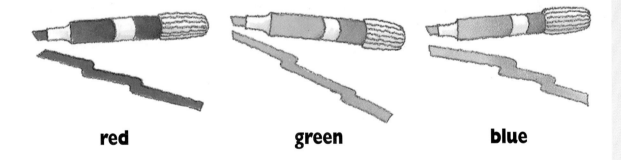

red   green   blue

4. Look. Listen. Sing.

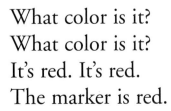

What color is it?
What color is it?
It's red. It's red.
The marker is red.

5. Read. Point. Say.

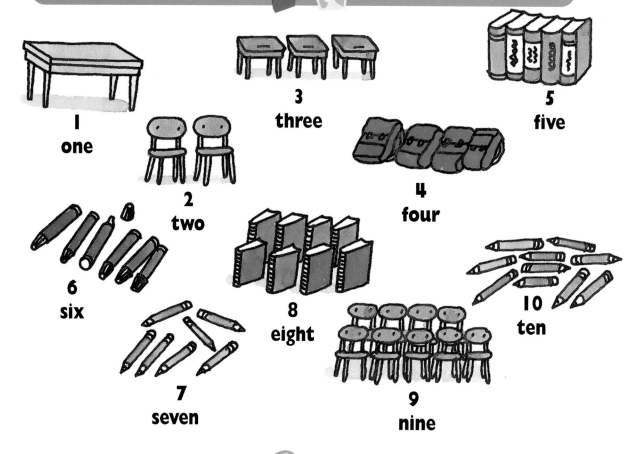

1 one

2 two

3 three

4 four

5 five

6 six

7 seven

8 eight

9 nine

10 ten

6. Listen and circle.

1.

2.

3.

Objectives

to identify the numbers *1–10*
to identify circles
to answer questions with *what* plus *is*
to answer questions with *what color* plus *is*
to understand sequence
to make associations

Key Vocabulary

- one, two, three, four, five, six, seven, eight, nine, ten
- circle, what, what color
- the

PRESENTATION

Using the Page

ACTIVITY 5

Read. Point. Say.

1. Read the number words for the numerals 1–10 several times for the students to repeat.

2. 🔆 Say the numbers in random order and ask the students to point to the correct word.

3. Point to an object and ask the students to identify it and its color by asking, "What's this?" and "What color is it?"

Reaching All Students

🔆 📧 **Number Sequence** Have the students count off from one to ten. Have all the (ones) get together and each make a flashcard of their number. Then have a series of ten students stand across the front of the room in mixed-up numerical order. The rest of the class must give instructions to put them in the correct numerical order, "Carlos is three. Ana is four. "

Workbook

Page 3, Activity 5: Count and write. Have the students count the objects in each set and write the correct number word on the line. Have the students present their pages and say what the items are and how many items are in each set. ANSWERS: three books, seven markers, four desks, one table, ten pencils, two chairs

---

PRACTICE

ACTIVITY 6

Listen and circle.

1. Give each student a piece of string. Draw a circle on the board. Then have them curve and join the string to make a circle.

2. 🎧 Model the sample exercise. Play the audio or say, "Circle the number two." Then play the tape or read the tapescript aloud two or three times for the students to complete the activity.
   AUDIOSCRIPT: 1. Circle the number three. 2. Circle the number seven. 3. Circle the number ten.

3. ⬜ Point to a numeral. Ask, "What is it? What color is it?"

Reaching All Students

⬜ **Vocabulary Check** Have the students identify the objects in the Picture Dictionary on pages 4–5.

Workbook

🎧 **Page 4, Activity 6: Listen and circle the number.** Model the sample exercise, "Circle the number three." Then play the audio or read the audioscript aloud two or three times for the students to complete the activity.
AUDIOSCRIPT: 1. Circle the number nine. 2. Circle the number one. 3. Circle the number eight.

Objectives

to identify classroom objects
to identify *red, green,* and *blue*
to understand simple classroom language
to use the simple present tense of *be*
to answer questions with *yes/no*
to answer questions with *what* plus *is*
to draw pictures of classroom objects
to count

Key Vocabulary

• book, chair, desk, marker, pencil, table
• it's, what's, a
• this
• blue, green, red

PRACTICE

Warm Up

Write *How do you say (eraser) in English?, What does (door) mean?,* and *I don't understand* on the board. Explain what each means and how it is to be used in the class. Encourage the students to use this language instead of their native language when asking for help. Prepare sign cards with these expressions written on them. Refer to them every time the expression is given in a student's native language.

Using the Page

ACTIVITY 7

Draw and answer.

1. Have the students draw pictures in the correct square for the labels *table, chair, desk,* and *marker.*

2. Have them color their pictures either red, blue, or green.

3. Focus attention on Hanna and Homer. Play the audio or read their conversation aloud two or three times for the students to repeat.

4. Call out each classroom object word and have the students point to the picture of the object. Say, "What's this?" Encourage the students to answer together, "It's a (table)."

Reaching All Students

Puppet Conversation Ask the students to present their drawings by using their Homer and Hanna puppets from page 93.

Guess the Object Students work in pairs. Present and tape on the board six classroom objects. Give one student in each pair one of the same classroom objects or a picture of the object. Make sure the students don't see each other's object. Have them hold their objects behind their backs. Explain that they are going to take turns guessing which of the six items the other is holding. For example, "Is it a marker?" "No."

Vocabulary Matching Game Distribute six pieces of cardboard the size of an index card. Ask the students to draw one classroom object on each. You may want to write the names of the objects on the board. Put the students into pairs and have them combine their "packs" of cards. Have them lay the cards face-down and mix them up. The pairs play a matching game by turning over any two cards. As they turn over the card, they must identify the object pictured. If the cards match and the student identifies the object correctly, the student keeps the pair. If the cards match, but the student incorrectly identifies the object, the cards must be turned over again. Play continues with the students taking turns. The student with the most pairs wins.

Workbook

Page 4, Activity 7: Match the numbers and pictures. Model the first answer. Have the students point to the word *two.* Have them trace the line from the *two* to the picture of the two chairs. Then have the students count the objects in the other sets and draw a line from each number word to the correct picture of the objects.

Language Activities Section, page 81
ANSWERS: 1. yes 2. yes 3. no 4. yes 5. yes 6. no 7. no

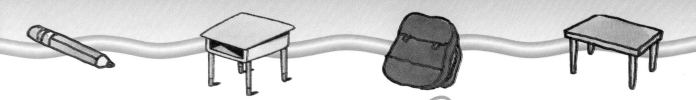

7. Draw and answer.

table

chair

desk

marker

What's this?

It's a book.

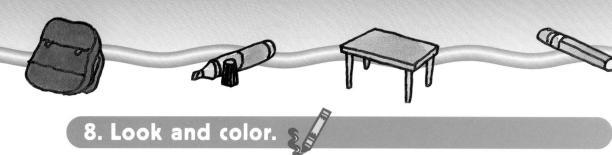

8. Look and color.

1 = 2 = 3 =

Objectives

to identify *red, green,* and *blue*
to identify classroom objects
to use simple classroom language
to classify by color
to make associations

Key Vocabulary

• blue, green, red

APPLICATION

Using the Page
ACTIVITY 8
Look and color.

Introduce or review the playground items in the picture: *swing, slide, jungle gym, merry-go-round.* (You may wish to display Picture Cards of playground, swing, and slide.) Then have the students color the picture. All the 1s should be red, all the 2s should be blue, and all the 3s should be green.

Reaching All Students

Vocabulary Enrichment This may be an appropriate time to present or review additional vocabulary the students need to know such as *scissors* and *Can I go to the bathroom?*

What color are you wearing? Prepare color cutouts of red, green, and blue for the students to pin on their clothing. Have the students say what color they are wearing and show the class their clothes. As a class, count how many people are wearing red, blue, and green. Illustrate the results by writing a chart on the board with the colors in the left column and the numbers of students along the top.

I Spy Explain to the students that they will be detectives and look for things in the room. You may want to tape up cutouts of particular objects that are visible to all children. Select one object and say, "I spy something (blue)." Students should look around the room and name (blue) objects that they think you see. If the vocabulary is not known, the students may point to it or touch the object. The student who correctly guesses what you "spy" begins the next round with "I spy something _____."

Colorful Classroom Objects Distribute to the students sheets of paper that are labeled *Red, Green,* and *Blue.* Have the students draw classroom objects of their choice on each sheet using the color. Then have the students present their pictures to the class.

Color Game Make a "color road" by taping pieces of red, blue, and green paper to the floor. Have the students take turns hopping down the road on one foot as the class chants and claps in rhythm: "Hop on red! Hop on blue! Hop on green too!"

Folders Make folders out of folded construction paper or ask each student to bring a blank folder to class. Have the students write their names on their folders and draw a picture of their school. The students can keep their English work for the year in this folder. This portfolio can be collected at the end of each unit. The contents can be assessed and recorded on the student assessment chart on page xxiii.

Workbook

Page 5, Activity 8: Make cards. Have the students color the cards using their red, green, or blue markers. Make sure they use only one color for each picture. Then have the students cut out the cards and write the name of each object pictured on each card. Then the students can use the cards as flashcards to review the words for classroom objects and the colors *red, green,* and *blue.*

Language Activities Section, page 82
ANSWERS: 1. blue 2. red 3. green

Story Summary

A mother helps a boy pack his book bag to get ready for a busy day at school.

Key Unit Vocabulary

a, book, book bag, good morning, I'm, is, markers, pencils, red

Word Bank

ready, write, draw

BEFORE READING

WARM UP

Invite the students to unpack some items from their book bags or backpacks and place the items on their desks. Then ask them to name the common objects they unpack, such as pencils, markers, books, and crayons.

PUT TOGETHER THE LITTLE BOOK

Ask the students to take pages 7–8 out of their books. Have them fold the pages in half to make the Little Book, *Ready for School!*

PREVIEW THE LITTLE BOOK

1. After the books are folded, the students can look at the pictures and point out objects they recognize.

2. After previewing the pictures, read the title aloud. Ask, "What is this story about?" Let the students look at the pictures and tell what they see the boy doing. Then ask them to predict what the boy does to get ready for school.

SHARE NEW WORDS

Write the Word Bank words on the board. Say and point to each word and ask the students to raise their hands if they know the word. Have them repeat the words after you. Use TPR to show the meanings of the action words.

DURING READING

READING THE LITTLE BOOK

After the students have previewed the Little Book, *Ready for School!* model reading the story. They can listen to the story as you read it or play the audio. Tell them they can ask questions and talk about the story when you read it again.

GUIDED READING

Read the story aloud as the students follow along. Point to each word as you say it and encourage the students to track the print in their books as they read.

TEACHER TIPS

Read the story with expression, especially the exclamations. As you read, you may also wish to point to real-life objects that are mentioned in the story, or to Picture Cards of apple, bananas, and ball.

REREADING

Return to the students' predictions about the story and have them compare their predictions with what actually takes place. Go back through the book and let volunteers retell what happens in the story. Then assess their comprehension with questions such as these:

Page 1 *What is the boy getting ready for?*
Page 2 *What does the boy use to write and draw?*
Page 3 *What does the boy pack?*
Page 4 *What can happen next?*

Point out objects in the picture on each page that will help the students understand the comprehension questions.

Good morning, Mother.
I'm getting ready for school.

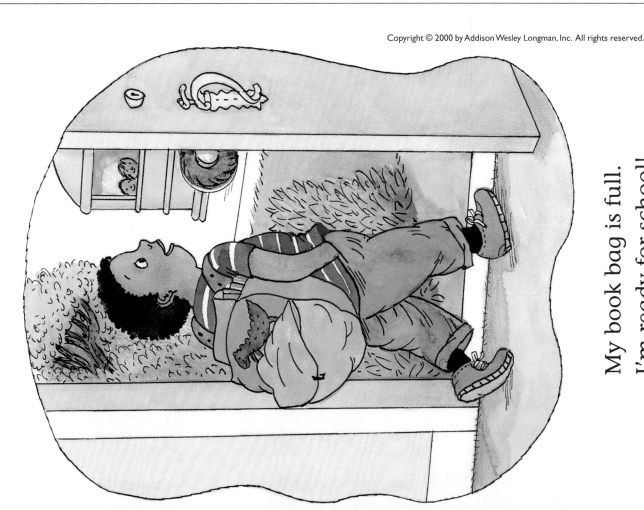

My book bag is full.
I'm ready for school!

Books to read.
Pencils and markers
to write and draw.

An apple, a banana,
a little red ball!

AFTER READING

Activities for Developing Language

RETELL THE STORY

Pairs can work together to use the illustrations to retell the story to each other.

CONTEXT CLUES

Reread the story aloud, pausing before key words such as *pencils, markers, write, draw, ball,* and *school* so the students can supply the missing word.

CLASSIFYING

Have the students gather the following objects: an apple, a banana, a little red ball, markers, and pencils. Then have the students classify the items by telling what things they can eat, what things they can write with, and what things they can play with.

ACT IT OUT!

The students can gather props that are used in the story. Then let pairs work together to act out the story. One partner can be the boy and the other can be the mother. The students can use the pictures to help them recall what the boy says or retell the dialogue in their own words.

MATH CONNECTION

Ask each student to take one thing out of his or her book bag. Then tally how many students took out a pencil, a marker, a book, or another object. Make a simple bar graph and have the students tell what the graph shows.

WRITE ABOUT IT!

Brainstorm with the students the different things they like to take to school. List their ideas on the board. Then write the following on the board and have volunteers fill in the blanks with words from the list.

1. I color with _____.

2. I read the _____.

3. I eat the _____.

GRAMMAR CONNECTION: EXCLAMATION MARKS

Point out the exclamation marks in the story. Explain that when they see this mark, it means the speaker says the sentence with a lot of feeling. Model reading these sentences and invite the students to read with you.

WORKBOOK

Little Book Comprehension, page 83.

BULLETIN BOARD IDEAS

You may wish to have the students decorate a bulletin board titled *Our Book Bags* with drawings of objects they carry in their own bags. They can label each item.

FAMILY CONNECTION

Invite the students to take their Little Books home and share them with their friends and family members.

Objectives

to identify classroom objects
to identify *red, green,* and *blue*
to classify classroom objects
to answer questions with *yes/no*

Key Vocabulary

- blue, green, red
- circle
- book, book bag, chair, desk
- marker, pencil, table
- no, yes

APPLICATION

Using the Project Page

Draw. Color. Sort.

1. Have the students look at the pictures in order. Make sure they understand what is happening in the pictures and that they are going to label bags/boxes and classify objects by their colors.

2. Have the students work in pairs or in small groups. Supply three paper bags or boxes for each pair or group.

3. The students draw classroom objects and color them red, green, or blue. They may also use the pictures on the cards from Workbook page 5.

4. Have each pair or group color a circle on each bag/box. One should be red, one blue, and one green.

5. Have each pair or group work together to identify each picture. Ask, "Is it a (pencil)?" and have the students answer, "Yes" or "No."

6. Focus attention on Homer and Hanna. Play the audio or read their conversation two or three times for the students to repeat.

7. Then have each pair or group classify the pictures of the objects by color and put them into the correct bag or box. Ask, "Is this (red)?" and have the students answer, "Yes" or "No." If the answer is "Yes," they should put the picture in the (red) bag/box.

Reaching All Students

Color Sorting Label large boxes *red, green,* and *blue.* Collect as many things as possible for each color—toys, pieces of cloth, clothing, pictures from magazines, classroom objects, buttons, balloons, and so on. Hold up each item and have the class identify the color and tell you which box to put it in. You may want to have the students count how many items are in each box. Ask, "How many red things are there?"

Listening to the Beat Give each student a set of number cards 1–10 or have them make the cards themselves. Then clap your hands 2, 4, or 6 times and ask the students to hold up the card that represents the number of times you clapped. Then have the students say the number aloud.

Puppet Conversation Have the students use their Homer and Hanna puppets to identify objects in the classroom. For example, Hanna asks, "What's this?" Homer answers, "It's a (book)."

Workbook

Page 7, Activity 9: Draw a line from one to two to three, and so on. Color the picture. Point to the page and say, "What's this? I don't know." Point to the dots and say, "Dots." Point to the numbers and say, "Numbers." The students join numbers in sequence. Then they color the picture *(table)* red, green, or blue.

Page 7, Activity 10: Write your answer. When the students have finished joining the dots, ask, "What is it?" The students should answer, "It's a table." Help them write *table* on the line provided. You many want the students to present their pictures to the class. Have them identify the object and ask, "Is it (red)?" Encourage the students to answer, "Yes" or "No."

PROJECT

Draw. Color. Sort.

1.

2.

3. **Is this red?**

Yes.

 Count and say.

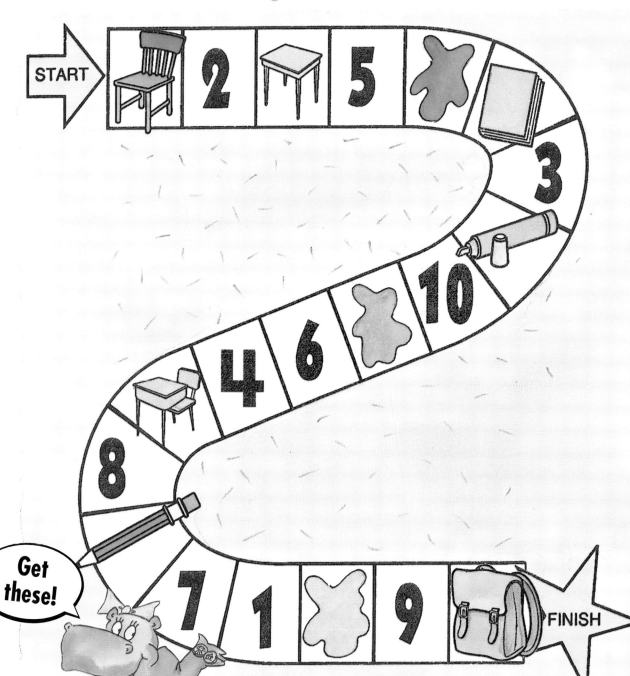

Get these!

1 =   2 =

Objectives

to identify classroom objects
to identify *red, green,* and *blue*
to use the simple present tense of *be*
to answer questions with *what color* plus
   is
to answer questions with *yes/no*
to count

Key Vocabulary

• book, book bag, chair, desk, marker, pencil,
   table
• it
• is
• it's, what's
• what color
• blue, green, red
• a

ASSESSMENT

Using the Page

Count and say.

1. [icon] Play the audio or read what Hanna is saying several times for the students to repeat. Get playing pieces and coins for the students to play with. A playing piece can be any small object such as an eraser, bottle cap, paper clip, or a piece of paper.

2. Have the students play in pairs or groups of three. Decide which side of the coin will be worth one point and which will be worth two. The students take turns tossing their coins and moving their playing pieces two, three, or four spaces on the board. They must identify the object or color that they land on, "It's a (desk)." If they answer incorrectly, they go back to where they were before their turn. The other players decide if the answers are correct. The first person to finish wins.

3. [icon] Go around and monitor the groups. Check for the use of the key vocabulary words. Record observations on the Student Oral Assessment Checklist on page xxi.

4. [icon] Point to a square on the game board. Ask a student to identify it and its color. "What's this?" *(It's a marker).*"What color is it?" *(It's blue.)* Then have that student point to another square on the game board and ask another student to identify it and its color.

Reaching All Students

Color Bingo Give each student a Bingo card (a card or paper divided into a 9-square grid). Have the students color each box red, green, or blue as they choose. Explain that they should not color a whole row the same color. Have the students tear up little pieces of paper to use as game pieces. As you call out a color, have the students put a game piece over that color on their Bingo card. The first student to get a straight line of game pieces wins.

[icon] **Writing Numbers** Distribute a sheet of writing paper to each student. Tell the class to listen and count the number of sounds you make, such as knocks on the desk. Call on volunteers to tell how many sounds they heard. If the rest of the class agrees on the answer, have the students write that number on their papers. Continue the activity with other numbers.

[icon] **Counting by Doing** Have the students practice counting by doing exercises. First, model hopping as you direct children to hop (7) times. Then lead them in doing other exercises such as (3) toe touches, (5) sit ups, and so on. During each exercise, the students should count aloud together.

What Color? Give each student a colored card (red, green, or blue). Ask the students questions about their cards, "What color is Patricia's card? Is it blue?" Encourage the students to answer, "Yes" or "No."

Objectives

to identify the numbers *1–10*
to identify circles
to identify classroom objects
to identify oneself
to exchange leave-takings

Key Vocabulary

- book bag, chair, desk, pencil
- circle, name
- good-bye
- blue, green, red

ASSESSMENT

Using the Page

Listen and circle.

1. 🎧 Play the audio or read the following sentences aloud. Have the students circle the objects or numbers they hear. Use the assessment chart on page xxiii to record how each student has done.
   AUDIOSCRIPT: 1. Circle the chair. 2. Circle the pencil. 3. Circle the number four. 4. Circle the desk. 5. Circle the book bag. 6. Circle the number six.

2. ✍️ Point to the objects and numbers in the Picture Dictionary on pages 10–11. Have the students identify them and their colors. Use the Student Oral Assessment Checklist to record each student's oral presentation on page xxi.

I can.

1. Read the statement for number 1 aloud to the students. Ask individuals, groups, or the whole class to identify the colors. Have them circle the pictures for the colors they can say.

2. Read the statement for number 2 aloud to the students. Ask individuals, groups, or the whole class to identify the numbers. Have them circle the numbers they can say.

3. Read the question. Have the students answer by writing their names on the line.

4. Quickly note oral production in these activities on the Student Oral Assessment Checklist on page xxi.

5. Focus attention on Homer and his "good-bye." You may wish to end each class by having your students wave and say, "good-bye."

Reaching All Students

Linked Response Give each student one of the classroom objects—real or a picture of one. Begin by pointing to a student's object and asking, "What's this?" That student answers, "It's a (book)." After answering, that student turns to the next and asks the question.

➗ **Arithmetic** If your students already know how to add, write some simple addition problems with pictures of groupings of items to illustrate the meaning of each numeral. Tell the students how to read them in English. For example, *1 + 3 = 4* "One and three are four." Ask individuals to read the equations aloud.

Unit Mural Elicit all the words and expressions the students remember from this unit. Write them on mural or poster paper. Have the students illustrate the vocabulary. Use this to review vocabulary in subsequent classes.

Unit 1 Test See page xxxi.

Workbook

🎧 ✍️ **Page 8, Listen and circle.** Play the audio or read the audioscript aloud two or three times for the students to complete the activity.
AUDIOSCRIPT: 1. Circle the book. 2. Circle the pencil. 3. Circle the table. 4. Circle the marker. 5. Circle the number nine. 6. Circle the number ten. 7. Circle the number seven.

 Listen and circle.

1.
2.
3.
4.
5.
6.

 I can.

Good-bye!

1. I can say colors.

2. I can say numbers. 1 4 5

3. What's your name?
   I'm _____.

2 My Family

Communication Objectives

to identify people
to identify family members
to talk about one's family
to say the letters of the alphabet
to distinguish between capital and lowercase letters
to identify the numbers *0–10*

Language Objectives

to use the simple present tense of *be*
to answer simple information questions: *Who's this?* and *How many?*
to use the simple present tense of *see*
to use the simple present tense of *have*
to use plural nouns
to pronounce /f/, /m/, /w/, and /s/

Learning Strategies and Thinking Skills

to apply prior knowledge
to classify
to make associations
to understand sequence
to use illustrations
to draw conclusions

Content Connections

Art: to draw a family tree
Literature/Language Arts: to distinguish between capital and lowercase letters of the alphabet; to spell key words
Mathematics: to count
Music: to sing a song
Social Studies: to make and read graphs

Materials

New Parade 1 Student Book, pages 12–21
New Parade 1 Workbook, pages 9–16; 84–86
New Parade 1 Audio: Tape/CD
New Parade 1 Video and Video Guide
New Parade 1 Posters
Old magazines, old newspapers, scissors, poster paper
Optional Materials: New Parade Picture Cards—family, monkeys, elephant, giraffe, lion; drawing paper, cardboard, pictures of families; *Little Celebrations— Jeb's Barn* by Andrea Butler, *Sharing Danny's Dad* by Angela Shelf Medearis, and *The Four Getters and Arf* by Helen Lester

Key Vocabulary

• boy, girl, man, woman
• baby, brother, family, father, mother, sister
• zero
• good-bye, hello
• how many, who's this
• do
• is
• have, see
• he's, I'm, she's
• Come here. Go to (your desk). Jump. Point to (the chair). Sit. Show me (the book). Walk.
• you
• my, this

Picture Dictionary

boy girl man woman baby
brother and sister   brothers   family

Setting Up the Classroom

Take some time before class to read through Unit 2. Collect the materials listed on page T2A. If possible, collect some magazine pictures or photos of families to show the students. You might want to prepare a list of TPR commands for the Warm Up on page T12. In advance, ask the students to bring in old magazines and newspapers, as well as some family photos, if possible. Read the Little Book, *Around Me!* to plan how you will read the story to the students.

Using the Video and the Video Guide

Show the video at the beginning of the unit to introduce language the students will be learning in context. The students may not understand everything at first. You should help them to get a general idea of what is happening. You can show the video again, especially at the beginning of each week of the unit. The students will understand more each time they view it and as they learn the words and patterns in the unit. The Video Guide will suggest where to stop and start the video. Encourage the students to interact with the video by answering the questions, singing, and doing the actions along with the children in the video.

Julia, Nora, and Sam are at Nora's house, talking about their families in this segment. Julia counts the number of people in her family and introduces some of the words for family members (*mother, father, sister*). Sam and Nora look at each other's family pictures, counting each person and saying, "This is my/your mother, This is my/your brother," and asking, "Who's this?" and "How many do you see?" Sam and Nora talk about how many people are in their families.

Family Connections

Encourage the students to teach "The Alphabet Song" to friends and family members. Family members and friends might also help the students to find and cut out magazine and newspaper pictures of families to bring to school for the bulletin board.

Bulletin Board Ideas

Place the title *Family* on the bulletin board. Then put up a picture or a Picture Card of a family enjoying something together. As the students learn more vocabulary words about families, encourage them to add other pictures of families doing things together. Later, you may want to use the bulletin board to help the students review words for people and family members. You may also want to use it to review numbers. For example, you might point to a picture and ask, "How many girls do you see?"

Little Book: Around Me!

Summary: A boy looks at the world around him—at school, at the playground, at the zoo, and at home. He tells whom he sees and what they're doing.

Workbook
Page 15, Activity 9

B	O	Y	X	X	X	X	X	X	X	X	X
A	X	X	X	X	W	X	X	X	X	X	X
B	X	X	X	X	O	X	X	X	X	X	X
Y	X	X	X	X	M	O	T	H	E	R	X	X
X	F	X	X	X	A	X	X	X	X	B	X
X	A	X	M	A	N	X	A	X	G	I	R	L
X	M	X	X	X	X	X	X	X	X	O	X
S	I	S	T	E	R	X	X	X	X	X	T	X
X	L	X	X	X	X	X	X	X	X	H	X
X	Y	X	X	X	X	X	F	A	T	H	E	R
X	X	X	X	X	X	X	X	X	X	X	R	X

2 My Family

1. Listen and chant.

My family has five people.
One, two, three, four, five.
We like to walk together,
One, two, three, four, five.
We like to sit together,
One, two, three, four, five.
We like to jump together,
One, two, three, four, five.

2. Listen. Count. Circle.

   1   2   ③   4   5

1.   1   2   3   4   5

2.   1   2   3   4   5

3.   1   2   3   4   5

4.   1   2   3   4   5

UNIT 2 • My Family

Objectives

to identify people and family members
to answer questions with *how many*
to use the simple present tense of *see*
to pronounce /f/, /m/, and /w/
to count

Key Vocabulary

- boy, family, girl, man, woman
- jump, see, sit, walk
- how many
- my

WARM UP

1. [X] Use TPR to introduce or review *show me (the book), point to the (chair), jump, walk, come here,* and *go to your desk.* See page ix for more information.

2. Show photographs of various families to the class, and check if any students know such words as *family* and *mother.*

3. Display the Poster for Unit 2.

PRESENTATION

Using the Page
ACTIVITY 1
Listen and chant.

1. Show a picture or Picture Card of a family with a mother, father, sister, brother, and a baby. Point to each family member as you say the word.

2. Focus attention on the pictures of the fingers. Make sure the students understand they are to do the fingerplay as they chant.

3. [audio] Play the audio or chant the poem to the class as you act out the fingerplay. Then have the students repeat several times. To practice pronunciation, focus on /f/ in *family* and *five,* /m/ in *my,* and /w/ in *we.*

4. Have groups of five work together to act out the chant. They should link arms and walk, sit, and jump together as they say the chant.

ACTIVITY 2
Listen. Count. Circle.

1. Introduce or review the words *boy, girl, man, woman,* using pictures.

2. To present the plurals of these words, write *1 boy/2 boys, 1 girl/2 girls, 1 man/2 men, 1 woman/2 women* on the board. Use Picture Cards or real people to illustrate each word.

3. [audio] Model the sample exercise. Play the audio or say, "How many boys do you see?"

(three) Then play the audio or read the audioscript aloud two or three times.
AUDIOSCRIPT: 1. How many girls do you see? *(four)* 2. How many girls do you see? *(two)* 3. How many boys do you see? *(one)* 4. How many girls do you see? *(two)*

Reaching All Students

Chant Expansion Have the students rewrite the chant, substituting the number of people in their families and the things they like to do.

Workbook

Page 9, Activity 1: Color and match. Have the students color the picture. Ask them who they think the various people are. Model the sample answer. Have the students draw lines from the words to the pictures of the family members.

[audio] **Page 10, Activity 2: Listen. Count. Circle.** Play the audio or read aloud to model the sample exercise: "How many girls do you see?" *(two)* Then play the audio or read the audioscript aloud two or three times for the students to complete the activity. The answers are in parentheses.
AUDIOSCRIPT: 1. How many boys do you see? *(five)* 2. How many girls do you see? *(three)* 3. How many men do you see? *(one)* 4. How many women do you see? *(two)* 5. How many boys do you see? *(four)* 6. How many girls do you see? *(two)*

Objectives

to identify people
to identify family members
to talk about one's family
to answer the question *Who's this?*
to use plural nouns
to use the simple present tense of *be*

Key Vocabulary

- baby, boy, brother, family, father, girl,
- man, mother, sister, woman
- is
- he's, I'm, she's
- my
- who's this
- this

PRESENTATION

Warm Up

Write *How do you say (_____) in English?* on the board. Encourage the students to use this question instead of their native language when asking for the meaning of a word they don't understand.

Using the Page

ACTIVITY 3

Look. Listen. Say.

1. Focus attention on the first picture. Say, "Show me the baby."

2. Have the students point to the first picture as you play the audio or say the sentences, "I'm David. This is my family." Then have the students point to the other pictures as you play the audio or read the sentences, "This is my (mother)."

3. Point to the pictures in random order and ask, "Who's this?" Have the students identify the family member and say if the person is a man, woman, boy, or girl. (*She's a girl.*)

4. Read to the students what Hanna is saying. Ask volunteers to tell about their own families, using the sentences as a model. You may want to have the students use the pictures of the families they make on Workbook page 11 or family photographs the students bring from home as visual aids. Have the students show their pictures to the rest of the class and identify their parents and brothers and sisters. Have them say their names as well.

Reaching All Students

Vocabulary Expansion Focus attention on the Picture Dictionary on pages 12–13. Have the students point to each and repeat the words *(boy, girl, man, woman, baby, boy and girl, two boys, family).*

Family Activities Ask the students, "What does your family like to do together?" Write their answers on the board. Take a survey of the students to find out what the most popular family activities are. You may want to illustrate the results with a bar graph.

Family Tree Draw a simple family tree on the board for David's family. Have the class choose names for his family members. Then have the students draw family trees for their own families. Help them as necessary. You may want them to illustrate the picture with activities they like to do with their families. Have them present their family trees to the class.

Workbook

Page 11, Activity 3: Draw and color. Say. Ask the students to draw and color a picture of their families. Because some students may want to include extended family members in their pictures, make sure to present the necessary vocabulary. This can be determined easily by checking over the students' drawings. Have the students share their pictures with the rest of the class. Have them say the sentence, "This is my family." Have them identify their family members and say their names, "This is my (father). His name is (Robert)."

I'm David. This is my family.

This is my mother.

This is my father.

This is my sister.

This is my brother.

This is my baby brother.

Please tell me about your family.

4. Count. Say.

> **How many brothers do you have?**

> **How many sisters do you have?**

5. Listen and say.

Aa Bb Cc Dd Ee Ff Gg Hh Ii

Jj Kk Ll Mm Nn Oo Pp Qq Rr

Ss Tt Uu Vv Ww Xx Yy Zz

Objectives

to identify family members
to identify the numbers *0–10*
to understand the simple present tense
   of *have*
to say the letters of the alphabet
to distinguish between capital and lowercase
   letters
to count

Key Vocabulary

- baby, boy, brother, family, father, girl
- man, mother, sister, woman
- you
- zero
- how many
- do, have

PRESENTATION

Using the Page

ACTIVITY 4

Count. Say.

1. Ask, "What numbers do you already know?"
   (1–10)

2. To present *zero,* hold up one finger and say,
   "I see one." Then fold the finger down and say,
   "Now I see zero."

3. Have the students look at picture 1. Point to
   the girl and read what Homer is saying, "How
   many brothers do you have?" Have them count
   the boys and say, "One." Continue asking how
   many sisters *(two),* mothers *(one),* and fathers
   (one) the girl has.

4. Continue with picture 2. Point to the boy and
   read what Hanna is saying, "How many sisters
   do you have?" The students should answer,
   "One." Then point to the boy and say, "How
   many brothers do you have?" Help the
   students decide that the answer is zero or none.

ACTIVITY 5

Listen and say.

1. 🎧 Point to each capital and lowercase letter
   to present the letters of the alphabet. Have the
   students repeat after you or the audio, "It's an
   A" and so on.

2. 🔊 Explain that each letter of the alphabet
   has a large and small form. Illustrate this point
   by pointing to a capital letter and then its
   corresponding lowercase letter.

3. Ask, "What color is the (C)? Which letters
   are (red)?"

4. Have the students cut out the alphabet cards
   on pages 95, 97, and 99.

5. Have the students hold up the correct alphabet
   card for each letter as they say the chant in
   Activity 6. Afterwards the students can store
   their set of alphabet cards in their English class
   folders (see page T6).

Reaching All Students

✓ **Vocabulary Check** Point to the people in
the Picture Dictionary at the top of pages 14–15.
Have the students identify them as *man, woman,
boy, girl,* or *baby.*

Letter Dictation Have the students use their
alphabet cards to practice comprehension of the
names of the letters. Call out letters in random
order and have the students hold up their
matching letters.

Workbook

**Page 12, Activity 4: Circle the same letters.
Say. Count.** Focus attention on the letter *A* in
the left column. Ask the students to look at the
letters in the right column and circle the letters
that are the same as the *A.* Check to make sure
everyone has circled the three *As.* Have the
students complete the activity. You may want the
students to work in pairs to compare their
answers. Then have the students say the names of
the letters that are the same.

Objectives

to identify family members
to talk about one's family
to say the letters of the alphabet
to identify the numbers *0–10*
to use the simple present tense of *have*
to pronounce /s/

Key Vocabulary

- baby, boy, girl, brother, family
- father, girl, man, mother, sister, woman
- you
- do, have, see

PRACTICE

Using the Page

ACTIVITY 6

Listen. Write. Say.

1. 🎧 Play the audio or read the chant several times.

2. Have the students fill in the missing letters. Then have them name the letters.

3. Finally, lead the students in saying all of the letters of the alphabet and the chant. To practice pronunciation, focus on /s/ in *sister, see,* and *say.*

ACTIVITY 7

Listen and circle.

1. Have the students review the numbers by reading them aloud.

2. 🎧 Play the audio or read, "How many brothers do you have? Circle the number." "How many sisters do you have? Circle the number."

3. 🔄 You may want to make a class chart of how many students have each number of brothers and sisters. Encourage each student to say, "I have (two) (sisters)."

ACTIVITY 8

Count and name.

1. Model the sample. Have the students count the number of people in the family. *(four)* Preteach the question, "How many (mothers) do you see?" *(one)* Have the students count the number of brothers, sisters, babies, mothers, and fathers in the picture.
ANSWERS: 1 brother, 1 sister, 1 mother, 1 father, 0 babies

2. Have the students count the number of brothers, sisters, babies, mothers, and fathers in the next three pictures.
ANSWERS: 1. 2 brothers/2 babies, 1 sister, 1 mother, 1 father; 2. 1 brother, 1 sister, 1 mother; 3. 4 brothers (1 baby), 1 mother, 1 father

Reaching All Students

💡 **Alphabet Sequence** Have twenty-six students hold up one letter of their set of alphabet cards. Have them stand in front of the room in mixed-up order. Have the remaining students tell them where to stand to be in the correct alphabetical order. If your class is smaller, divide the alphabet and only sequence half the alphabet at a time.

Workbook

🎧 **Page 12, Activity 5: Listen. Write. Say.** Play the audio or read aloud to model the sample exercise: "Fill in the missing letter." Then play the audio or read the audioscript aloud two or three times for the students to complete the activity. (The letters in italics are the answers.)
AUDIOSCRIPT: 1. E, F, *G;* 2. H, *I,* J, K; 3. L, M, *N,* O; 4. *P,* Q, R, S; 5. T, *U,* V, W; 6. X, *Y, Z.*

Page 13, Activity 6: Count and write. Model the sample exercise. Have the students count the number of brothers in the picture. *(two)* Have the students count the sisters, brothers, mothers, and fathers in each picture and write their answers in the blanks.
ANSWERS: 1. 3 2. 0 3. 1 4. 1 5. 0 6. 3 7. 1 8. 0

6. Listen. Write. Say.

A, B, _____, D, E, F, G,

H, I, J, K, L, M, _____, O, P,

Q, R, _____, T, U, V,

_____, X, Y, Z.

Mother, father, sister see
How I say my ABCs.

7. Listen and circle.

1. brothers 0 1 2 3 4 5 6 7 8 9 10

2. sisters 0 1 2 3 4 5 6 7 8 9 10

8. Count and name.

1.

2.

3.

9. Play and match.

It's a "D"!

They match!

10. Listen. Chant. Find.

A B CDE
This is my family.
F G HIJ
I love them every day.
K L MNO
Mother, father, baby, oh
P Q RST
Brother, sister, you can see
U V W X Y Z
All the people in my family.

Look!
Here's "B"!

Objectives

to say the letters of the alphabet
to identify family members
to count

Key Vocabulary

• baby, brother, family, father, mother, sister
• my, this

APPLICATION

Warm Up

1. Review the alphabet by having the students say the chants from Activities 6 and 10.

2. Invite volunteers to take turns naming the letters of the alphabet until they reach *z.*

Using the Page

ACTIVITY 9

Play and match.

1. Have the students take out their alphabet cards.

2. Put the students into pairs and have the pairs combine their alphabet cards, mix them up, and lay them facedown on a flat surface.

3. Focus attention on the picture. Read what the girl in purple and Hanna are saying. Explain that the students are to take turns turning over pairs of cards. The object is to match two identical cards. As they turn over a card, they are to identify it, "It's an *M.*" The player with the most pairs of matching cards wins.

ACTIVITY 10

Listen. Chant. Find.

1. 🎵 Play the audio or read the chant several times for the students to repeat.

2. Read what Homer is saying. Then have the students look at the picture and find, say, and count the number of "hidden" letters.
ANSWERS: There are 10 hidden letters in the picture. They are *A, B, F, I, L, M (upside-down)* or *W, O, P, S, Y*

Reaching All Students

Alphabet Bingo Have the students draw two horizontal and two vertical lines on sheets of paper so they are divided into nine boxes. Have them write a letter in each box. Have the students tear up nine little pieces of paper to use as game pieces. Call out letters of the alphabet in random order. The students cover up that letter on their Bingo cards with the pieces of paper. The first person to get three spaces in a row covered in any direction says, "Bingo!" and wins.

🎵 📼 **Alphabet Song** Play the audio or teach the "The Alphabet Song" to the students.

A, B, C, D, E, F, G,
H, I, J, K, L, M, N, O, P,
Q, R, S and T, U, V,
W, X, and Y, and Z
Now I know my ABC's
Tell me what you think of me.

Workbook

Page 14, Activity 7: Draw a line from A to B to C, and so on. Have the students connect the letters in the correct alphabetical order to form a baby in a stroller. Have the students color their pictures and present them to the class.

Page 14, Activity 8: Circle your answer. Read the question. Have the students circle their answer. (*Yes.*)

Language Activities Section, page 84
ANSWERS: 1. am 2. is 3. is 4. am 5. is

Language Activities Section, page 85
ANSWERS: 1. She 2. He 3. He 4. She 5. He 6. She

Story Summary

A boy looks at the world around him—at school, at the playground, at the zoo, and at home. He tells whom he sees and what they're doing.

Key Unit Vocabulary

do, family, go to, my, see

Word Bank

classmates, home, tree, waiting

BEFORE READING

WARM UP

Ask the students to walk to the window. Suggest that they look around outside and tell what they see. Then they can walk back to their desks and look around them. Invite the students to tell what they see in the classroom.

PUT TOGETHER THE LITTLE BOOK

Ask the students to take pages 17–18 out of their books. They can fold the pages in half to make the Little Book, *Around Me!*

PREVIEW THE LITTLE BOOK

1. Ask the students to tell about the pictures on each page. Then ask them to find the main character of the story who is shown on each page.

2. After previewing the pictures, read the title aloud. Ask, "Who is telling this story?" Then ask them to look at the pictures and tell what the boy is doing. Encourage them to identify animals, objects, and people they see in the pictures. Then invite the students to tell what the story is about.

SHARE NEW WORDS

Write the Word Bank words on the board. Say each word and ask the students to repeat it after you. Use pictures in the story to show the meanings of these words. Then invite the students to go on a word hunt and find each of these words in the Little Book.

DURING READING

READING THE LITTLE BOOK

After the students have previewed the Little Book, *Around Me!* read the story aloud or play the audio. You may tell the students that they can ask questions and talk about it when you read it again.

GUIDED READING

Read the story aloud, tracking the print as the students follow along. Some students may wish to track the print in their own books as they read.

TEACHER TIPS

Point out the words that are repeated in the story. *I go to _____ and what do I see? I see _____. They _____.* As you read aloud, emphasize these phrases and say them in the same rhythmical pattern.

REREADING

Talk with the students about their story predictions. Have them compare what happens in the story with what they predicted. Then ask a student to use the illustrations to retell the story. Assess the students' comprehension with questions such as these:

Page 1 *Where is the boy and what does he see?*
Page 2 *What are the boy and his friends doing?*
Page 3 *What are the monkeys doing?*
Page 4 *Who is waiting for the boy?*

Point out any objects in the picture on each page that will help the students understand the setting and comprehension questions.

AROUND ME!
by Mario Herrera

I go to school and what do I see?
I see my classmates.
They read with me.

1

Then I go home and what do I see?
I see my family.
They are waiting for me!

4

I go to the playground and
what do I see?
I see my friends. They play with me.

I go to the zoo and what do I see?
I see monkeys.
They climb up a tree.

AFTER READING

Activities for Developing Language

RETELL THE STORY

Invite volunteers to take turns pretending they are the boy in the story. Ask them to point to each illustration and retell what the boy is saying.

CLASSIFYING

Write the word *school* in the center of a word map. Invite the students to work in groups to add words having to do with school to the map. For example, they might write *classmates, books, classroom,* and *teacher.* Then you may want the students to make other word maps starting with *home* and *zoo.*

SETTING

Talk about the different places pictured in the story. Then ask the students to choose one setting from the story and draw a picture of it. Then help them to label objects on the picture they drew.

DRAMA CONNECTION

As you reread the story aloud, the students may role play the actions of the classmates, friends, monkeys, and family.

SCIENCE CONNECTION

Tell the students that many animals in zoos live in the wild in South America and Africa. You might provide picture books of animals from these places, or display Picture Cards of monkeys, elephant, giraffe, and lion. Then have groups work together to draw a mural of the animals. Encourage them to label each one.

WRITE ABOUT IT!

Reread the story, emphasizing the repeated phrases. (*I go to the _____ and what do I see? I see _____.*) Then write these sentences with blanks on the board. Invite the students to think about places they like to go and things or people they like to see. Ask a volunteer to write his or her ideas in the blanks and to read the sentences aloud. Then erase the words and give other volunteers the opportunity to write and read aloud their ideas.

GRAMMAR CONNECTION: QUESTION MARKS

Point out the first sentence in the story. Explain that the question mark shows the speaker is asking a question. Model how the tone of voice rises at the end of most questions.

WORKBOOK

Little Book Comprehension, page 86.

BULLETIN BOARD IDEAS

You may wish to have the students decorate a bulletin board titled *What We See on the Playground* with labeled drawings of things they see on the playground.

FAMILY CONNECTION

Invite the students to take their Little Books home and read them to their friends and family members.

Objectives

to identify people
to identify family members
to use plural nouns
to classify

Key Vocabulary

• baby, boy, family, girl, man, woman

APPLICATION

Using the Project Page

Make a poster.

1. Bring to class or have the students bring old magazines and newspapers that they can cut out.

2. 💡 Tell the students that they are going to classify people into the following categories—men, women, babies, boys, girls, families. Put the students into groups of two or three. Assign a category to each group. Have the students go through the newspapers and magazines and cut out pictures of people that represent their category.

3. Give each group a large sheet of paper. Write the words *Men, Women, Boys, Girls, Babies,* and *Families* on the board for the students to copy as headings on the appropriate sheet of paper. Then have the students paste their pictures on the paper.

4. Have each group of students present their poster to the rest of the class. You may want to display the posters in the room during the unit and refer to them to reinforce the vocabulary.

5. On the family posters, have the students in each group identify the mother, father, sister, and/or brother in their pictures and have the students classify the people into the categories—men, women, girls, boys, or babies.

Reaching All Students

👤 **He's/She's Linked Response** Have the students stand up. While pointing to the person next to them, have them say, "(He's) a boy. *(He's Michael)*." Tell students to pay attention to *he's* and *she's*.

💡 **Drawing Conclusions** Have the students work independently, in pairs, or in groups to look at the families in the family poster and decide what the different families like to do. After the students have described each family in the family poster, the class may want to recite the poem on page 12, substituting with information from the poster.

👥 **Family Trees** Draw a simple family tree on the board for one of the families in the family poster. Have the class name all the people in the family.

👥 **Reading Flashcards** Have the students make flashcards by writing the key vocabulary words, singular and plural, on small pieces of cardboard. Put the students into pairs and have them take turns reading each other's flashcards.

👥 **Reading Bee** Divide the class into two teams. Show a flashcard to a member of one team. If that person reads the word correctly, his or her team scores a point and it's the next team's turn. If the person doesn't read the word correctly, the other team gets a chance to read it. The team with the most points wins.

Workbook

Page 15, Activity 9: Find the words. Circle the words. Read each of the words at the top of the word puzzle aloud to the students. Explain that they are to find these words in the puzzle. Encourage them to cross the words off the top as they find and circle them in the puzzle. See page T2B for the answers.

PROJECT

Make a poster.

Boys

Girls

Say the letters in order.

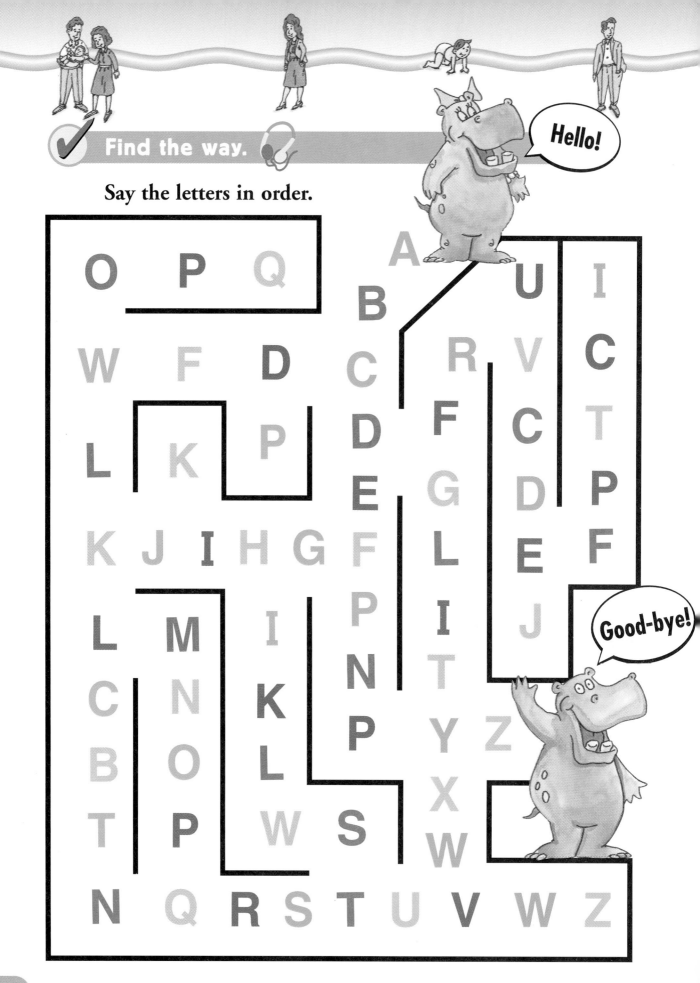

Hello!

Good-bye!

Objectives

to say the letters of the alphabet
to understand sequence

Key Vocabulary

• good-bye, hello

Using the Page

Find the way.

1. Play the audio or read what Homer and Hanna are saying several times for the students to repeat. Explain to the students that they will begin following the maze where Hanna is saying *Hello,* and they will finish where Homer is saying *Good-bye.*

2. Have the students use their markers to trace the correct path through the maze. Tell them to follow the correct alphabetical order.

3. After the students have completed their routes, have volunteers trace their routes and say the letters. As the students describe their routes, check for objectives: (1) the oral identification of the letters of the alphabet and (2) the correct sequence of the letters. Record your observations on the Student Oral Assessment Checklist on page xxi.

Reaching All Students

Scrambled Words Write some of the key vocabulary words with the letters in mixed-up order on the board, for example, *iglr, abyb, thafer,* and so on. (You may want to include key vocabulary from Unit 1.) Have the students work individually, in pairs, or in groups to unscramble them.

Spelling Dictation Spell aloud key vocabulary words from this unit and Unit 1. Have the students write the words as you dictate them on sheets of paper. Repeat each word two or more times.

Family Trees Draw an imaginary family tree on the board using names. Make sure there are plenty of brothers and sisters. Give a clue to the students such as "I am Maria's sister." Have the students say the name of the person.

Chant for the Only Child Find out if there are any students who have no brothers or sisters. Write this alternative chant on the board for those students to copy. Give these students the opportunity to say this chant.

I don't have a brother.
I don't have a sister.
I sing!
I jump!
I play!
I dream!
I like to be with me!

Objectives

to identify the numbers *0–10*
to identify family members
to say the letters of the alphabet
to answer questions with *how many*
to use the simple present tense of *see*

Key Vocabulary

- baby, boy, brother, father, girl, man, mother, sister, woman
- you
- how many
- do, see

ASSESSMENT

Using the Page

Listen. Count. Circle.

1. Have the students point to the people in the picture as you play the audio or say, "This is the (mother). She's a (woman)."

2. Play the audio or read the questions. Have the students circle the correct numbers.
   AUDIOSCRIPT: 1. How many mothers do you see? 2. How many babies do you see? 3. How many brothers do you see? 4. How many sisters do you see? 5. How many fathers do you see? 6. How many boys do you see?
   ANSWERS: 1. 1 2. 1 3. 2 4. 2 5. 1 6. 2

3. Point to different people in the picture and ask individuals to identify the family member and if that person is a man, woman, boy, or girl.

4. Point to the family members in the Picture Dictionary on pages 20–21. Have the students identify them. Use the Student Oral Assessment Checklist on page xxi to record each student's oral presentation.

I can.

1. Read the statement for number 1 aloud to the students. Ask individuals, groups, or the whole class to identify the letters of the alphabet. Have them circle the pictures for the letters they can say.

2. Read the statement for number 2 aloud to the students. Ask individuals, groups, or the whole class to identify the members of the family. Have them circle the pictures of the family members they can say. Quickly note oral production in these activities on the Student Oral Assessment Checklist on page xxi.

Reaching All Students

Family Members Display a picture of a family in front of the class. You may want to use one from this unit. Ask individuals to show you different people in the picture, "Show me the (mother)." "Point to the (baby)."

Tallest to Smallest Have the students draw a picture of their families with the family members in line from smallest to tallest. Have the students show the class their families, say who's the smallest, tallest, and so on and show where they fit in.

Unit Mural Elicit all the words and expressions the students remember from this unit. Write them on mural or poster paper. Have the students illustrate the vocabulary. Use this to review vocabulary in subsequent classes.

Unit 2 Test See page xxxii.

Workbook

Page 16, Listen. Count. Circle.
Have the students point to the people in the picture as you say, "This is the (father). He's a (man)." Then play the audio or read the following. Have the students circle the correct number for the eight examples.
AUDIOSCRIPT: 1. How many mothers do you see? 2. How many babies do you see? 3. How many sisters do you see? 4. How many brothers do you see? 5. How many fathers do you see? 6. How many women do you see? 7. How many men do you see? 8. How many girls do you see?
ANSWERS: 1. 2 2. 1 3. 4 4. 2 5. 1 6. 2 7. 1 8. 4

Listen. Count. Circle.

1. 0 1 2 3 4 5 6

2. 0 1 2 3 4 5 6

3. 0 1 2 3 4 5 6

4. 0 1 2 3 4 5 6

5. 0 1 2 3 4 5 6

6. 0 1 2 3 4 5 6

 I can.

1. I can say my ABC's. **C D K T**

2. I can say mother, father, brother, sister, and baby.

3 My Body

Communication Objectives

to identify and describe parts of the body
to say how many parts of the body one has
to identify colors
to differentiate between *big* and *little*
to differentiate between *long* and *short*

Language Objectives

to use plural nouns including the irregular *feet*
to use possessive adjectives *his* and *her*
to use predicate adjectives
to use the simple present tense of *be*
to use the simple present tense of *have*
to answer information questions: *What color?* and *How many?*
to pronounce /h/, /n/, /w/, and /θ/

Learning Strategies and Thinking Skills

to apply prior knowledge
to relate parts to the whole
to compare and contrast
to classify
to use illustrations

Content Connections

Art: to create a monster and masks
Music: to sing songs
Science: to identify the parts of the body
Social Studies: to make and read graphs

Materials

New Parade 1 Student Book, pages 22–31
New Parade 1 Workbook, pages 17–26; 87–89
New Parade 1 Audio: Tape/CD
New Parade 1 Video and Video Guide
New Parade 1 Posters

Pieces of colored paper—brown, orange, purple, and yellow; thin, chart-size paper; markers; crayons; paper plates; Bingo materials
Optional Materials: New Parade Picture Cards—clown; drawing paper, cutouts of donkey body parts, old magazines, poster paper; *Little Celebrations—Animal Stretches* by Marcia Vaughan, *Keep the Beat* by Carolina Ortega, *Keeping Fit* by Sonya Dunn, and *A Wiggly, Jiggly, Joggly Tooth* by Bill Hawley

Key Vocabulary

- arm, body, ear, eye, face, finger, foot (feet), hair, hand, head, knee, leg, mouth, nose, shoulder, thumb, toe
- clown, monster
- how many, what color
- are, have, move, pick up, put down, touch
- they, they're
- her, his
- big, little, long, short
- brown, color, orange, purple, yellow

Picture Dictionary

hand   leg   foot   finger   eye   ear   nose   clown   face

Setting Up the Classroom

Beforehand, prepare a list of TPR commands that include the parts of the body to be taught in this unit. For example, "Touch your head. Move your foot." You might also want to introduce a few more for comprehension such as "Shake your head." and "Bend your leg." The students need not write or say these verbs at this point; just have them follow the commands. Make sure you have the materials listed on page T3A. Read the Little Book, *Who Am I?* to find some objects you may want the students to point out in the pictures.

Using the Video and the Video Guide

Begin by showing the video to set the stage for the unit. This will give the students a preview of the language they will be learning about parts of the body. Let the Video Guide suggest where to stop and start the video. Use the video often. You may want to show it at the beginning of each week during the four-week unit. Encourage the students to interact with the video by answering the questions, singing, and doing the actions along with the children in the video.

In this video segment, Julia, Ana, and Sam are dressed up as clowns. Then we hear the body song "One Finger, One Thumb," as we see the body parts mentioned. Sam and Ana are dressed up as funny clowns and talk about clown features, using adjectives and colors, "His hair is long. Her nose is big. It's red." Later, Scott and Ana show that they have six little clown ears, two long feet, and ten little feet.

Family Connections

After the students have completed the Project on page 29 in class, encourage them to tell their friends and families at home about it. Suggest that the students may want to teach them words they used to make the graph such as *brown eyes* and *long hair*.

Bulletin Board Ideas

Encourage the students to cut out pictures of eyes, nose, ears, mouth, and hair from old magazines. Then have them glue these pictures onto paper and use crayons to create a face. Display the students' work on a bulletin board. Use the bulletin board, as you work through the unit, to review the vocabulary. For example, say, "Her hair is long." Then ask volunteers to point to a picture that shows long hair.

Little Book: Who Am I?

Summary: Children follow colorful hints in this riddle book to discover a funny clown.

Workbook

Page 23, Activity 8

H	A	I	R	X	X	X	X	X	X	X	X
A	X	X	X	X	H	X	X	T	H	U	M	B
N	X	X	X	X	E	X	X	O	X	X	O	X
D	X	X	X	X	A	X	X	E	X	X	U	X
S	H	O	U	L	D	E	R	S	X	X	T	X
X	X	X	X	E	X	A	X	X	X	X	H	X
X	F	I	N	G	E	R	X	X	X	X	X	X
X	A	X	O	X	X	S	X	X	X	X	X	X
X	C	X	S	X	X	X	X	X	X	X	X	X
X	E	Y	E	S	X	X	X	X	X	X	X	X

3 My Body

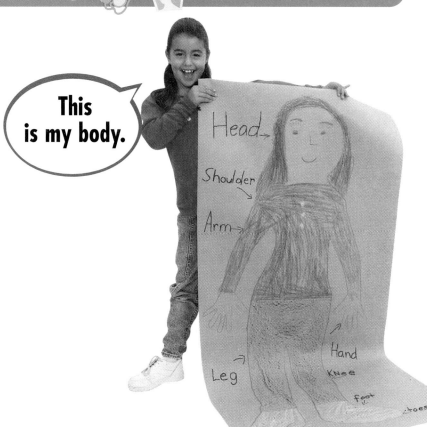

This is my body.

Head

Shoulder

Arm

Leg

Hand

Knee

foot

toes

2. Listen and sing.

Head and shoulders, knees and toes,
Knees and toes, knees and toes;
Head and shoulders, knees and toes,
Eyes, ears, mouth, and nose.

Objectives

to identify parts of the body
to use plural nouns
to use the simple present tense of *be*
to relate parts to the whole
to pronounce /h/ and /n/

Key Vocabulary

• **arm, body, foot (feet), hand, head, knee, leg, shoulder, toe**
• **her, his**

WARM UP

1. 🏃 Review TPR from Units 1 and 2. Say, "Touch your (eye). Move your (hands)." and model the actions. Continue, asking the students to touch and/or move their heads, legs, mouths, and so on.

2. 🏃 Pick up a pencil and then put it down as you model, "Pick up the pencil. Put down the pencil." Continue with other classroom objects. See page ix for more information.

3. Display the Poster for Unit 3.

PRESENTATION

Using the Page

ACTIVITY 1

Look. Listen. Say.

1. Preteach the key vocabulary by pointing to yourself and saying, "This is my body." and naming parts of your body such as *head, arm, hand*, and so on. Say the words several times for the students to repeat.

2. Ask a boy and a girl to come to the front of the class or use pictures of a girl and a boy. Point to different parts of the body and say, "Her (hair) is brown. His hair is (black)." Emphasize *her* and *his*. You may want to present *blond* at this time.

3. 🎧 💡 Have the students point to the parts of the pictured body as you play the audio or read the labels several times for the students to repeat. Then read what the girl is saying several times for the students to repeat.

4. ✅ Name different parts of the body and have the students point to the correct part of the picture.

ACTIVITY 2

Listen and sing.

1. 🎧 🔊 Play the audio or sing the song "Head and Shoulders" for the students as you do the motions illustrated in the book.

2. Have the students form a circle in the classroom. Have them sing along with you or the audio and touch the corresponding parts of their bodies as they sing. You may want to speed up the song and the motions as the students become more proficient with the song. To practice pronunciation, focus on /h/ in *head* and /n/ in *knees*.

3. Encourage the students to create new versions of the song for the class and move accordingly.

Reaching All Students

Vocabulary Expansion Focus attention on the Picture Dictionary on pages 22–23. Have the students point to each and repeat the words (*hand, leg, foot, finger, eye, ear, nose, clown face*).

Workbook

Page 17, Activity 1: Match. Say. Color. Read the words in dark type several times for the students to repeat. The students draw a line from the word to the part of the body in the picture. Then they color the picture and talk about it.

UNIT 3 • My Body

Objectives
to identify colors
to identify and describe parts of the body
to differentiate between *big* and *little*
to differentiate between *long* and *short*
to use possessive adjectives *his* and *her*
to answer questions with *what color*
to compare and contrast

Key Vocabulary
• ear, eye, face, hair, mouth, nose
• clown
• big, little, long, short
• brown, orange, purple, yellow
• what color

PRESENTATION

Using the Page
ACTIVITY 3
Look. Point. Say.

1. Give each student a piece of paper that is brown, orange, purple, or yellow. Introduce the name of each color and ask the students with a certain color to follow commands such as "Purples, stand up."

2. Point to the first pictured marker and identify its color, "It's yellow." Do this for the other markers. Repeat several times for the students to repeat.

3. Point to the markers in a random order and ask the students to identify the colors. Ask, "What color is it?" (*It's purple.*)

ACTIVITY 4
Listen. Point. Say.

1. Have the students point to the parts of the face as you play the audio or read the labels for the students to repeat.

2. Name different parts of the face and have the students point to the correct part of the picture or their own faces.

ACTIVITY 5
Look. Listen. Read.

1. Introduce the word *clown,* using pictures or Picture Card. Identify the male and female clown.

2. Play the audio or read Homer and Hanna's conversation several times for the students to repeat. Then play the audio or read the text as the students look at the picture in their books.

3. Point to or say the words for different parts of the clowns' bodies and ask the students to say what color each part is and whether it is big or little. "It's a nose. It's red. It's big."

Language Note: Point out that *they're* means *they are.*

4. Point to the (nose) of the male clown. Say, "His nose is green." Then point to the female clown's nose and say, "Her nose is yellow." Continue by pointing to parts of the clowns' faces and having students describe them by using a possessive adjective and a color or a size.

Reaching All Students
Classifying Have the students make vocabulary cards, or supply them with real objects or pictures of things that are long or short, big or little. Have them work in pairs to sort the objects by size or length.

Workbook
Page 18, Activity 2: Draw your face. Say. Match. Have the students complete the picture of their faces. Then read the words several times for the students to repeat. Have the students draw a line from the word to the part of the face in their pictures.

Page 18, Activity 3: Write the missing word. Point to several students' pictures and say, "This is your face." Help the students write the word *face* on the line provided.

3. Look. Point. Say.

yellow **brown** **orange** **purple**

4. Listen. Point. Say.

hair

eye

ear

nose

mouth

5. Look. Listen. Read.

What color are his ears?

They're yellow.

Look at this clown.
His mouth is big. It's orange.
His hair is short. It's blue.

Look at this clown.
Her mouth is little. It's red.
Her hair is long. It's purple.

6. Draw and say.

1.

2.

3.

My hair is long and brown.

7. Listen and color.

Objectives

to identify and describe parts of the body
to identify colors
to use plural nouns
to use predicate adjectives
to use possessive adjectives *his* and *her*

Key Vocabulary

• arm, ear, hair, leg, nose
• big, little, long, short
• brown, orange, purple, yellow

PRACTICE

Using the Page

ACTIVITY 6
Draw and say.

1. Review the parts of the body by singing the song "Head and Shoulders."

2. Have the students look at the three pictures. Make sure they understand that they are to make a tracing of one another's bodies. Supply them with thin chart-size paper and markers or crayons. If paper is scarce, you may want to have only a few students make tracings.

3. Read what the girl is saying several times for the students to repeat. Then have the students show their pictures to the class and identify the body parts.

4. ⊘ ◄▣ Display the students' drawings in the room. Throughout the week, point to a picture and ask the students to name the body parts, "It's a (leg)."

ACTIVITY 7
Listen and color.

1. 🎧 Play the audio or read the audioscript aloud to the students. Have them use the correct marker or crayon to color the body parts of the boy clown.
AUDIOSCRIPT: 1. Color his hair yellow. 2. Color his eyes green. 3. Color his hands purple. 4. Color his nose orange. 5. Color his legs brown. 6. Color his mouth red.

2. Point to different parts of the clown's body and have the students identify each body part and name its color, "It's his nose. His nose is orange."

Reaching All Students

⊘ **Picture Dictionary** Review words for parts of the body by having the students name the parts on pages 24–25.

🏃 **Following TPR Directions** Play Simon Says using action vocabulary your students have learned. Remind the students to do the action only when you say "Simon says" first.

🏃 **TPR Game** Play a version of "Pin the Tail on the Donkey." Draw a picture of a donkey. Tape the donkey's "body" to the wall. Make, in separate pieces, a head, eyes, nose, mouth, ears, and feet. Model and practice the name of each body part. Then have them take turns attaching the parts in the correct position while they are blindfolded.

🎧 ◄▣ **Chant** Write the chant on the board. Say the chant with the students. Substitute different students' names and hair or eye color.

> Celebrate (child's name)
> Celebrate!
> She has (red hair).
> Isn't that great?

Workbook

Page 19, Activity 4: Read. Color. Read the sentences for number 1 several times for the students to repeat. Have them color the head next to the sentences accordingly. Repeat for number 2. Have them write the answers about themselves for number 3 on the lines provided and color the head to look like themselves. Ask individuals to describe the faces to the class.

Language Activities Section, page 87
ANSWERS: 1. face, nose 2. arms, feet 3. fingers, toes

Objectives

to identify and describe parts of the body
to say how many parts of the body one has
to identify colors
to answer information questions: *What color?*
How many?
to use the simple present tense of *have*
to pronounce /w/ and /θ/

Key Vocabulary

- arm, eye, finger, foot (feet), hair, hand, leg, mouth, nose, thumb, toe
- monster
- how many
- have, they're

PRACTICE

Using the Page

ACTIVITY 8

Look. Point. Say.

1. Introduce the word *monster* by showing the students a picture of one.

2. Have the students look at the picture of the monster. Then play the audio or read Homer and Hanna's conversation several times for the students to repeat.

3. Have the students answer similar questions about different parts of the body. Have them say how many and what color of each body part the monster has.

ACTIVITY 9

Draw and say.

1. Read what the girl is saying about her monster picture several times for the students to repeat.

2. Have the students draw a funny monster picture like the one the girl is holding. Encourage them to use their imaginations. Have them use their red, green, blue, yellow, orange, brown, and purple markers or crayons. Then have the students describe their monsters.

3. Have the students work in pairs to ask each other questions about their monster pictures. A student should hold his or her picture where the partner can't see it. Have them ask questions such as "How many eyes does it have? What color are its eyes? Are the legs long or short?"

ACTIVITY 10

Listen and sing.

1. Play the audio or sing the song to the students. As the song is being sung, do the motions illustrated in the book.

2. Have the students stand up and move the corresponding parts of their bodies as they sing the song. To practice pronunciation, focus on /w/ in *one* and *we'll* and /θ/ in *thumb*.

3. Have the students keep adding body parts as they sing. For example, "One finger, one thumb, one hand keep moving . . ." It becomes increasingly difficult to do all the actions, so the students should know that the song is done in fun.

Reaching All Students

Matching Have the students create their own set of word cards—face, hair, eyes, nose, and so on. Ask them to match the words from their cards with the word cards of a partner. Then have the students make picture cards for the same words. Have the students match their picture cards and their word cards. Have the students keep their sets of cards for future practice.

Workbook

Page 20, Activity 5: Count. Write the number word. Model the sample answer by saying, "I have (two) (eyes). How many eyes do you have?" Help the students reply with a complete sentence. Say, "Write the word *one, two,* or *ten* on the line." ANSWERS: 1. one 2. one 3. two 4. ten 5. two 6. two 7. ten

8. Look. Point. Say.

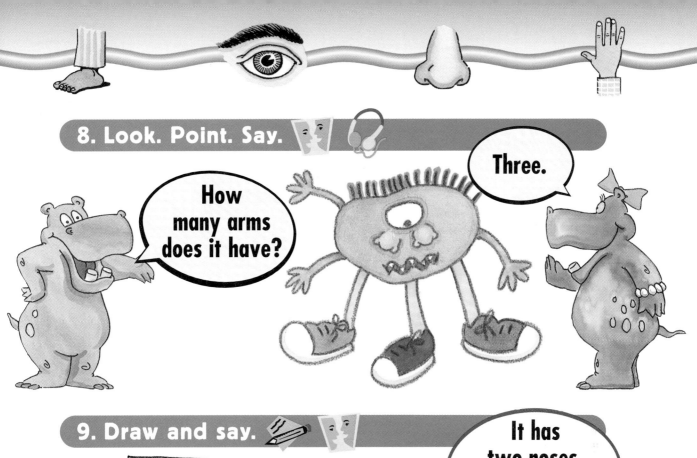

9. Draw and say.

It has two noses. They're big and green.

10. Listen and sing.

One finger, one thumb keep moving.
One finger, one thumb keep moving.
One finger, one thumb keep moving.
And we'll all be happy today.

11. Play the game.

1   2   3   4

His nose is blue and his hair is green.

It's number 4.

12. Listen. Circle.

1.

2.

3.

Objectives

to identify and describe parts of the body
to identify colors
to differentiate between *big* and *little*
to differentiate between *long* and *short*
to use possessive adjectives *his* and *her*
to use the simple present tense of *be*
to compare and contrast

Key Vocabulary

- ear, eye, finger, foot (feet), hair, hand, mouth, nose
- big, little, long, short
- brown, orange, purple, yellow

APPLICATION

Using the Page

ACTIVITY 11

Play the game.

1. 🎧 Play the audio or read the conversation several times for the students to repeat.

2. Choose one of the pictured clowns to describe. Describe the clown. Have the students guess the number of the clown that you are describing.

3. If your students are able, you may want them to work in pairs to play the game. One person chooses a clown to describe without telling the partner. The person describes the clown. The partner tries to guess the number of the clown that is being described. Or, you may want to ask individuals to stand up and describe a clown to the class. If a classmate correctly identifies the clown, he or she gets to choose and describe the next clown.

ACTIVITY 12

Listen. Circle.

1. 🎧 Model the sample exercise. Have the students point to the first two pictures as you play the audio or read aloud the sentence, "His hair is long. Circle the clown with long hair." Point out the answer circle.

2. 🎧 Play the audio or read the audioscript aloud two or three times. Have the students circle the answers. Then check the students' work.
   AUDIOSCRIPT: 1. Her nose is big. 2. Her ears are little. 3. His mouth is big.

Reaching All Students

🔄 **Let's Draw** Have the students divide and number a sheet of paper into four sections. Dictate long and short, big and little things for the students to draw in each section. Then have them color their pictures. You may want to have the students work in pairs and guess what's in each section, "Is the (long pencil) in number 1?" *(Yes.)* "Is it (purple)?" *(No.)* "Is it (green)?" *(Yes.)*

Workbook

🎧 **Page 21, Activity 6: Listen. Draw a line. Say.** Play the audio or read the audioscript several times for the students to repeat. Model the sample exercise by saying, "His hands are little." Have the students follow the answer line. Then have the students draw a line from each numbered balloon to the corresponding picture and body part. Then have the students talk about the pictures.
AUDIOSCRIPT: 1. His hands are little. 2. His hair is long. 3. Her hair is short. 4. Her feet are big. 5. His nose is big. 6. Her mouth is big.

Page 22, Activity 7: Draw and color. Write.
Have the students finish the clown faces by drawing in the missing parts using their markers or crayons. Then have the students write the words for the parts that are missing.
ANSWERS: 1. eye 2. nose 3. hair 4. mouth

Language Activities Section, page 88
ANSWERS: 1. His 2. His 3. Her 4. Her 5. His 6. Her

Story Summary

Children follow colorful hints in this riddle book to discover a funny clown.

Key Unit Vocabulary

are, big, brown, clown, color, eye, face, hair, have, little, mouth, nose, shoes, yellow

Word Bank

clothes, many

BEFORE READING

WARM UP

Look around the classroom and say, "I see brown." Then ask volunteers to find a brown object and point it out to the class. Repeat the activity using other colors, including blue, white, and yellow. Try to include all of the students in the activity.

PUT TOGETHER THE LITTLE BOOK

Ask the students to remove pages 27–28 from their books. They can fold the pages in half to make the Little Book, *Who Am I?*

PREVIEW THE LITTLE BOOK

1. After the books are folded, invite the students to point to and name the colors they see in one or more of the illustrations.

2. Read the title aloud. Then have the students look at the pictures and describe what they see there. Encourage them to predict what they think the answer to the title is.

SHARE NEW WORDS

Write the Word Bank words on the board. Say each word and ask the students to repeat it after you. Use pictures in the story or objects in the classroom to illustrate the meanings of these words. Ask the students to look for the Word Bank words and to point to them in their Little Books.

DURING READING

READING THE LITTLE BOOK

Play the audio or read the story aloud. Tell the students they can ask questions and talk about it when you read the story again.

GUIDED READING

Read the story aloud, tracking the print as you go. Some students may wish to track the print in their own books as they read along.

TEACHER TIPS

Help the students distinguish between *face* and *head* and have them point to each. You might also ask volunteers to gather objects in the classroom that are blue, white, brown, or yellow. Ask them to hold up each object they found and say aloud the name of the color.

REREADING

Ask the students if they thought that the answer to the title question would be a clown and what clues made them guess that. Then invite volunteers to take turns looking at each illustration and retelling the text. You may assess their comprehension with questions such as these:

Page 1 *What color is the hair?*
Page 2 *What is on the face?*
Page 3 *What is big and brown?*
Page 4 *Is the clown happy or sad?*

Point out objects and colors in the illustrations that may help the students understand the comprehension questions.

WHO AM I?

by Mario Herrera

I have yellow hair and a little hat.

Who am I?
I'm a clown!

My face has white eyes, a red nose,
and a blue mouth.

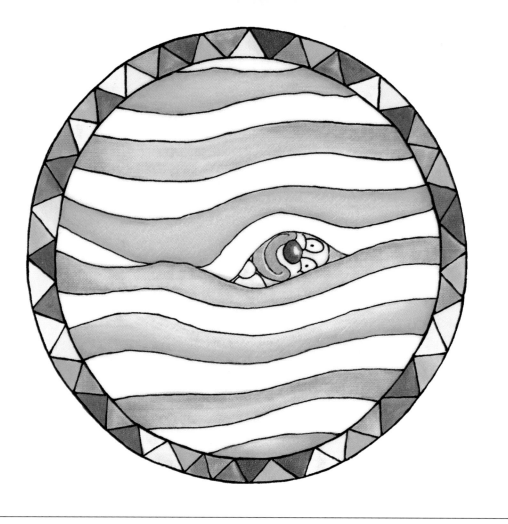

My clothes have many colors.
My shoes are big and brown!

AFTER READING

Activities for Developing Language

PREDICTING

Reread the story with the students. After you read aloud each page, ask them who they thought the speaker was. Ask what clues helped them decide that.

CONTEXT CLUES

Reread the story, pausing before you say key words so the students can fill in the blanks. After the reading, ask them to point to clues in the story and pictures that helped them know which words completed the sentences.

CHARACTER

Draw a word map and label it *Clown.* Display a picture or Picture Card. Then have the students add to the map some words and phrases that describe a clown.

PHYSICAL EDUCATION CONNECTION

Invite the students to march, raising their knees high as you clap in rhythm. Stop and point to your knees. Say the word *knees.* Have them say the word and point to their knees. Do this again, pointing to your feet and saying *feet.* Then jump with legs apart and arms over your head. Jump again, bringing legs together and arms at your sides. Repeat this jumping-jack motion several times with the students. Point to your arms and say *arms.* Then have the students follow you as they did before.

ART CONNECTION

You might want to display pictures of clowns and have the students describe each, pointing out the different colors of their hats and clothing. Then invite the students to draw their own funny clown. Encourage them to use their drawing to describe the clown.

WRITE ABOUT IT!

Ask the students to describe themselves. Then suggest they write a riddle that gives special clues, ending with *Who Am I?* Read aloud their riddles and ask the class to guess the answers. They can add their riddles to their portfolios.

GRAMMAR CONNECTION: ENDING MARKS

Point out the exclamation marks, periods, and question mark in the story. Then give three students index cards, each with one of the marks. Reread the book, pausing at the end of every sentence. Then the student holds up the card that should end that sentence.

WORKBOOK

Little Book Comprehension, page 89.

BULLETIN BOARD IDEAS

You may wish to have the students decorate a bulletin board titled *Clowns* with pictures of clowns they drew.

FAMILY CONNECTION

Invite the students to take their Little Books home and read them to a family member. Encourage them to have the family member guess the answer to the title's question before the reading.

Objectives

to identify and describe parts of the body
to identify colors
to differentiate between *big* and *little*
to differentiate between *long* and *short*
to use possessive adjectives *his* and *her*
to make and read graphs

Key Vocabulary

- ears, eyes, feet, hair, mouth, nose
- her, his
- long, short

APPLICATION

Using the Project Page

Make a graph.

1. Read Homer's question several times for the students to repeat. Make sure the students understand that they are going to find out how many boys and girls have long or short hair and how many have green, blue, or brown eyes.

2. Survey the students in the class to find out how many have green, blue, or brown eyes and long or short hair. Ask, "How many have (blue eyes)?" Show the students how to make a bar graph to illustrate the results.

3. Have the students talk about what the graph shows. Ask, "Do more boys and girls have long hair or short hair? What color eyes do most boys and girls have?"

Color. Make. Say.

1. Have the students color and cut out the face features on page 101. Help the students paste the features they want on the back of a paper plate or on a round piece of paper. Then help the students tie strings to their masks.

2. Have the students look at the picture while you read the conversation several times. Make sure the students understand that they are to describe one of the masks.

3. Divide the class into two teams. Ask four students to put on their masks and come to the front of the class. Let members of each team take turns describing one of the masks.

The other team decides if the description is correct. For each correct answer, that team gets a point. The team with the most points wins.

4. Have the students keep their masks for future practice.

Reaching All Students

What do You Use? Name an action such as *running, jumping, swimming* and ask the students what part of the body they use in that action. You may want to divide the students into two teams and ask the questions to a member from each team. The first person to answer correctly scores a point for his or her team. Ask (running in place), "What do you use?" Answer, "My (legs)."

Sequence of Commands Present the students, together and individually, with a sequence of commands that incorporate both singular and plural parts of the body. "Touch your toes. Raise your hand. Raise two hands. Move your eyes. Move your legs."

Workbook

Page 23, Activity 8: Find the words. Circle the words. Read each of the words at the top of the word puzzle for the students to repeat. Explain that they are to find these words in the puzzle. Encourage them to cross the words off the top as they find them and circle them in the puzzle. See page T3B for the answers.

PROJECT

Make a graph.

Is his hair short or long?

	1	2	3	4	5	6	7	8	9	10

Color. Make. Say.

It's Tony. His nose is orange. It's little.

Yes!

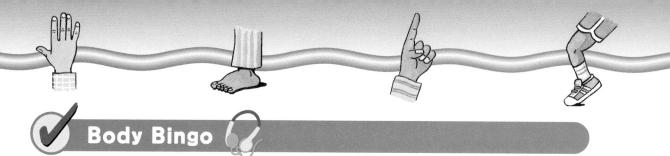

✓ Body Bingo 🎧

Listen and color four more.

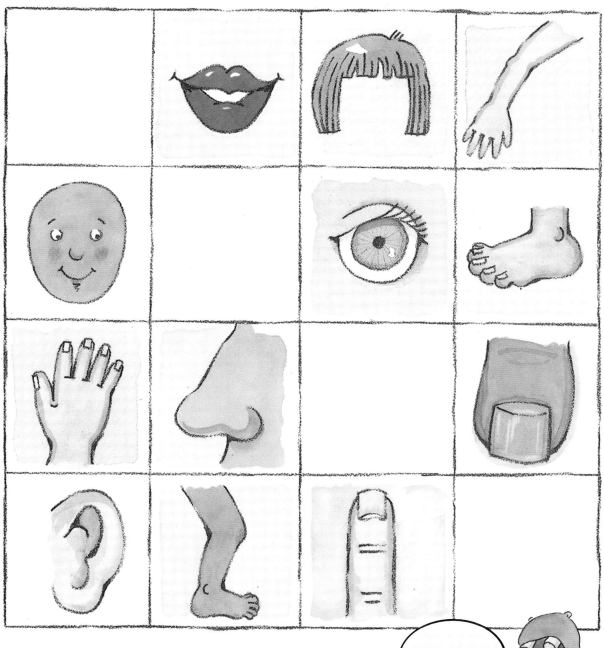

BINGO!

Objectives

to identify and describe parts of the body
to identify colors
to classify
to use illustrations

Key Vocabulary

- arm, ear, eye, face, finger, foot, hair, hand, head, leg, mouth, nose, toe
- brown, orange, purple, yellow

ASSESSMENT

Using the Page

Body Bingo

1. Have the students color any of the four empty squares yellow, brown, orange, and purple.

2. Have the students cut or tear 16 small pieces of paper large enough to cover the squares on the Bingo card.

3. To introduce Bingo, read what Homer is saying for the students to repeat. Tell the students to yell "Bingo!" as soon as they complete a row across or up and down, after listening and covering each picture.

4. ▶ Play the audio or read the audioscript aloud. Have the students cover the correct pictures with a piece of paper.
   AUDIOSCRIPT: 1. mouth 2. hand 3. toe 4. eye 5. yellow 6. nose 7. purple 8. face 9. ear 10. leg 11. orange 12. hair 13. arm 14. finger 15. foot 16. brown

5. ✓ After a student has filled a row, have him or her describe each picture in the Bingo row. Record your observations on the Student Oral Assessment Checklist on page xxi.

Reaching All Students

▶ ⟵⟶ **Right and Left Hand Chant** Copy the poem onto the board or make copies for the students. Read it aloud as you do the motions. Then have the students say the poem and do the motions. Repeat as often as desired.

Raise your left hand.
Raise your right hand.
Stand up. Sit down.
Right, Right, Right!

▶ ⺭ **Body Poem** Read the following poem verses and have the students say them with you. You may want to have the students stand in pairs and point to their partner's body parts as they say the poem together.

Two ears
two eyes
one nose
two hands
ten fingers
ten toes
It's you!

Two eyes
two ears
one nose
ten fingers
two hands
ten toes
It's me!

💡 **Parts of the Body Posters** Have the students cut out pictures of the parts of the body from old magazines. You may want to put the students into groups and assign each group a different body part. When they have cut out a lot of pictures, help each group paste the pictures onto a poster board to make a human body or a monster's body out of the pictures. You may want to have them label the posters. Let each group present its poster to the class. "These are (arms)."

Objectives

to identify and describe parts of the body
to identify colors
to use possessive adjectives *his* and *her*

Key Vocabulary

• arm, ear, eye, face, finger, foot, hair, hand, head, leg, mouth, nose, toe
• brown, orange, purple, yellow

ASSESSMENT

Using the Page

Listen and color.

1. 🌐 Play the audio or read the audioscript aloud to the students. Have them use the correct marker or crayon to color the body parts. Use the assessment chart on page xxiii to record how each student has done.
AUDIOSCRIPT: 1. Color her hair purple. 2. Color her nose brown. 3. Color her arms yellow. 4. Color her feet orange. 5. Color her legs red. 6. Color her mouth green.

2. Point to different parts of the clown's body. Have the students identify the body part and name its color, "It's her nose. It's brown. It's her leg. It's red." Invite the students to finish coloring the drawing as they wish.

I can.

1. Read the statement for number 1 aloud to the students. Ask individuals, groups, or the whole class to identify the parts of the body. Have them circle the parts of the picture of the clown's face for the words they can say.

2. Read the statement for number 2 aloud to the students. Ask individuals, groups, or the whole class to identify the colors. Have them circle the pictures for the words they can say.

3. Read the statement for number 3 aloud to the students. Ask individuals to hold up and talk about the masks they made. Quickly note oral production in these activities on the Student Oral Assessment Checklist on page xxi.

Reaching All Students

🖊 **Vocabulary Checklist** Have the students identify the pictures in the Picture Dictionary on pages 30–31.

Unit Mural Elicit all the words and expressions the students remember from this unit. Write them on mural or poster paper. Have the students illustrate the vocabulary. Use this to review vocabulary in subsequent classes.

Unit 3 Test See page xxxiii.

Workbook

🌐 🖊 **Page 24, Listen and color.** Play the audio or read the audioscript aloud to the students. Have them use the correct marker or crayon to color the body parts of the two clowns. Then point to the different parts of one clown's body and have the students identify them.
AUDIOSCRIPT: 1. Color her hair yellow. 2. Color his ears green. 3. Color his hair purple. 4. Color his eyes orange. 5. Color her legs red. 6. Color her feet brown. 7. Color her mouth orange. 8. Color his hands yellow. 9. Color his feet blue.

The following Workbook pages are a practice test for Units 1–3. Have the students do pages 25–26 as a practice test. Check the students' answers. You may want to review areas with which they had difficulty before they take the test on pages xl–xli.

🖊 **Page 25, Match the numbers and pictures.** Have the students count the people or objects in each picture and draw a line from each number word to the correct picture.

🌐 🖊 **Page 26, Listen and circle.** Play the audio or read the audioscript aloud two or three times for the students to complete the activity.
AUDIOSCRIPT: 1. Circle the book. 2. Circle the chair. 3. Circle the leg. 4. Circle the number three. 5. Circle the ear. 6. Circle the mother. 7. Circle the boy.

✔ Listen and color.

✔ I can.

1. I can say eyes, ears, nose, and mouth.

2. I can say colors.

3. I can make a mask.

4 My Clothes

Communication Objectives

to identify items of clothing
to tell what one is wearing
to name one's favorite color and clothes
to identify colors
to follow directions

Language Objectives

to use adjectives before nouns
to use the present progressive tense
to use plural nouns
to use possessive adjectives *his/her*
to understand *this/these*

Learning Strategies and Thinking Skills

to classify
to sequence
to use selective attention
to apply prior knowledge
to pronounce /p/, /ð/

Content Connections

Art: to make paper dolls; to make collages;
  to draw clothes
Mathematics: to count
Music: to sing songs
Social Studies: to take a survey; to make
  charts and graphs

Materials

New Parade 1 Student Book, pages 32–41
New Parade 1 Workbook, pages 27–34;
  90–92
New Parade 1 Audio: Tape/CD
New Parade 1 Video and Video Guide
New Parade 1 Posters
Toy telephones, crayons or markers, scissors,
  old magazines, old newspapers, old
  catalogs, poster paper, glue, pictures of
  different colored clothes, game pieces,
  coins

Optional Materials: New Parade Picture
  Cards—dress, skirt, shirt, pants, jacket,
  sweater, hats; adult-sized clothes, clothing
  box, drawing paper, paper for a mural;
  Little Celebrations—This Hat by Eve
  Feldman, *Lin's Backpack* by Helen Lester,
  Sneakers! Sneakers! by Angela Shelf
  Medearis, and *The Crazy Quilt* by Kristin
  Avery

Key Vocabulary

- clothes, dress, hat, jacket, pants, shirt,
  shoe, skirt, sock, sweater
- what, what color, what's
- are, is
- wearing
- Put on your (hat).; Take off your (shoes).;
  Hang up the (dress).; Fold the (shirt).; Put
  the (shirt) away.
- he, it, she
- these, this
- black, pink, white

Picture Dictionary

dress shoes skirt sweater pants hat
jacket shirt socks

Setting Up the Classroom

Read Unit 4 before you begin, so that you are familiar with the material you will be covering. Make sure that you gather the supplies you will need to teach the lessons. Using adult-sized clothes will make the lessons more fun, since most children love dressing up in them. Prepare TPR commands using the articles of clothing introduced in this unit for the Warm Up on page T32. If you do not have enough toy telephones for Activity 5, you could use cardboard cutouts of telephone receivers or cell phones. Read the Little Book *Helping* to decide what tone of voice you will use when you read it aloud to the students.

Using the Video and the Video Guide

Show the video to start this new unit. The students will get an idea of the topic and a preview of the language they will be learning. Help them to understand what is happening. Encourage the students to interact with the video by answering the questions, singing, and doing the actions along with the children in the video. Plan to use the video often, especially at the beginning of each week. The students will understand more and more each time. Use the Video Guide to give you ideas about where to start and stop the video.

This video segment focuses on clothes, colors, *this* and *that,* and actions such as *put on, take off,* and *fold.* Sam receives a phone call from Nora. He puts on his shoes and goes to her house to help her unpack a bag of clothes. The children act out the chant from the Student Book, "Are these blue pants?" Nora gives Sam funny socks, "These are socks. Put on your socks." and they talk about the clothes in the bag and their colors as they fold and hang them, "What's this? This is a shirt. These are pants."

Family Connections

Ask the students to find out a friend or family member's favorite articles of clothing and then have them draw that person wearing those clothes. Have the students bring their pictures to class and encourage them to talk about the person and his or her favorite clothes.

Bulletin Board Ideas

On strips of construction paper write the names of the items of clothing covered in this unit in a column down the left side of the bulletin board. Challenge the students to find magazine pictures of those items in colors they have learned and to hang them beside the name of each item of clothing. For example, when you finish the unit, there might be red, green, blue, black, pink, purple, yellow, and white shirts beside the word *shirt* on the bulletin board. When the bulletin board is complete, have the students say the colors and items of clothing they see.

Little Book: Helping

Summary: While a boy is helping his mother put away clothes, his younger sister is pulling them out and putting them on. Then both children put on warm jackets to play outside on a chilly day.

4 My Clothes

1. Listen and chant.

Are these blue pants?
No, they're not.
Are these green pants?
No, they're not.
What color are they?
Can you say?
They're orange!

2. Look and say.

BLACK

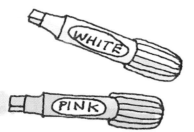

WHITE

PINK

What colors do you know?

Objectives

to identify items of clothing
to identify colors
to pronounce /p/ and /ð/
to apply prior knowledge

Key Vocabulary

- dress, hat, jacket, pants, shirt, shoe, skirt, sock, sweater
- what color
- black, pink, white

WARM UP

1. 💡 Display Picture Cards of dress, skirt, shirt, pants, hats, jacket, sweater or pictures from a clothing catalog, or fill a box with the clothing items in the key vocabulary list. Hold up each picture or clothing item and invite the students to identify any clothing items and colors they can. Then name each item for the students to repeat.

2. 🕴 As a warm up at the beginning of each class do some TPR activities. Using the clothes from the clothing box, demonstrate: *Put on your (hat). Take off your (shoes). Hang up the (dress). Fold the (shirt). Put the (shirt) away.* For an explanation of TPR, see page ix.

3. Display the Poster for Unit 4.

PRESENTATION

Using the Page

ACTIVITY 1

Listen and chant.

1. Ask the students to say what the teacher is doing in the picture.

2. 🎧 Play the audio or read the chant aloud several times for the students to repeat. To practice pronunciation, focus on /p/ in *pants* and /ð/ in *these*.

3. The students substitute other clothing items in additional verses. On the board, write *Is this a (pink sock)? No, it isn't. What color is it? It's (yellow).* Make sure the students know to substitute these lines for singular items of clothing.

ACTIVITY 2

Look and say.

1. Focus attention on Hanna. Read what she is asking. Have the students name the colors they already know and show you the appropriate matching markers. Then point to a marker on the page and introduce or review its color, "It's (black)." Do this for the other markers.

2. Show pictures of clothing items that are black, white, or pink. Ask, "What color is the (shirt)?" *(It's white.)*

Reaching All Students

Vocabulary Expansion Focus attention on the Picture Dictionary on pages 32–33. Have the students point at each piece of clothing and identify it *(dress, shoes, skirt, sweater, pants, hat, jacket, shirt).*

Workbook

Page 27, Activity 1: Match. Say. Color. Model the first answer. Have the students point to the word *skirt*. Have them trace the line from the word *skirt* to the picture of the skirt. Then have the students draw a line from each remaining word to the picture of that item. Then dictate a color for each item, for example, "Color the shirt red."

Page 28, Activity 2: Color the spaces. Read the numbers and the colors they represent several times. Have the students color the shapes using the color key. If your students can't read the color names, you might want to use a bulletin board to post circles of the different colors and then the corresponding numbers next to them.

Page 28, Activity 3: Write your answer. When the students have finished coloring the picture, ask, "What is it?" The students should answer, "It's a jacket." Help them write *jacket* on the line provided.

Objectives

to identify items of clothing
to tell what people are wearing
to identify colors
to use adjectives before nouns
to use plural nouns

Key Vocabulary

- clothes, dress, hat, jacket, pants, shirt, shoe, skirt, sock, sweater
- wearing
- black, pink, white

PRESENTATION

Using the Page

ACTIVITY 3

Listen. Point. Say.

1. ☀ Ask the students to look at the first clothesline and name any items they can in English.

2. 🎧 Point to the clothes on the first clothesline. Play the audio or say the word for each singular item. Have the students repeat each word. Repeat this procedure for the plural items on the second clothesline.

ACTIVITY 4

Look. Listen. Read.

1. Introduce or review *hat* and *shoes* by displaying pictures or the real clothing items from your clothing box.

2. 🎧 Have the students look at the picture. Play the audio or read the conversation aloud several times for the students to repeat.

3. Ask individual students to identify the other clothes that each person in the picture is wearing such as "He's wearing blue pants."

4. Read aloud what Homer is asking. Have the students answer his question by saying, "She's wearing (pink shoes). He's wearing (blue pants)."

5. Ask individuals to stand up and say what they are wearing. Encourage them to say what colors their clothes are.

Reaching All Students

🧍 **Clothes Game** Play a TPR game. Substitute your students' clothing items in the following chant:

Look around, look around.
Look around and see.
If you're wearing a (pink dress),
Come and stand by me!

Singular to Plural Game Divide the class into two teams. Say a singular sentence to one member from each team. The first person to correctly change the singular sentence into a plural sentence scores a point for his or her team. For example, "This is a shoe" becomes "These are shoes." The team with the most points wins.

🎧 🔀 **Students' Clothing** Have the students sing about their own clothing. Play the audio or sing the song (tune of "Mary Had a Little Lamb") for the students to repeat. Have them sit in a circle and have the class sing a verse for each student.

(Mario's) wearing a yellow shirt,
A yellow shirt, a yellow shirt,
(Mario's) wearing a yellow shirt,
This fine day!

Introduce new clothing words as you come to a student wearing these items.

Workbook

Page 29, Activity 4: Match. Say. Color. Model the sample answer. Have the students trace the line from *dress* to its picture. Read the words in the center column several times for the students to repeat. Have the students draw a line from the word to the pictured piece of clothing. Then have the students color the pictures.

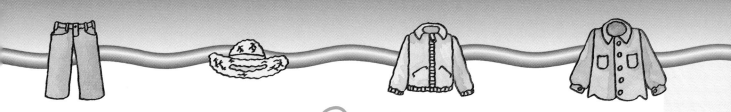

3. Listen. Point. Say.

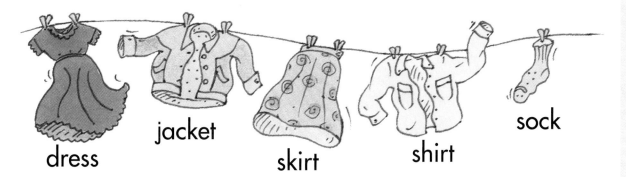

dress

jacket

skirt

shirt

sock

dresses

jackets

skirts

shirts

socks

4. Look. Listen. Read.

I'm wearing a yellow hat.

I'm wearing black shoes.

What else are they wearing?

5. Look. Listen. Say.

What are you wearing?

A shirt and pants.

What are you wearing?

A sweater and a skirt.

6. Listen and circle.

1.

2.

3.

4.

5.

Objectives

to identify items of clothing
to tell what one is wearing
to name one's favorite color
to use plural nouns
to understand *this/these*

Key Vocabulary

* clothes, dress, hat, jacket, pants, shirt, shoe, skirt, sock, sweater
* what
* is, are, wearing
* these, this

PRACTICE

Using the Page

ACTIVITY 5

Look. Listen. Say.

1. Focus attention on the pictures. Ask, "What are the girls doing?" *(talking on the phone)*

2. 🎧 Play the audio or read their conversation several times for the students to repeat.

3. Give pairs of students toy telephones and ask them to act out the conversation from the book, substituting the clothes they are wearing for those mentioned in the conversation. Help with any additional vocabulary the students might need.

ACTIVITY 6

Listen and circle.

1. 🎧 Model the sample exercise. Play the audio or say, "These are hats. Circle the hats." Make sure the students understand why the two hats are circled.

2. Play the audio or read the audioscript several times. Have the students circle the picture that stands for what they hear.
   AUDIOSCRIPT: 1. These are jackets. 2. This is a shirt. 3. These are socks. 4. This is a shoe. 5. These are sweaters.
   ANSWERS: 1. The blue jacket and the black jacket are circled. 2. The blue shirt is circled. 3. The orange socks are circled. 4. The white tennis shoe is circled. 5. The brown sweaters are circled.

3. Point to each picture of the clothing items and ask the students to say the correct singular or plural word. You might also want to have the students identify the color of each item.

Reaching All Students

Singular and Plural Nouns Continue Activity 6 on a separate sheet of paper by naming singular and plural vocabulary for classroom objects, body parts, and family members.

🎧 🔊 **My Favorite Color** Play the audio or read the following poem several times to the students. Then ask the students what their favorite colors are.

Do you have some shoes?
　Yes, I do. Yes, I do.
What color are they?
　They're blue. They're blue.

Do you have a T-shirt?
　Yes, I do. Yes, I do.
What color is it?
　It's blue. It's blue.

Is blue your favorite color?
Did I guess? Did I guess?
　Blue's my favorite color!
　Yes! Yes! Yes!

Poem Expansion Have the students substitute other clothing items and colors in the poem. You may want to hold up real clothing items to prompt responses.

🔊 **Counting the Clothes** Have the students count the articles of clothing in Activity 6. You may want to help them make a graph to illustrate the results.

Objectives

to identify items of clothing
to identify colors
to follow directions
to use possessive adjectives *his/her*
to use selective attention

Key Vocabulary

• clothes, dress, hat, jacket, pants, shirt, shoe, skirt, sock, sweater
• it
• is
• wearing

PRACTICE

Warm Up

1. ☑ Use pictures or Picture Cards of clothes and real clothes to review the key vocabulary words. Check to see how many words the students can say.

2. Have the students say the chant on page 32.

Using the Page

ACTIVITY 7

Listen and color.

🎧 Play the audio or read the audioscript aloud to the students. Have them use the correct marker or crayon to color the clothes.
AUDIOSCRIPT: 1. Color the boy's jacket red. 2. Color the girl's skirt green. 3. Color his pants blue. 4. Color his shoes black. 5. Color her shoes brown. 6. Color her hat yellow. 7. Color her jacket purple. 8. Color his hat orange. 9. Color her socks white.

ACTIVITY 8

Play the game.

1. Focus attention on the pictures. Ask, "What kind of game do you think the students in the picture are playing?" *(guessing game)*

2. 🎧 💡 Play the audio or read the conversation aloud several times for the students to repeat. Make sure the students understand that the boy and girl are guessing who the third boy is describing.

3. Read aloud what Hanna is saying several times for the students to repeat.

4. Secretly pick a person in the class to be described and say one clue. Have the students guess who it is. Continue adding clues and having them guess until someone correctly guesses. Let the person who correctly guesses silently pick the next person to be described.

Reaching All Students

Pair Activity If your students are linguistically able, have pairs of students play the guessing game. Ask one to silently pick a person in the class to be described and to say one clue. Have the partner guess who it is. Have them continue adding clues and guessing until the partner correctly guesses. Continue with other pairs.

☑ **Vocabulary Check** Have the students identify the pieces of clothing in the Picture Dictionary on pages 34–35.

Workbook

🎧 Page 30, Activity 5: Listen and color. Play the audio or read the audioscript aloud several times. Have the students use their markers or crayons to color the appropriate clothing.
AUDIOSCRIPT: Color the shirt red and the hat blue. Color the pants blue and the jacket black. Color the socks pink and the shoes purple. Color the sweater green and the skirt orange. Color the dress red and the sweater yellow. Color the shoes pink and the pants orange.

Language Activities Section, page 90
ANSWERS: Answers will vary.

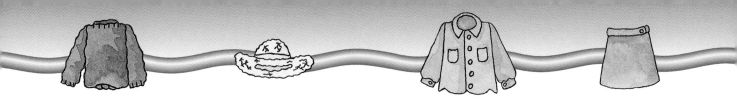

7. Listen and color.

8. Play the game.

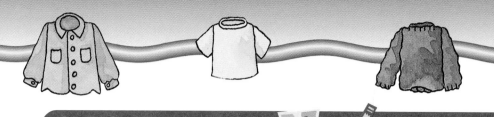

9. Ask. Count. Color.

What's your favorite color?

	Favorite Color									
	1	2	3	4	5	6	7	8	9	10
blue										
brown										
green										
orange										
pink										
purple										
red										
white										
yellow										

What are your favorite clothes?

How many boys and girls like hats?

	Favorite Clothes									
	1	2	3	4	5	6	7	8	9	10
dresses										
hats										
jackets										
pants										
shirts										
shoes										
skirts										
socks										
sweater										

Objectives

to identify items of clothing
to tell what one is wearing
to name one's favorite color
to identify colors
to use adjectives before nouns
to count
to make charts and graphs

Key Vocabulary

- clothes, dress, hat, jacket, pants, shirt, shoe, skirt, sock, sweater
- wearing
- black, pink, white

APPLICATION

Using the Page

ACTIVITY 9

Ask. Count. Color.

1. Read what Homer and Hanna are asking several times for the students to repeat. Have the students tell what their favorite color is and what their favorite clothes are.

2. Divide the class into groups of 10 or fewer. Have the students in each group ask one another what their favorite colors and clothes are. For each response, have the students check or color a box. Show the students how to use a marker to color in the rows to make the survey look like a bar graph.

3. Reread what Homer is asking about the bottom graph. You may want to have volunteers from each group report their results as you compile all the groups' results in a "favorite color" graph and a "favorite clothes" graph for the whole class. As a class, discuss the results of the survey. Ask, "How many boys and girls like (blue)? How many boys and girls like (sweaters)?"

Reaching All Students

Dress Up Game Bring into class two of each of the following adult-sized items and put into separate piles: hats, shirts, sweaters, pairs of socks, pairs of shoes. Divide the class into two teams. Have a student from each team put on one set of the clothing as fast as he or she can. All buttons must be buttoned and shoelaces tied. The student who finishes first and who can name all the clothing items with the help of his or her teammates wins a point for his or her team. The team with the most points wins. For larger classes, you may want entire teams to dress up at a time. Each correctly dressed student who can identify the clothing scores a point for the team.

Let's Draw Have each student fold and number drawing paper into eight sections. Ask the student to draw and color a clothing item in each section. Then have the students work in pairs and ask each other what they have in each numbered section, "What's in your number two box?" *(pink socks)*

Workbook

Page 31, Activity 6: Make cards. Have the students color the pictures using any color they choose. Then have the students cut out the cards and write the name of each item of clothing pictured on each card. Then the students can work in pairs to ask and answer questions about their cards. One student can hold up a card and ask, "What is this? What color is it?" The other can answer, "It's a (red hat)." Or the pairs can combine their cards and match the words with the pictures.

Language Activities Section, page 91
ANSWERS: 1. wearing 2. taking 3. folding
4. hanging

Story Summary

While a boy is helping his mother put away clothes, his younger sister is pulling them out and putting them on. Then both children put on warm jackets to play outside on a chilly day.

Key Unit Vocabulary

fold the (skirt), hang up the (dress), pants, put on your (jackets), put the (shirt) away, these

Word Bank

help, now

BEFORE READING

WARM UP

Invite all students wearing brown pants to stand. Say *brown pants* and ask the students to repeat the words. Then ask the students wearing white socks to stand. Say the words and have the students repeat them. Continue this activity using other colors and items of clothing until everyone is standing.

PUT TOGETHER THE LITTLE BOOK

Ask students to remove pages 37–38 from their books. They can fold the pages in half to make the Little Book, *Helping*.

PREVIEW THE LITTLE BOOK

1. After the books are assembled, ask the students to tell what articles of clothing and other objects they see on each page.

2. Read the title aloud and encourage the students to look at the pictures, telling what the children are doing on each page. Ask: "How are the children helping?" Then encourage them to describe what is happening in the pictures. Finally, ask the students to predict what will happen in the story.

SHARE NEW WORDS

Write the Word Bank words on the board. Say the words and invite the students repeat them after you. Use illustrations in the story or role play to explain the words' meanings.

DURING READING

READING THE LITTLE BOOK

Invite the students to listen quietly as you play the audio or read the story aloud. Tell the students to save their questions to ask when you read the story again.

GUIDED READING

Read the story aloud as the students follow along. Ask a volunteer track the print as you read.

TEACHER TIPS

Invite the students to role play actions such as *hang up, put away, fold, go out,* and *put on.*

REREADING

Ask students to compare their predictions about what would take place in the story to what actually occurred. Quickly review what happens in the story. You may assess their comprehension with questions like these:

Page 1 *What does the mother ask the children to do?*
Page 2 *What is the boy doing to help?*
Page 3 *What is the girl doing?*
Page 4 *Where do the children go?*

Point out actions in the illustrations that help students understand the comprehension questions.

Fold these skirts and pants.
Hang up these shirts.

Put these shoes away.

AFTER READING

Activities for Developing Language

SUMMARIZING

Have volunteers take turns using their own words to tell what happens in the story.

MAIN IDEA

The students can work in pairs and tell each other what happens on each page. Encourage them to use the illustrations to help them. They can also listen again to the audio.

SEQUENCING

Invite students to draw three boxes and number them from 1 to 3. In the boxes, the students can draw pictures that show what the children in the story do first, next, and last.

SOCIAL STUDIES CONNECTION

Have small groups work together to create a poster or mural of ways they can help out at home. They can draw illustrations and write captions to go underneath each picture.

ART CONNECTION

Ask the students to cut out articles of clothing from magazines or catalogs. They may choose one item to paste on construction paper. Then suggest the students use crayons to add a head, arms, legs, and feet to make a picture of themselves wearing the clothing they cut out. Help them to add a label to the clothing such as *shirt, dress,* or *hat.*

WRITE ABOUT IT!

Have students draw a picture of a time they helped out at home. Then have them write or dictate what they are doing in the picture. Add their writing to their portfolios. Invite the students to draw a picture for each new word for their own Picture Dictionary.

GRAMMAR CONNECTION: IMPERATIVE SENTENCES

Write on the board *Please help me. Hang up these dresses.* Explain to the students that these sentences tell someone what to do. Then have them suggest other sentences that give commands. Point out how these sentences all end in periods.

WORKBOOK

See Little Book Comprehension, page 92.

BULLETIN BOARD IDEAS

You may wish to have students draw pictures of themselves doing jobs at home. Hang the pictures on a bulletin board titled *Helping at Home.*

FAMILY CONNECTION

Invite the students to take their Little Books home and share them with their friends and family members. Suggest that when they help out at home, the students might want to tell family members how to say the task.

PROJECT

Cut. Color. Play.

What's he wearing?

He's wearing blue pants.

Make a collage.

① ②

③

These are my favorite clothes.

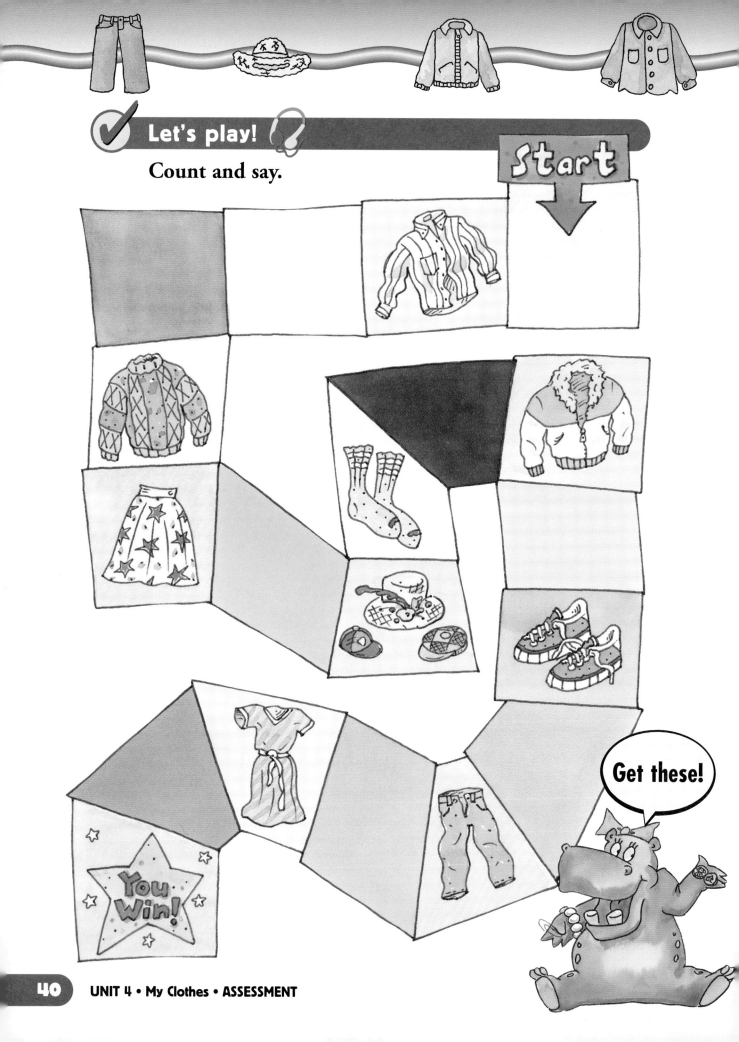

Let's play!

Count and say.

Start

Get these!

You Win!

Objectives

to identify items of clothing
to identify colors
to follow directions
to use adjectives before nouns
to understand *this/these*
to classify

Key Vocabulary

- clothes, dress, hat, jacket, pants, shirt, shoe, skirt, sock, sweater,
- black, pink, white
- these, this

ASSESSMENT

Warm Up

1. Review the words for clothes by showing pictures of different colored clothes for the students to describe. Encourage the students to say sentences such as "This is a white sock."

2. Have the students sort clothes or pictures of clothes by color. Elicit from the students sentences such as "These are pink."

Using the Page

Let's play!

1. Play the audio or read what Hanna is saying several times for the students to repeat. Get playing pieces and coins for the students to play with. A playing piece can be any small object such as an eraser, bottle cap, paper clip, or a piece of paper.

2. Have the students play in pairs or groups of three. Decide which side of the coin will be worth one point and which will be worth two. The students take turns tossing their coins and moving their playing pieces two, three, or four spaces on the board. They must identify the clothes and their colors or the color swatch that they land on. For example, for a white shirt, a student might say, "It's a (white shirt)" or "It's a shirt. It's white." For plural items, a student might say, "These are pink socks." If they answer incorrectly, they go back to where they were before their turn. The other players decide if the answers are correct. The first person to finish wins.

3. As the students play the game, walk around the room and observe how individual students are using the key vocabulary words. Check for objectives: (1) the identification of items of clothing and (2) the use of descriptive colors. Record your observations on the Student Oral Assessment Checklist on page xxi.

4. Point to a square on the game board. Ask a student to identify the picture in it and its color. "What's this?" *(It's a green dress.)* Then have that student point to another square on the game board and ask another student to identify the pictured item and its color.

Reaching All Students

Memory Card Game Have the students get the clothing cards they made in Workbook, Activity 6. Put the students into pairs and have them combine their cards and turn them all facedown. Then have them take turns turning over pairs of cards and trying to match the items. Make sure the students say the items pictured as they turn the cards over. If they don't match a pair, they must turn them facedown again. The person with the most pairs wins.

Clothes Sorting Collect as many pictures of clothing as possible. Label boxes—dresses, hats, jackets, pants, skirts, shoes, shirts, socks, and sweaters. Hold up each picture and have the class identify the clothing and tell you which box to put it in.

UNIT 4 • My Clothes

Objectives
to identify items of clothing
to tell what one is wearing
to identify colors
to use plural nouns
to understand *this/these*

Key Vocabulary
• clothes, dress, hat, jacket, pants, shirt, shoe, skirt, sock, sweater
• black, pink, white
• these, this

ASSESSMENT

Using the Page

Listen and circle.

Play the audio or read the following sentences aloud. Have the students circle the pictures they hear. Use the assessment chart to record how each student has done.
AUDIOSCRIPT: 1. These are blue pants.
2. These are black shoes. 3. This is an orange skirt. 4. This is a red hat. 5. This is a brown jacket. 6. This is a pink sweater.
ANSWERS: 1. The blue pants are circled.
2. The black shoes are circled. 3. The orange skirt is circled. 4. The red hat is circled.
5. The brown jacket is circled. 6. The pink sweater is circled.

I can.

1. Read the statement for number 1 aloud to the students. Ask individuals, groups, or the whole class to identify the colors. Have them circle the pictures for the words they can say.

2. Read the statement for number 2 aloud to the students. Ask individuals, groups, or the whole class to identify the pieces of clothing *(dress, shoes, pants)*. Have them circle the pictures of the words they can say. Quickly note oral production in these activities on the Student Oral Assessment Checklist on page xxi.

Reaching All Students

Vocabulary Checklist Point to the clothes in the Picture Dictionary on pages 40–41. Have the students identify them.

Mary Wore a Red Dress Write this song on the board or make a copy for the students. Play the audio or sing the song several

times for the students to repeat. Hold up a red dress as you sing. Then ask a student to hold up another piece of clothing from the clothing box (or a clothing card) and have the students substitute the name, clothing, and color in the song. The student gets to choose the next person for the song.

Mary wore a red dress, red dress, red dress. Mary wore a red dress all day long.

Fashion Show Put on a fashion show. Let the students dress up in adult-sized clothes and parade around the front of the classroom. Play commentator of the outfits, "Here's Ana. She's wearing a yellow dress and a pair of green shoes." After you have talked about several students, ask individuals to be the commentator.

Unit Mural Elicit all the words and expressions the students remember from this unit. Write them on mural or poster paper. Have the students illustrate the vocabulary. Use this to review vocabulary in subsequent classes.

Unit 4 Test See page xxxiv.

Workbook

Page 34, Listen and circle. Play the audio or read the audioscript aloud two or three times for the students to complete the activity.
AUDIOSCRIPT: 1. This is a skirt. 2. These are socks. 3. This is a dress. 4. This is a shirt.
5. This is a sweater. 6. These are pants. 7. These are hats.
ANSWERS: 1. The skirt is circled. 2. The socks are circled. 3. The dress is circled. 4. The shirt is circled. 5. The sweater is circled. 6. The pants are circled. 7. The hats are circled.

✔ Listen and circle. 🎧

1.

2.

3.

4.

5.

6.

✔ I can.

1. I can say colors.

2. I can say clothes.

5 My House

Communication Objectives

to identify rooms and objects in a house
to describe a home
to identify family members
to identify actions
to identify locations
to identify shapes—circle, square, triangle, rectangle
to identify colors

Language Objectives

to use adjectives before nouns
to use the preposition *in*
to use the simple present tense of *be*
to use the present progressive tense
to answer questions with *what, where,* and *how many*
to use singular and plural nouns
to pronounce /l/, /r/, and /d/

Learning Strategies and Thinking Skills

to apply prior knowledge
to relate part to whole
to classify
to compare and contrast
to use illustrations
to follow directions

Content Connections

Art: to make a house with cutout shapes; to draw houses
Literature: to say poems
Mathematics: to recognize shapes; to count; to use simple coordinates
Social Studies: to draw a map of a house; to locate objects using simple coordinates

Materials

New Parade 1 Student Book, pages 42–51
New Parade 1 Workbook, pages 35–42; 93–95
New Parade 1 Audio: Tape/CD
New Parade 1 Video and Video Guide
New Parade 1 Posters
Box, pictures of houses and people in houses, crayons or markers, glue, scissors, colored construction paper, big and little rectangles, squares, circles, and triangles
Optional Materials: New Parade Picture Cards—house, eat, cook; doll house; felt board "house"; drawing paper; old newspapers, catalogs, and magazines; poster paper; *Little Celebrations—Shape Walk* by Anita Parks, *Take a Guess* by Terry Briggs, and *Off to Grandma's House* by Mary Patton

Key Vocabulary

- bathroom, bathtub, bed, bedroom, bookcase, chair, closet, dining room, house, kitchen, lamp, living room, sofa, stove, table, TV
- circle, rectangle, square, triangle
- how many, what, what's, where, who
- are, do, is, put, see
- cooking, doing, eating, playing, reading, sleeping, watching TV
- he's, she's, they're
- in

Picture Dictionary

chair   table   sofa   bookcase   bathtub   bed   lamp   stove

Setting Up the Classroom

Prepare for this unit by reading through the material and gathering the supplies and materials for the activities. Collect some magazine pictures of people cooking, eating, sleeping, and watching TV or use Picture Cards if you would like to extend Activity 2. For the Warm Up on page T42, prepare written TPR commands to review some of the material from Units 1–4. Be sure to include commands that use *in*. For example, "Put your hand in your pocket." and "Put the shoe in the box." Read the Little Book *Fluffy Is Missing!* to anticipate some questions the students might ask.

Using the Video and the Video Guide

Begin the unit by showing the video, in order to give the students a preview of the language they will be learning in context. You may want to repeat the video segment often, especially at the beginning of each week. The Video Guide will suggest places to stop and start the video. Encourage the students to interact with the video by answering the questions, singing, and doing the actions along with the children in the video.

This video segment focuses on the rooms of the house, furniture, and questions such as "Where do you eat?" "How many lamps are in your living room?" "What's this?" and "Do you like reading in the living room?" It also features the verb *like*—"I like the chair," and activities—*reading, eating,* and *playing*. First, we see Sam making a sandwich in the kitchen, then eating in the dining room. Nora and Sam read books in Sam's living room and Nora counts and talks about objects in the living room. Then Sam takes Nora on a tour of his house. They look in the bathroom, the closet, and Sam's room—with his toy box full of toys!

Family Connections

Ask the students to observe their families and then draw pictures at home of them doing activities in various rooms. Encourage them to label each picture with the name of the room. They might use these pictures to teach their families the names of the rooms.

Bulletin Board Ideas

With thin strips of paper, make the outline of a simple five-room house on the bulletin board. Encourage the students to make labels for each room and "furnish" the house with pictures cut out from magazines over the course of the unit.

Little Book: Fluffy Is Missing!

Summary: Mary is sad. She can't find her cat, Fluffy, anywhere—not in the kitchen, not in the living room. When she finds him outside on the roof, she is happy again.

5 My House

Hanna, where's the father?

bathroom

bedroom

closet

kitchen

dining room

living room

In the kitchen, I think.

Objectives

to identify rooms and objects in a house
to describe a home
to review family members
to answer questions with *where*
to use the preposition *in*
to use illustrations

Key Vocabulary

- bathroom, bathtub, bed, bedroom, bookcase, chair, closet, dining room, house, kitchen, lamp, living room, sofa, stove, table, TV
- where
- is, put

WARM UP

1. **[X]** Use TPR to review the classroom commands the students have learned in earlier units. Then ask individuals to put things in something such as a box as you say, "Put the (pencil) in the (box)." See page ix for more information.

2. Place a small box on your desk and ask the students to identify it. Place a pencil inside the box and say, "The pencil is in the box." Repeat, and then ask, "Where's the pencil?"

Help the students answer, "It's in the box." Continue placing other objects in boxes, desks, and so on.

3. **[bulb]** Say, "Now we will talk about what is in our houses." Show photographs of the insides of various houses to the class, and check if any students know such words as *kitchen*.

4. Display the Poster for Unit 5.

PRESENTATION

Using the Page
ACTIVITY 1
Listen. Point. Say.

1. **[audio]** Play the audio or read the names of the different rooms in the house several times for the students to repeat. Then have the students point to the rooms as you name them.

2. Introduce the preposition *in* by pointing to the father and saying, "This is the father. He's in the kitchen." Then point to other family members in the house and identify in which room he or she is.

3. **[audio]** Play the audio or read Homer and Hanna's conversation several times for the students to repeat. Guide the students in answering similar questions about the location of each member of the family in the picture.

4. Point to the furnishings in the house to present *bathtub, bed, bookcase, lamp, sofa, stove, table, chairs,* and *TV*. Then have the students point to each item as you name it. Then help the students identify what furnishings are in the

bedroom, dining room, and living room. Ask, "Where's the bed?" *(It's in the bedroom.)*

Reaching All Students

Vocabulary Expansion Focus attention on the Picture Dictionary on pages 42–43. Have the students point to the different pieces of furniture as you say the words for them to repeat several times *(chair, table, sofa, bookcase, bathtub, bed, lamp, stove)*. You may also want the students to say what color each piece of furniture is.

Model House Bring in a doll house, make a felt board "house," or draw a house. Have the students take turns placing "people" in the house and identifying the people, rooms, and furniture.

[icon] My Family and Me Have the students make take-home books. Help them make front and back covers. As the students go through the unit, have them create pages about their families, rooms in their homes, and what family members do in each room. Encourage the students to write family member's names and names of places and objects in their books.

Objectives

to identify rooms in a house
to describe a home
to identify actions
to identify family members
to apply prior knowledge
to pronounce /l/ and /r/
to use the present progressive tense
to answer questions with *what*

Key Vocabulary

- bedroom, dining room, house, kitchen, living room
- what
- is
- cooking, doing, eating, playing, sleeping, watching TV

PRESENTATION

Warm Up

1. Have the students say rhymes or chants from previous units such as on pages 12 and 16.

2. Review the names of the rooms in a house by pointing to the rooms in a doll house or a picture of a cut-away view of a house. Have the students name each room as you point to it.

3. Show pictures of people cooking, eating, sleeping, and watching TV to introduce those words. For example, say, "The (mother) is cooking. The baby is (sleeping)."

Using the Page
ACTIVITY 2
Listen. Repeat. Do the actions.

1. Focus attention on the pictures. Ask, "What do you think the boy is doing?" (*cooking, watching TV, eating, sleeping*)

2. Play the audio or read the poem aloud several times for the students to repeat. As the students say the poem, have them also do the hand motions shown in the picture.

3. You may want to divide the class into groups of four and have each group do just one of the motions.

4. To practice pronunciation, focus on /l/ in *let's* and /r/ in *rooms.*

Reaching All Students

Guess the Action Have the students take turns pantomiming actions for the other students to guess.

Room Classifying Provide old magazines or catalogs for pairs of students. Assign a different room to each pair. The students are to find as many pictures as they can of things that belong in that room. Each pair can make a collage of its pictures. Have the pairs label their pictures and display and discuss them. Supply the students with any language they need to discuss the things in their rooms.

Workbook

Page 35, Activity 1: Cut and listen. Have the students cut out the people at the bottom of the page. Play the audio or read the audioscript aloud several times for the students to complete the activity. Check to see that the students have glued the people into the correct rooms. You may want to have the students work in pairs and ask each other where the people are in the house. AUDIOSCRIPT: 1. Put the father in the kitchen. 2. Put the mother in the living room. 3. Put the baby in the bedroom. 4. Put the sister in the dining room. 5. Put the brother in the bathroom.

Language Activities Section, page 93
ANSWERS: 1. closet 2. bedroom 3. bathroom 4. bookcase 5. kitchen 6. living room

Objectives

to identify items of clothing
to tell what one is wearing
to name one's favorite color and clothes
to use the present progressive tense
to use adjectives before nouns
to classify

Key Vocabulary

• clothes, dress, hat, jacket, pants, shirt, shoe, skirt, sock, sweater
• what's
• wearing
• he, she

APPLICATION

Using the Project Page

Cut. Color. Play.

1. Focus attention on the pictures. Ask, "What are the children doing in the pictures? Has anyone ever played with paper dolls before?"

2. Have the students color and then cut out the dolls and their clothing on pages 103 and 105.

3. Read the conversation several times for the students to repeat. Make sure the students understand that they are going to dress the dolls and talk about what the dolls are wearing.

4. Have the students work in pairs, small groups, or as a class to ask and answer questions about what their dolls are wearing. Make sure they include the colors.

5. Point to pictures of people from magazines or catalogs and ask the students about their clothing, "What's he/she wearing? Is he/she wearing a (pink shirt)?"

Make a collage.

1. Introduce the word *favorite*. Ask the students to tell you what their favorite clothes, food, movies, and so on are.

2. Focus attention on the pictures and ask the students to say what they think the girl is doing. Ask, "Has anyone ever made a collage before?" Explain that a collage is a group of pictures showing one idea. Point out the finished collage in Step 3. Help the students understand the steps they will follow to complete the activity.

3. Supply the students with old magazines, newspapers, and store catalogs that have a lot of pictures of people and clothing. Make sure the students understand that they are to look for their favorite clothes, cut them out, and paste them on poster paper to make a collage.

4. Help the students make their collages. Write *My Favorite Clothes* on the board for the students to copy at the top of their papers.

5. Read what the girl is saying several times for the students to repeat. Then ask them to describe the clothing in their collages with the rest of the class.

Reaching All Students

Class Survey Help the students identify everyone's favorite clothes. Then have the students count the number of students in the class who like shoes, and so on to determine which kind of clothing is the most popular in the class.

Workbook

Page 33, Activity 7: Draw a line from A to B, to C, and so on. Color the picture. Point to the page and say, "What's this? I don't know." Point to the dots and say, "Dots." The students join letters in the correct order. When the students finish, ask, "Who is it?" The students should answer, "It's a boy." Then they color the picture.

Page 33, Activity 8: Read. Write your answer. When the students have finished coloring, ask, "What's he wearing?" Read each sentence several times for the students to repeat. Have them write their answers on the lines provided. Their answers will depend on how they colored the picture.

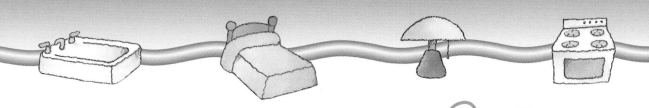

2. Listen. Repeat. Do the actions.

My House
Let's go to my house.
Let's go today.
I'll show you all the rooms
Where we work and play.

Here is the kitchen
Where Mother cooks for me.
Here is the living room
Where I watch TV.

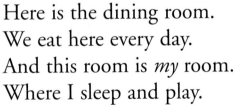

Here is the dining room.
We eat here every day.
And this room is *my* room.
Where I sleep and play.

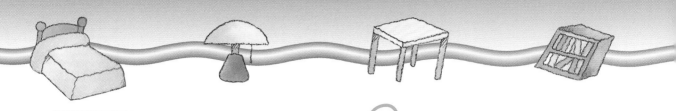

3. Listen. Draw your house.

4. Listen. Say the actions.

He's playing.

He's sleeping.

She's reading.

She's watching TV.

They're cooking.

UNIT 5 • My House

Objectives

to identify rooms in a house
to describe a home
to identify actions
to identify family members
to apply prior knowledge
to use the simple present tense of *be*
to use the present progressive tense

Key Vocabulary

- bathroom, bedroom, dining room, house, kitchen, living room
- he's, she's, they're
- are
- cooking, playing, reading, sleeping, watching TV

PRESENTATION

Using the Page
ACTIVITY 3
Listen. Draw your house.

1. Play the audio or read the audioscript several times.
   AUDIOSCRIPT: (1) Draw your house or apartment. (The students can draw pictures of the insides of their houses or apartments. They can draw a blue print or a cut-away view as in the house on page 42.) (2) Draw your bed. (3) Draw your family in the rooms. What are they doing?

2. Have the students show and discuss their drawings with the rest of the class. Have them say what each room is and identify the furniture in it. Have them say what activities take place in each room. (*This is my house. This is a bedroom. This is a bed. My brother is sleeping.*)

ACTIVITY 4
Listen. Say the actions.

1. Play the audio or read the labels several times for the students to repeat. Introduce the word *playing*. Then have the students point to the pictures and identify each activity.

2. Point to the pictured activities and ask the students to identify what the people are doing.

Reaching All Students

Vocabulary Check Have the students review the words for the furniture in the Picture Dictionary on pages 44–45.

Looking Back Have the students turn to page 42 and say what each person is doing.

Family Activities Divide the class into pairs and have the students question each other about where they are and what they are doing. For example, "Where are you?" (*I'm in the kitchen.*) "What are you doing?" (*I'm eating.*)

Workbook

Page 37, Activity 2: Draw your favorite house. Color. Have the students create a picture of their "dream" house. Encourage them to be imaginative and make interesting, fun houses. Then have them display their pictures and discuss their "dream" houses with the class. You may want to have them do this in pairs or groups.

Page 37, Activity 3: Write the number. Have the students choose the number of rooms, bedrooms, kitchens, TVs, and sofas in their "dream" house and write their answers in the blanks. Answers will vary depending on the students' choices.

Page 38, Activity 4: Read and match. Model the first answer. Have the students point to the word *eating*. Have the students trace the line from the word to the picture of the girl eating. Then have the students draw lines from each word to the correct corresponding picture.

Language Activities Section, page 94
ANSWER: 1. sleeping 2. reading 3. cooking 4. eating 5. playing 6. watching

T44

Objectives

to identify shapes
to answer questions with *how many*
to identify colors
to relate part to the whole
to count
to use singular and plural nouns

Key Vocabulary

• circle, rectangle, square, triangle
• how many
• do, see

PRESENTATION

Warm Up

Show models or pictures of the four different shapes to the class, and check in their own language to see if any students know how the four shapes are different. (*A circle is round like a ball. A triangle has three sides. A rectangle has four sides, like a door or the cover of a book. A square has four sides all the same length.*)

Using the Page
ACTIVITY 5

Look. Match. Draw a line.

1. Focus attention on the shapes at the top of the page. Point to each shape and say its name several times for the students to repeat.

2. Model the sample. Have the students draw a line from each word to the shape it represents.

Reaching All Students

Locate and Group Shapes in the Classroom Have the students look for objects in the classroom that are round, square, rectangular, and triangular. Have them tape a paper circle, rectangle, square, or triangle on each object. Encourage them to talk about each object. For example, "The (door) is like a (rectangle)."

PRACTICE

ACTIVITY 6

Count. Write the number.

1. Make sure the students understand that they are to count the number of different colored shapes and write the number on the line.

2. Read what Hanna is asking the students several times for them to repeat. Have the students count the red circles in the picture. Model the sample exercise: "Write *one*." Have the students count the other shapes and write in their answers to complete the activity.
ANSWERS: 1. 2 2. 4 3. 4 4. 1 5. 1 6. 2

Reaching All Students

Using Shapes Have the students draw and cut out red, blue, green, and yellow circles, rectangles, squares, and triangles. Then have the students use the colored shapes to make houses and people. Encourage the students to talk about their pictures. For example, "It's a big house. The rooms are rectangles. The girl has red hair."

Workbook

Page 39, Activity 5: Cut and match. Have the students cut out the shapes at the bottom of the page. Have them glue them above the matching words in the squares above. You may want to have the students color the shapes at the bottom of the page before they cut them out. Then have them play Bingo. Make sure the students tear up little pieces of paper with which to cover the shapes. Describe a possible shape on the page either as "A (big) (square). It's (red)." or "A (big) (red) (square)." The students cover that picture if they have it. The first to cover three in a row in any direction wins.

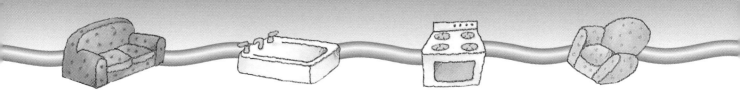

5. Look. Match. Draw a line.

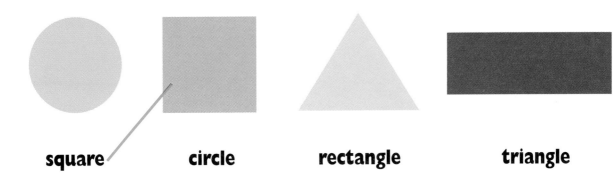

square   circle   rectangle   triangle

6. Count. Write the number.

How many red circles do you see?

1

1.____   2.____   3.____

4.____   5.____   6.____

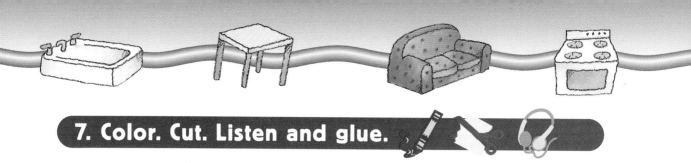

7. Color. Cut. Listen and glue.

1.

2.

3.

UNIT 5 • My House

Objectives

to identify rooms in a house
to describe a home
to identify locations
to use the preposition *in*
to answer questions with *what* and *where*
to apply prior knowledge
to follow directions

Key Vocabulary

- bathroom, bed, bedroom, chair, closet, dining room
- house
- living room, sofa, table, TV
- what, where
- is
- in

APPLICATION

Warm Up

1. Have the students say the poem from page 43.

2. ⊘ Use a doll house or pictures of the rooms of a house or an apartment to review the key vocabulary words. Check to see how many words the students can say.

Using the Page
ACTIVITY 7
Cut. Color. Listen and glue.

1. Have the students look at the three pictures. Ask them, "What do you think the boy is doing?" *(cutting and gluing)*

2. Have the students color and cut out the furniture on page 107.

3. 🖉 💡 Have the students glue the furniture in the different rooms following your directions. Play the audio or read the sentences below several times for the students to complete the activity. Then check to see that they followed the instructions. For example, ask, "What is in the living room? Where is the bed?"

AUDIOSCRIPT: 1. The sofa is in the living room. 2. The bed is in the bedroom. 3. The big table is in the kitchen. 4. The little table is in the living room. 5. The two little chairs are in the kitchen. 6. The TV is in the living room. 7. The clothes are in the closet. 8. The big chair is in the living room.

Reaching All Students

Shape and Color Patterns Have the students make 5 green triangles and 5 red squares. Model a pattern—triangle, square, triangle, square, triangle, square. Ask the students, "What is the pattern?" *(triangle, square, triangle, square, triangle, square* or *green, red, green, red, green, red)* Ask the students to show the shape that comes next in the pattern. *(triangle)* Have the students work in pairs and make and talk about their own patterns.

🖉 ⬌ **Shapes Poem** Write the following poem on the board or make a copy for each student. Play the audio or say the poem with the students several times. Then say it again, and have them draw the shapes as they recite.

Shapes
Draw a circle, draw a circle.
Round as can be.
Draw a circle, draw a circle.
Just for me.

Draw a square, draw a square.
A square is my name.
Draw a square, draw a square.
A block looks the same.

Draw a triangle, draw a triangle.
With corners three.
Draw a triangle, draw a triangle.
Just for me.

T46

Story Summary

Mary is sad. She can't find her cat, Fluffy, anywhere—not in the kitchen, not in the living room. When she finds him outside on the roof, she is happy again.

Key Unit Vocabulary

in, is, kitchen, living room, where, who

Word Bank

missing, roof, not, again

BEFORE READING

WARM UP

Put up pictures of living room, kitchen, bedroom, and bathroom. Point to the pictures. Ask the students to go to the living room. Then in turn, call out each of the other rooms and ask the students to go to that room.

PUT TOGETHER THE LITTLE BOOK

Ask the students to remove pages 47–48 from their books. They can fold the pages in half to make the Little Book, *Fluffy Is Missing!*

PREVIEW THE LITTLE BOOK

1. After the students put their books together, have them point to pictures that show the living room and the kitchen.

2. Point to the roof of the house. Model the word *roof* and ask the students to repeat it. Have them point to the roof of the house in their books or on the Picture Card.

3. Read the title aloud and preview the first three pictures together. Invite the students to tell what they see happening in each illustration. Ask, "Who is Fluffy? Why is the girl sad?" Encourage them to tell where the story is taking place on each page. Then have the students predict where the girl will find Fluffy.

SHARE NEW WORDS

Write the Word Bank words on the board. Say the words aloud and have the students repeat them after you. Use each word in a sentence and have the students find the word in their books.

DURING READING

READING THE LITTLE BOOK

The students can listen as you play the audio or read the story aloud. Tell them they can ask questions and talk about the story when you read it again.

GUIDED READING

Read the story aloud, tracking the print as you read. Pause before you read the last page and ask the students to predict again where they think Fluffy could be.

TEACHER TIPS

Point out phrases that repeat in the story such as *Where is Fluffy?* and *Fluffy is not in the _____.* As you reread the story, have the students join in as you repeat these phrases.

REREADING

Together discuss the students' predictions and compare them with what actually happened in the story. Quickly review what the story is about. You may assess their comprehension with questions such as these:

Page 1 *What is missing?*
Page 2 *Where is Mary looking for Fluffy?*
Page 3 *Where does Mary's father thinks Fluffy is?*
Page 4 *How does Mary feel?*

Guide the students in using the illustrations to help them understand what is happening in the story.

Fluffy Is Missing!

by Mario Herrera

Mary is sad. Her cat Fluffy is missing.
Where is Fluffy? Where is Fluffy?

1

Fluffy is on the roof!
Now Mary is happy again!

4

Fluffy is not in the kitchen.
Mary's mother is in the kitchen.
Where is Fluffy? Where is Fluffy?

Fluffy is not in the living room.
Mary's father is in the living room.
Where is Fluffy? Where is Fluffy?

AFTER READING

Activities for Developing Language

RETELL THE STORY

To assess their understanding of the story, ask the students to take turns retelling it to a small group. They can use the illustrations to guide them.

PLOT

Ask the students to recall where Mary looked for Fluffy. Draw three boxes labeled *1, 2,* and *3.* Suggest that the students draw a picture to show the order of events in the story. Then have them use their pictures to retell the story.

SETTING

Display the illustrations for each page. Ask the students to identify each setting. Then discuss the setting by telling what people do there and what objects they see there.

ACT IT OUT!

The students can assume the roles of Mary and her mother and father to act out the story. Ask one group to role play the story as it is read aloud. Another group might improvise what the characters would say and do in another situation.

MAKE A MODEL

Use cereal boxes to have the students make models of the different rooms in the house. You may also want them to make finger puppets of Fluffy, Mary, and her parents. Encourage the students to use the figures to act out what happens in the story.

WRITE ABOUT IT!

Discuss different settings where Fluffy could have gone other than the roof. Then list other places Mary could have looked for her pet. The students can write or dictate their ideas to change the story. Invite them to draw a picture of each word for their own Picture Dictionary. You may wish to create a class Big Book with their finished ideas.

GRAMMAR CONNECTION: EXCLAMATORY SENTENCES

Write *Fluffy is on the roof! Now Mary is happy again!* on the board and read the sentences aloud. Tell the students that these sentences show excitement. Point out how these sentences both end in exclamation points.

WORKBOOK

Little Book Comprehension, page 95.

BULLETIN BOARD IDEAS

You may wish to have the students draw pictures of their cats or any cats they like for a bulletin board titled *Cats.*

FAMILY CONNECTION

Invite the students to take their Little Books home and share them with their friends and family members.

Objectives
to identify shapes
to answer questions with *how many*
to pronounce /d/
to use adjectives before nouns

Key Vocabulary
• circle, square, rectangle, triangle
• how many, who

APPLICATION

Using the Project Page

Make a house. Say.

1. Have the students look at the three pictures. Ask them, "What do you think the girl is doing?" *(cutting, gluing, making a picture)*

2. ✏️ Supply the students with colored construction paper or have them color white paper. Have them draw and cut out different kinds of circles, squares, rectangles, and triangles. Ask them to name the shapes.

3. 🔁 Have the students create houses out of the shapes. Let them glue their houses on a sheet of paper.

4. Read the teacher's question in the picture several times for the students to repeat. Encourage the students to answer the question about their own "houses."

5. Have the students display their houses for the rest of the class. Ask each student to say how many of each shape is in their picture.

6. You may want to have the students work in pairs and have them exchange their shape houses. Then have each student count the number of different-colored shapes in their partner's picture.

Listen. Act out. Say.

1. 🎧 Focus attention on the pictures. Play the audio or read the poem several times for the students to repeat.

2. Distribute big and little rectangles, squares, circles, and triangles of each of the colors to the students. As the students say the poem, have them hold up the corresponding shape.

3. 🎧 Play the audio or read Homer's and Hanna's directions. Then have the students make additional verses by substituting different shapes, different-sized shapes, and different colors.

4. To practice pronunciation, focus on /d/ in *do*.

Reaching All Students

🔁 **Class House** Have the students draw a "class house" on a large sheet of paper or poster paper. Pictures of furniture cut from magazines or catalogs can be glued on the drawing. Then have the students dictate sentences describing the "class house" for you to write on the board.

Workbook

Page 41, Activity 6: Say the alphabet. Color the spaces. Direct the students' attention to the alphabets that border the picture. They may work in pairs to take turns saying the alphabet to each other. Next, from the list, read the letters and the colors they represent several times. Have the students color the lettered shapes in the picture using the color key. They can use colors of their own choice for the unlettered shapes.

Page 41, Activity 7: Write your answer. When the students have finished coloring, have them write the name of the object on the line. ANSWER: It's a TV.

PROJECT

Make a house. Say.

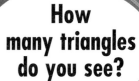

How many triangles do you see?

(1).

(2).

(3).

Listen. Act out. Say.

Who has a big circle?
I do! I do!
Who has an orange circle?
I do! I do!

Say other colors!

Say other shapes! Are they big or little?

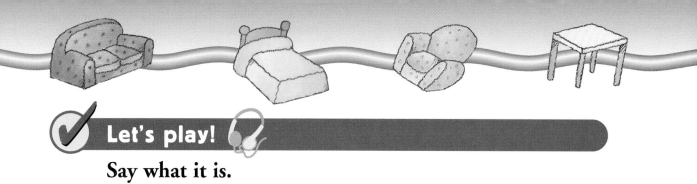

✓ Let's play! 🎧

Say what it is.

What's in A1?

It's a sofa.

UNIT 5 • My House

Objectives

to identify objects in a house
to identify shapes
to identify actions
to use the present progressive tense
to use simple coordinates
to answer questions with *what*

Key Vocabulary

- circle, rectangle, square, triangle, bed, chair, sofa, table, TV
- what, what's
- cooking, eating, playing, reading, sleeping, watching TV

ASSESSMENT

Warm Up

1. ⊘ Review key vocabulary words by showing pictures of rooms of a house, shapes, and actions for the students to identify. Check to see how many words the students can say.

2. Review the shapes chant activity (see page T49).

Using the Page

Let's play!

1. Draw a grid on the board like the one in the book but without pictures. Point to the numerals across the top of the grid and the letters down the lefthand side of the grid. Then point to the number 2 with one finger and the letter B with another finger. Move your two fingers until they meet. Then say, "This box is *B2*."

2. Focus attention on the grid in the book. Have the students practice putting their fingers on a letter and a number and then moving their fingers together. Have them identify the box, "It's (*C3*)."

3. 🎧 Focus attention on Homer and Hanna. Play the audio or read their conversation several times for the students to repeat. Have the students point to *A1*. Ask, "What's in *A1*?" Have the students look and answer, "It's a sofa."

4. Call out coordinates and ask individuals to say what is pictured there. For the pictures of the actions, say, "Look at *C3*. What's the man doing?" The students should look and answer, "He's eating."

5. You may want to divide the class into two teams. Take turns calling out coordinates and having alternating team members identify the pictures. Teams get one point for each correct identification. The team with the most points wins.

6. ⊘ As the students give their answers, check for objectives: (1) the identification of objects in the home, (2) the identification of shapes, and (3) the identification of actions. Record your observations on the Student Oral Assessment Checklist on page xxi.

Reaching All Students

⊘ **Using Shapes** Provide the students with different-colored shapes, or have them draw, color, and cut out paper shapes. To start the activity, the students should have their shapes on their desks. Then they must listen and follow your instructions. For example, "Show me a triangle. Show me a purple shape. Who has a blue shape? Put a pink shape on your nose. If it's a circle, say 'Hooray!'"

💡 **Houses Around the World** Bring books from the library about houses from different countries. Have the students discuss and describe the houses. Ask, "How are the houses like the ones in your country? How are the houses different from the ones in your country? Who would like to live in each house?"

Objectives

to identify rooms and objects in a house
to describe a home
to identify locations
to identify shapes
to use the preposition *in*
to count

Key Vocabulary

• bathroom, bed, bedroom, chair, closet, dining room, living room, sofa, table, TV
• circle, rectangle, square, triangle

ASSESSMENT

Using the Page

Count. Write the number.

1. Model the exercise.

2. ⟨⟩ Have the students do the activity. They are to count the number of different rooms or pieces of furniture and write the number on the line.
ANSWERS: 1. 1 living room 2. 2 closets 3. 4 chairs 4. 3 beds 5. 1 bathroom

3. ☑ Have the students name the rooms and furniture in the picture of the house. Use the Student Oral Assessment Checklist on page xxi to record each student's oral presentation.

I can.

1. Read the statement for number 1 aloud to the students. Ask individuals, groups, or the whole class to identify the rooms in the house *(kitchen, bedroom)*. Have them circle the pictures for the words they can say. You might ask individuals to name rooms in their homes. You also may want to have individuals say where objects are located in their homes such as "The sofa is in the living room."

2. Read the statement for number 2 aloud to the students. Ask individuals, groups, or the whole class to name the shapes *(triangle, square, circle, rectangle)*. Have them circle the pictures for the words they can say. Quickly note oral production in these activities on the Student Oral Assessment Checklist on page xxi.

Reaching All Students

☑ **Vocabulary Check** Point to the furniture in the Picture Dictionary on pages 50–51. Have the students identify each piece.

⟨⟩ **Collecting Data from a Picture**
Distribute drawing paper and markers. Have each student draw a picture of a room in a house that contains various numbers of objects, for example: 2 beds, 1 closet, 1 table, 3 books, and so on. Have the students work in pairs. Tell them to exchange drawings and take turns discussing what objects are in the room and how many of each they see in the drawing.

Unit Mural Elicit all the words and expressions the students remember from this unit. Write them on mural or poster paper. Have the students illustrate the vocabulary. Use this to review vocabulary in subsequent classes.

Unit 5 Test See page xxxv.

Workbook

☑ **Page 42, Count. Write the number. Match.** Have the students count the number of different rooms or pieces of furniture and write the number on the line. Then have them draw lines from the words to the corresponding rooms or furnishings.
ANSWERS: a. 1 bedroom b. 1 kitchen c. 4 chairs d. 2 beds e. 3 tables f. 1 bathroom

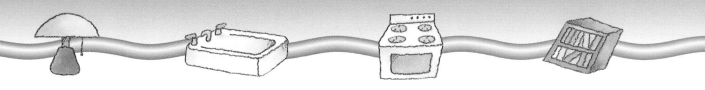

 Count. Write the number.

_____1_____ dining room   1. _____ living room

2. _____ closets   3. _____ chairs

4. _____ beds   5. _____ bathroom

 I can.

1. I can talk about my house.

2. I can name shapes.

6 Animals

Communication Objectives

to identify and describe animals
to identify what animals say
to identify animal actions
to identify colors
to identify the numbers *0–10*

Language Objectives

to use the simple present tense of *be, see,* and *say*
to use the present progressive tense with *it's* and *they're (eating)*
to use plural nouns
to pronounce /i/, /aɪ/, and /ɔ/

Learning Strategies and Thinking Skills

to classify
to make comparisons (*big* vs. *little*)
to make associations
to apply prior knowledge
to sequence
to use illustrations

Content Connections

Art: to draw animals; to make animal collages
Literature: to recite a nursery rhyme
Music: to sing a song
Science: to count number of legs different animals have; to explore animal life
Social Studies: to make graphs to present information

Materials

New Parade 1 Student Book, pages 52–61
New Parade 1 Workbook, pages 43–52; 96–98
New Parade 1 Audio: Tape/CD
New Parade 1 Video and Video Guide
New Parade 1 Posters

Pictures of key vocabulary animals, pictures of big and little animals, pictures of animal and people actions, old magazines and newspapers, large sheets of paper, glue, scissors, crayons or markers, yarn, string, hole punch
Optional Materials: New Parade Picture Cards—bird, cat, cows, dog, ducks, fish, hippopotamus, horses, eat, crawl, jump; drawing paper, boxes or bags, poster paper; *Little Celebrations—Farm Day* by Sarah Tatler, *Thumbprint Critters* by Sarah Tatler, *I Wonder* by Viveka Wehtje, *What Do You Do?* by Suzanne Hardin, and *Animal Builders* by Jon Mudge

Key Vocabulary

• bird, bug, cat, cow, dog, duck, fish, frog, hippopotamus, horse, worm
• what
• is, say, see
• crawling, doing, eating, flying, jumping, running, sleeping, swimming
• it's, they're
• big, little

Picture Dictionary

horse bird cat dog frog duck cow fish bug

Setting Up the Classroom

Prepare for this unit by reading through the material and gathering the supplies for the activities. You will need many pictures of big and small animals. It is a good idea to prepare animal sounds for Warm Up 3 on page T52 and clues for Warm Up 2 on page T60 before starting the lessons. Read the Little Book *Carnival!* to plan the tone you might use when reading it aloud.

Using the Video and the Video Guide

You should show the video at the beginning of the unit to introduce the students to the language they will be learning in this unit in context. Help them use the context to get a general idea of what is happening. You can go back and show the video again, especially at the beginning of each week. The students will understand more every time they view it, as they learn the words and patterns in the unit. The Video Guide will suggest places to stop and start the video. Encourage the students to interact with the video by answering the questions, singing, and doing the actions along with the children in the video.

This video segment takes place at "Pet Day" in the park. The students are introduced to action verbs as Julia explains what the animals are doing *(running, jumping, crawling, eating)*. Nora and Bobby show off their pets. The characters also focus on the verb *see,* and compare their pets: "Do you see my frog?" "I see a running dog."

Family Connections

Encourage the students to have fun with the animal sounds they learn in English by teaching them to family and friends at home.

Bulletin Board Ideas

Write "activity" words from this unit such as *crawling, eating,* and *jumping* on slips of paper. Place them around the bulletin board. Encourage the students to cut out or draw pictures of people and animals doing those activities and put them up near the correct words on the board. Later you may want the students to tell what each one is doing.

Little Book: Carnival!

Summary: A class has fun when the children dress up as animals for a Carnival. They run, jump, and crawl until all they can do is fall asleep.

Workbook
Page 49, Activity 6

6 Animals

1. Listen and sing together.

Old MacDonald has a farm,
E-I-E-I-O.
And on this farm he has a dog,
E-I-E-I-O.
With a bow wow here
And a bow wow there,
Here a bow, there a wow
Everywhere a bow wow.
Old MacDonald has a farm,
E-I-E-I-O.

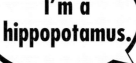

Objectives

to identify and describe animals
to identify what animals say
to make comparisons (*big* vs. *little*)
to pronounce /i/ and /aɪ/
to use the simple present tense of *be* and *see*

Key Vocabulary

• **bird, cat, cow, dog, duck, frog, hippopotamus, horse**
• **big, little**
• **is, say, see**

WARM UP

1. Have pictures or Picture Cards of the vocabulary animals on display at the beginning of class. Hold up each picture and invite the students to identify it if they know the word. Then say, "It's a (bird)." Ask, "Do you have a (dog)?"

2. Ask the students what cats, dogs, and so on, say in their language. Then say what the animals say in English. Have the students repeat these sounds several times.

3. Make the animal sounds in random order. Encourage the students to identify the animals by saying, "It's a (horse)."

4. 🔆 Provide pictures of the key vocabulary animals but include big and little examples of the same animal, for example, a big dog and a little dog. Have the students make two piles of pictures, one for big animals and one for little animals.

5. Display the Poster for Unit 6.

PRESENTATION

Using the Page
ACTIVITY 1
Listen and sing together.

1. Say the name of each animal as you point to it. Then point to the animals in random order and ask, "What animal do you see?" Have the students identify each one.

2. Have the students say a name of an animal and correctly point to it in the picture.

3. 🎧 🔲 Play the audio or sing the song. Then have the students sing it several times. Add new verses by substituting *dog* and *bow wow* with the other animals pictured and the sounds they make. To practice pronunciation, focus on /i/ and /aɪ/ in *E-I-E-I-O*.

4. 🎧 Play the audio or read the conversation between Hanna and the bird several times for the students to repeat.

5. Have the students look at the scene and ask, "What color is the (bird)?" The students should answer, "It's (blue)."

6. Have the students look at the scene and ask, "What animals are big? What animals are little?" Have the students point at the big animals and then at the little animals. The students should say, for example, "The horse is big. The frog is little."

Reaching All Students

Vocabulary Expansion Focus attention on the Picture Dictionary on pages 52–53. Have the students point to the different animals as you say the words for them to repeat several times *(horse, bird, cat, dog, frog, duck, cow, fish)*. After presenting page 53, you may want the students to identify the animals' actions.

Animal Sounds Have individual students make animal sounds. The rest of the class must guess which animal is being imitated. "It's a (cow)."

🔲 **Art Activity** Ask the students to draw a picture of their favorite animal. Then have them take turns showing their drawings as you ask the rest of the class, "What do you see?" "A (dog)." You may have to help with new vocabulary.

UNIT 6 • Animals

Objectives

to identify and describe animals
to identify animal actions
to use the present progressive tense with
  it's (eating)
to make associations
to use illustrations

Key Vocabulary

• bird, bug, cat, cow, dog, fish, frog, worm
• crawling, eating, flying, jumping, running, sleeping, swimming
• it's

PRESENTATION

Warm Up

1. Review the actions the students learned in Unit 5, emphasizing the actions that animals can do *(sleeping, eating)*.

2. Mime animals crawling, flying, jumping, running, sleeping, and swimming to introduce or review those words or display Picture Cards.

3. Act out eating, sleeping, crawling, jumping, running, flying, and swimming as you say the actions. Say a series of three of these actions and have the students respond individually, in groups, or as a class.

Using the Page

ACTIVITY 2

Listen. Point. Say.

1. Display pictures or draw pictures of a worm and a fish to present the key vocabulary.

2. Focus attention on the picture. Ask the students, "What animals do you see?" Have the students point to each animal and identify it. "It's a (cow)."

3. Point to each animal and play the audio and say what each animal is doing several times for the students to point and repeat.

4. Randomly point to the different animals and ask, "What's it doing?" "It's (jumping)."

ACTIVITY 3

Count the legs. Say.

1. Focus attention on the pictures. Point to the bug and identify it for the students. Have the students point to the other animals and identify them. *(cat, frog, fish)*

2. Then ask, "How many legs does the (cat) have?" *(cat—four, frog—four, fish—zero, bug—six)*

3. You may want to have the students make a chart showing the animals in the pictures and the number of legs each has. Encourage the students to add other animals they know.

Reaching All Students

Animal Collages Have the students make their own animal collages. The students can cut out pictures of animals doing different actions from old magazines and arrange the pictures in a collage. Then have the students display their collages to the class, describe the animals in their collages by color and size, and say what each animal is doing. Supply the students with any vocabulary they need to express their ideas.

Action Charades Whisper an action in an individual student's ear. Ask the student to act out the action for the other students to guess.

Workbook

Page 43, Activity 1: Circle the animals. Color. Say. Have the students find and color the ten hidden animals. *(bird, bug, cat, cow, dog, duck, fish, frog, horse, worm)* Then have them color the picture as they like. Ask individuals, groups, or the class to point to each hidden animal and name it and its color.

Page 44, Activity 2: Draw and color four animals. Have the students draw and color any four animals they choose. Then have them display their pictures and describe the animals they drew.

2. Listen. Point. Say.

It's sleeping.

It's swimming.

It's running.

It's eating.

It's crawling.

It's jumping.

It's flying.

3. Count the legs. Say.

①

②

③

④

Objectives

to identify and describe animals
to identify animal actions
to identify colors
to make comparisons (*big* vs. *little*)
to use plural nouns
to use the present progressive tense with *they're*

Key Vocabulary

- bird, cat, cow, dog, duck, frog, horse
- what
- doing, eating, flying, jumping, running, sleeping, swimming
- big, little
- they're

PRACTICE

Using the Page
ACTIVITY 4
Listen and color.

1. Play the audio or read the audioscript aloud several times. Check to see that the students use the correct marker or crayon to color the animals.
AUDIOSCRIPT: 1. Color the big horse brown. 2. Color the little duck yellow. 3. Color the little cat orange. 4. Color the big bird blue. 5. Color the big dog brown and white. 6. Color the little frog green. 7. Color the little horse black. 8. Color the big duck brown. 9. Color the big cat yellow. 10. Color the little bird red.

2. Play the audio or read Homer and Hanna's conversation several times for the students to repeat. Have the students look at the picture and see if Hanna's answer is correct.

3. Focus attention on the picture. Ask similar questions about the picture.

Reaching All Students

Vocabulary Check Have the students review the words for the animals and their actions in the Picture Dictionary on pages 54–55.

Animal Identification Divide the class into two teams. Ask members of each team to identify an animal, its color, and its size. Each correct answer scores a point for the team.

Drawing Dictation Have the students fold and number drawing paper into six sections. Read or play the following directions several times for the students to repeat:

AUDIOSCRIPT: 1. Draw a big dog. 2. Draw a little dog. 3. Draw a big cow. 4. Draw a little cow. 5. Draw a big cat. 6. Draw a little cat.

Sorting Game Provide pictures of big and little animals for the students to sort. Label two large boxes or bags with a big and little circle. Have a student name an animal and describe it, "It's a (horse). It's (big/little)."

Big/Little Have the students draw or paint pictures of animals that are big or little. Help the students write sentences about each picture. *This is a (horse). It's (brown). It's (big).*

Follow the Leader Ask the students to stand, watch, and listen while you say an action and act it out. Ask the students to follow your actions. Let individual students take turns being the leader. After the student calls out an action and acts it out, the rest of the class follows the leader's action.

Workbook

Page 45, Activity 3: Circle the same animals. Listen and color. Have the students look at the first animal in each row and circle the same-sized animal in that row. Then play the audio or read the audioscript several times for the students to complete the activity.
AUDIOSCRIPT: 1. Color the big birds green. Color the little birds yellow. 2. Color the little cats black. Color the big cats brown. 3. Color the little cows red. Color the big cows white and black. 4. Color the big fish blue. Color the little fish pink. 5. Color the big horses black. Color the little horses yellow. 6. Color the little dogs black. Color the big dogs brown and yellow.

Objectives

to identify and describe animals
to identify animal actions
to sequence
to pronounce /j̆/

Key Vocabulary

- bird, cat, frog, horse
- big, little
- green, orange

PRACTICE

Using the Page

ACTIVITY 5

Listen. Circle.

1. Model the sample exercise. Have the students point to the first two pictures as you play the audio or read aloud the sentence, "The horse is running." Point out the circled answer.

2. Play the audio or read the audioscript aloud two or three times. Have the students circle the answers. Then check the students' work.
   AUDIOSCRIPT: 1. The frog is jumping. 2. The bird is flying. 3. The cat is sleeping.

ACTIVITY 6

Listen and say together.

1. Focus attention on the pictures. Explain that the students will do the actions as they say the rhyme.

2. Play the audio or say the rhyme aloud to the students one time. Then say it again, but do the hand motions.

3. Have the students say the rhyme and do the hand motions. Repeat as often as necessary, perhaps on a daily basis, until the students know the rhyme and the motions. To practice pronunciation, focus on /j̆/ in *Jack* and *Jill*.

Reaching All Students

Action Song Play the audio or sing the following song (tune of "Battle Hymn of the Republic") several times for the students to repeat.
Little Peter Rabbit has a fly upon his ear.
Little Peter Rabbit has a fly upon his ear.
Little Peter Rabbit has a fly upon his ear.
And he flicks it 'till it flies away.

Then explain to the students that as they repeat the song they are going to substitute actions for the words: (1) instead of singing *rabbit*, have the students use their hands to make rabbit ears, (2) in addition, instead of singing *fly*, have them use their fingers to show flying away, (3) in addition, instead of singing *ear*, have them point to their right ear, (4) in addition, instead of singing *flick*, have them use their hands to flick their right ear.

Animal Pictures Write the sounds animals make on the board. Point to one sound and read it aloud. Have the students draw pictures of the animal that makes that sound. Have them copy the animal sound underneath their pictures. Do this for all the animals.

Actions Sequence Call out a series of actions such as *run, jump, walk*. Then have the students recall the order of the actions. You may want to have the students work in teams with individuals on each team taking turns doing and naming the actions.

Workbook

Page 46, Activity 4: Listen. Draw a line. Say. Show the students where to begin the maze. Point to the individual pictures and play the audio or say, "It's (flying)." Have the students find the picture of the (bird). Have them draw a line from the beginning of the maze to that picture. Continue until the students have found the path to each picture. Ask individuals to show the paths they made to the class and to identify the animals.
AUDIOSCRIPT: 1. It's flying. 2. It's swimming. 3. It's sleeping. 4. It's crawling. 5. It's running. 6. It's jumping. 7. It's eating.

5. Listen. Circle.

1.

2.

3.

6. Listen and say together.

Do the motions.

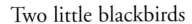

Two little blackbirds

Sitting on a hill.

One named Jack

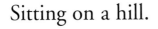

And one named Jill.

Fly away, Jack.

Fly away, Jill.

Come back, Jack.

Come back, Jill.

7. Look. Match. Draw a line.

Which animals are eating?

8. Listen and number.

1

Objectives

to identify and describe animals
to identify animal actions
to identify the numbers *0–10*
to apply prior knowledge

Key Vocabulary

• **bird, cat, cow, dog, duck, fish, frog, horse**
• **eating, running, sleeping, swimming**

PRACTICE

Warm Up

1. ☑ Use pictures or Picture Cards of animals and actions to review the key vocabulary words. Check to see how many words the students can say.

2. Have the students sing the song from page 52.

Using the Page

ACTIVITY 7

Look. Match. Draw a line.

1. Focus attention on the two columns of pictures. Ask, "What do you see?" Have the students identify each animal and the action it is doing. "It's a (fish). It's (swimming)."

2. Call attention to Hanna and read her question several times for the students to repeat and answer *(cow and bird)*. Then ask about each of the other actions, for example, "What animals are swimming?" *(duck and fish)*

3. Point to the sample line. Ask, "What is the fish doing? What is the duck doing?" *(swimming)* Have the students find other animals that are doing the same thing and draw a line between them.
   ANSWERS: dog and horse—running; cow and bird—eating; frog and cat—sleeping

ACTIVITY 8

Listen and number.

1. Have the students make the sounds for the pictured animals.

2. ✐ Model the sample exercise. Play the audio or make the sound of the dog barking several times. Point to the number 1. Make sure the students understand that they are to write the number they hear next to the picture of the animal that makes the sound.

AUDIOSCRIPT: (Dog barking.) Write number one. (Cat mewing.) Write number two. (Duck quacking.) Write number three. (Cow mooing.) Write number four.

3. The students name animals they numbered.
   ANSWERS: 2. cat 3. duck 4. cow

Reaching All Students

◄► **Shadow Drawings** Make shapes with your hands to make shadow drawings of different animals. Ask the students, "What is it?" The students can guess, "It's a (bird)." Ask, "What's it doing?" The students can answer, "It's flying." You may want to have the students work in small groups to talk about their own shadow drawings.

◄► **Favorite Animals** Have the students find out what animals are the most popular in the class. Ask, "What's your favorite animal?" Have them illustrate the results in a bar graph.

Workbook

Page 47, Activity 5: Color. Cut. Make cards.
The students color the cards and cut them out. Pairs of students combine and shuffle their sets of cards and lay them facedown on a table. The students take turns turning over two cards. As they turn over each card, the students must identify the animal, its color, and what it is doing. If they make a match, they keep the two cards. The student with the most cards wins.

Language Activities Section, page 96
ANSWERS: 1. jumping 2. running 3. crawling 4. swimming 5. flying

Language Activities Section, page 97
ANSWERS: 1. big 2. little 3. big 4. little 5. big

Story Summary

A class has fun when the children dress up as animals for a Carnival. They run, jump, and crawl until all they can do is fall asleep.

Key Unit Vocabulary

big, bird, crawling, dog, eating, fish, flying, frog, horse, jumping, little, running, sleeping, swimming, worm

Word Bank

today, suits, Carnival, tired

BEFORE READING

WARM UP

Show Picture Cards of bird, dog, fish, and horses or display drawings and have the students name them. Then show how each animal moves and have the students use TPR to show the actions with you.

PUT TOGETHER THE LITTLE BOOK

Ask the students to remove pages 57–58 from their books. They can fold the pages in half to make the Little Book, *Carnival!*

PREVIEW THE LITTLE BOOK

1. After the students have assembled the books, ask them to name the animals they see in the pictures.

2. Read the title aloud to the students and look at the pages together, describing what the children are doing in each illustration. Encourage the students to name each animal and say what the animal is doing. Then have them predict what the story is about.

SHARE NEW WORDS

Write the Word Bank words on the board. Ask the students to point to any words they know. Say the words and have the students repeat them after you. Use picture cues or TPR to explain the meanings of these words.

DURING READING

READING THE LITTLE BOOK

After the preview, have the students listen to the story as you read it aloud or play the audio. Tell them to hold their questions to discuss when you read the story again.

GUIDED READING

Read the story aloud, tracking the print as you read. Make sure the students use the pictures to help them understand what is happening in the text.

TEACHER TIPS

On a second or third reading of the story, have the students echo read the story, repeating each sentence after you.

REREADING

Review the students' predictions and compare them with what happened in the story. Quickly have the students tell what the story is about. You may assess their comprehension with questions such as these:

Page 1 *What are the children wearing?*
Page 2 *What are these animals doing?*
Page 3 *What are these animals doing?*
Page 4 *What are the children doing?*

As necessary, point to things in the illustrations to help the students answer the comprehension questions.

CARNIVAL!

by
Mario Herrera

The children are happy today.
They are wearing animal
suits for Carnival.

1

After Carnival the children are tired.
Now they are all sleeping!

4

Frogs are jumping.
Dogs are running.
And big worms are crawling.

Little horses are eating.
Birds are flying.
And fish are swimming.

AFTER READING

Activities for Developing Language

CHARACTER

Invite the students to take turns role playing the actions of each animal in the story while their classmates guess the animal's name.

MAKE MASKS FOR CARNIVAL

Help the students make their own masks for the animals in the Little Book story. Then invite them to have an animal parade in the classroom. Encourage them to role play the animals' actions.

ANIMAL RELAY

The students might enjoy racing in an animal relay. Divide the students into equal groups. Each group can pretend to be fish, birds, horses, or dogs. Then have a relay race to see which animals move the fastest.

WRITE ABOUT IT!

Display Picture Cards of dog, fish, and horse. Write these words on the board: *jumping, swimming, running.* Discuss with the students the different animals and the way they move. Then have them choose an animal and its action. Encourage them to write the name of the animal on paper and to illustrate it.

GRAMMAR CONNECTION: COMPLETE SENTENCES

Write *The children are wearing animal suits.* on the board. Tell the students this is a sentence. It tells who is doing something (the children) and tells what they are doing (are wearing animal suits). Then point out how this sentence begins with a capital letter and ends with a period.

WORKBOOK

Little Book Comprehension, page 98.

BULLETIN BOARD IDEAS

You may wish to have the students draw pictures of different animals moving. Help them to label their pictures. The students may add pictures as the unit progresses. Entitle the display *How Animals Move.*

FAMILY CONNECTION

Invite the students to take their Little Books home and share them with their friends and family members.

Objectives

to identify and describe animals
to classify
to apply prior knowledge

Key Vocabulary

• bird, bug, cat, cow, dog, duck, fish, frog, horse

APPLICATION

Warm Up

1. Review the animal names by showing pictures of animals and having the students name them.

2. ▓ Use TPR by writing an animal word on the board and having individuals select the corresponding picture or act like that animal. Invite the other students to say "Yes" or "No" depending on whether or not the individual selects the correct picture or performs the correct action.

Using the Project Page

Make a book.

1. Focus attention on the pictures. Make sure the students understand they are going to make a book of pictures of their favorite animals.

2. Supply the students with old magazines and newspapers they can cut up as well as sheets of paper that will serve as the pages in their books.

3. Have the students cut out pictures of their favorite animals. Have them sort the pictures and only put one kind of animal on each sheet of paper. Have them glue the animal pictures to the paper and write the name of the animal on the top. You may want to write the names of common favorites on the board for the students to copy. Have the students make a book cover of their favorite animals. Write *My Favorite Animals* on the board for the students to copy.

4. Punch three holes in each student's set of papers. Give the students six-inch pieces of yarn or string. Help them tie the pages together through the punched holes.

5. Have the students share their books with the class. Encourage them to talk about the color and size of the animals as well as what the animals say. Some may want to say what the animals in their pictures are doing. Have the students keep their books in their folders and use their animal books as review throughout the unit.

Reaching All Students

Pets Have the students talk about pets. Ask, "Who has a pet? What kind of animal is it? What's its name? What does it like to do?" The students might also bring in photos of their pets.

▓ **What Do Animals Do?** The students work in groups to categorize the animals they know. Which animals can be pets? Which are on a farm? Which are in a zoo? You may want to have the students draw animals in each category on sheets of paper and label the category. Display the sheets in the room and refer to them for review.

▓ **Looking at Animals** If possible, take the students for a nature walk or bring in a collection of bugs, worms, and so on for the students to examine with magnifying glasses. As a follow up, the students draw pictures and write the name of the animals they examine.

Workbook

Page 49, Activity 6: Find the words. Circle the words. Read each of the words at the top of the word puzzle for the students to repeat. Explain that they are to find these words in the puzzle. Encourage them to cross the words off the top as they find them and circle them in the puzzle. See page T6B for the answers.

PROJECT

Make a book.

1.

2.

3.

4.

MY FAVORITE ANIMALS

 Animal Bingo!

Listen and draw four more.

Bingo!

Objectives

to identify and describe animals
to identify animal actions
to identify colors
to use the simple present tense of *be* and *say*

Key Vocabulary

- bird, cat, cow, dog, fish, frog, worm
- flying, jumping, running, sleeping

ASSESSMENT

Using the Page

Warm Up

1. Review animal descriptions by showing pictures of different colored animals for the students to describe. Encourage the students to say sentences such as "This duck is white."

2. Give the students animal description clues for them to guess the animal, for example, "This animal is black. It has four legs. It says 'meow.'"

3. Review animal actions by showing pictures of animals in action or by acting out actions. Elicit from the students sentences such as "It's a bird. It's flying."

Animal Bingo!

1. Have the students draw a white duck swimming, an orange worm, a yellow duck, and a pink worm in any of the four empty squares.

2. Have the students cut or tear 16 small pieces of paper large enough to cover a square on the Bingo card.

3. To review the rules for Bingo, read what Homer is saying for the students to repeat. Tell the students to yell "Bingo!" as soon as they complete a row across or up and down, after listening and covering each picture.

4. ✏️ Play the audio or read the audioscript aloud. Have the students cover the correct pictures with a piece of paper.
   AUDIOSCRIPT: 1. This cat is black. 2. This worm is pink. 3. This dog is brown. It's running. 4. This duck is white. It's swimming. 5. This bird is red. It's flying. 6. This frog is green. It's sleeping. 7. This fish is yellow.

8. This cow is black and white. 9. This duck is yellow. 10.This frog is green. It's jumping. 11. This bird is blue. 12. This cow is purple. 13. This cat is sleeping. 14. This dog is sleeping. 15. This worm is orange. 16. This fish is purple.

5. ✅ After a student has filled a row, have him or her describe each picture in the Bingo row. Record your observations on the Student Oral Assessment Checklist on page xxi.

6. You may want to repeat the activity several times, changing the order of the sentences you read aloud each time.

Reaching All Students

✅ **Picture Dictionary** Have the students identify the pictures on pages 60–61. Then have them tell how many legs each animal has.

🏃 **Simon Says** Play Simon Says using action vocabulary your students have learned in this unit and Unit 3. Remind the students to do the action only when you say "Simon says" first. For example, (Simon says): *Point to your foot, touch your head, run, jump,* and *sleep.*

What Animal Am I? Hang or tape a picture or the name of an animal on the back of each student. Put the students into pairs or groups and have them ask *yes/no* questions to find out what animal they are. They can ask questions about color, size, and actions, "Am I big? Am I yellow? Am I flying?"

Objectives

to identify and describe animals
to identify animal actions
to identify colors
to use the present progressive tense with
  it's (eating)

Key Vocabulary

- bug, cat, cow, dog, fish, frog, horse, worm
- crawling, eating, jumping, running, sleeping, swimming

ASSESSMENT

Using the Page

Listen and circle.

Play the audio or read the audioscript several times. Have the students circle the answers. Use the assessment chart to record how well each student has done.
AUDIOSCRIPT: 1. It's sleeping. 2. It's jumping. 3. It's running. 4. The worm is crawling. 5. The horse is eating. 6. The fish are swimming.

I can.

1. Read the statement for number 1 aloud to the students. Ask individuals, groups, or the whole class to identify the animals *(dog, cat, cow)*. Have them circle the pictures for the words they can say.

2. Read the statement for number 2 aloud to the students. Ask individuals, groups, or the whole class to say what the animals are doing. Have them circle the pictures for the words they can say. Quickly note oral production in these activities on the Student Oral Assessment Checklist on page xxi.

Reaching All Students

Unit Mural Elicit all the words and expressions the students remember from this unit. Write them on mural or poster paper. Have the students illustrate the vocabulary. Use this to review vocabulary in subsequent classes.

What's in the picture? Display pictures of animals from magazine photos. Ask the students to identify the animals, their colors, and say if the animals are big or little.

TPR Give each student a picture of people or animals doing different actions. Ask individuals

to act out the action in his or her picture. Have the rest of the class guess what the student is doing. If you don't have pictures, you may just write the action on a sheet of paper which the student reads.

Unit 6 Test See page xxxvi.

Workbook

Page 50, Listen and circle. Play the audio or read the audioscript several times for the students to complete the activity.
AUDIOSCRIPT: 1. It's flying. 2. It's running. 3. It's swimming. 4. The dog is eating. 5. The worm is crawling. 6. The cat is sleeping.

The following Workbook pages are a practice test for Units 4–6. Check the answers. You may want to review areas with which they had difficulty before they take the test on pages xlii–xliii.

Page 51, Listen and circle. Play the audio or read the audioscript aloud several times for the students to complete the activity.
AUDIOSCRIPT: 1. Circle the skirt. 2. Circle the table. 3. Circle the shoes. 4. Circle the chair. 5. Circle the jacket. 6. Circle the triangle. 7. Circle the frog.

Page 52, Read and match. Have the students draw lines from each word to the correct corresponding picture.
ANSWERS: 1. horse—eating 2. cat—sleeping 3. boy—jumping 4. woman—cooking 5. man—reading 6. boy—playing ball 7. dog—running

Page 52, Say what each animal is doing. Have the students look at the pictures in the activity above and tell what the animals are doing, such as "The horse is eating."

 Listen. Circle.

1.

2.

3.

4.

5.

6.

 I can.

1. I can say animal names.

2. I can say what the animals are doing.

7 My Birthday

Communication Objectives

to say one's age
to name the days of the week
to talk about parties
to identify foods
to talk about things one has
to talk about things one wants
to identify actions
to identify numbers *1–10*

Language Objectives

to use the simple present tense of *have, want*
to use the present progressive tense
to answer *how old* questions with the present tense of *be*
to pronounce /b/, /y/, /g/, and /θ/

Learning Strategies and Thinking Skills

to sequence
to make associations
to apply prior knowledge
to use illustrations

Content Connections

Art: to make birthday hats; to make finger puppets; to draw birthday posters
Literature: to recite a poem
Mathematics: to count
Music: to sing a song
Social Studies: to make calendars; to use graphs to represent information

Materials

New Parade 1 Student Book, pages 62–71
New Parade 1 Workbook, pages 53–60; 99–101
New Parade 1 Audio: Tape/CD
New Parade 1 Video and Video Guide
New Parade 1 Posters

Photographs and pictures of children ages 1–8, birthday objects, and key vocabulary food, toys, calendars, crayons or markers, scissors, glue, construction paper, paper strips, tape, string, paper clips, game pieces, coins
Optional Materials: New Parade Picture Cards—cake, hamburger, hot dog, ice cream, milk, pizza, candles, presents; alphabet cards from Unit 2, sheets of paper, classroom objects, play food, stuffed animals, old magazines, poster paper, box or bag; *Little Celebrations— Peanut Butter*, and *On Top of Spaghetti* by Tom Glazer

Key Vocabulary

- cake, hamburger, hot dog, ice cream, milk, pizza
- balloon, birthday, candle, children, hat, kite, party, present
- fish
- Sunday, Monday, Tuesday, Wednesday, Thursday, Friday, Saturday
- day, week
- how old
- you
- are, have, is, want
- eating, opening, saying "Good-bye," saying "Hello," singing
- please
- happy

Picture Dictionary

cake   present   balloons   ice cream
hamburger   hot dog   milk   pizza

Setting Up the Classroom

Familiarize yourself with the material before starting this unit. Make sure you have the supplies you need to teach the unit. If possible, bring in plastic toy food rather than just pictures to provide the students with a more memorable experience. Prepare TPR commands for Warm Up 1 on page T62. If you are going to use Warm Up 3 on page T63, wrap the "present" beforehand. Read the Little Book, *Ana's Birthday Party*, so that you are familiar with the story.

Using the Video and the Video Guide

Show the video to start off this new unit. The students will get an idea of the topic and a preview of the language. Help them use the context to understand what is happening. Encourage the students to interact with the video by answering the questions, singing, and doing the actions along with the children in the video. Use the video often, especially at the beginning of each week. The students will understand more and more every time they watch. The Video Guide will suggest where to start and stop the video.

This video segment begins with Julia planning her birthday party, "I want a hat, cake and ice cream." We hear the "Happy Birthday" song. Later, Nora and Mike look at a calendar and talk about their ages, "How old are you? I'm eight." and their birthdays, which are both that week. They introduce some of the days of the week. They decide to have a party on Saturday and plan the food and activities they want. At the party, they open presents and talk about what they want and what they have.

Family Connections

Help the students make a one-week calendar, with the days of the week, to hang up at home. They should draw, and if possible, label, one activity their families do each day. Encourage the students to bring their calendars back to class the following week and talk about what they and their families did each day.

Bulletin Board Ideas

Write the words *Happy Birthday!* at the top of the bulletin board. Around the words, hang cutouts of balloons and wrapped presents. Encourage the students to bring in photographs of birthday parties. Photos might be from their own birthdays or from those of others. Also put up pictures of objects such as birthday cakes or birthday presents.

Little Book: Ana's Birthday Party

Summary: Saturday is Ana's birthday. She doesn't know that her friends and family are giving her a surprise party.

7 My Birthday

Happy Birthday to you!
Happy Birthday to you!
Happy Birthday, dear Carmen.
Happy Birthday to you!

Objectives

to say one's age

to answer *how old* questions with the present tense of *be*

to talk about parties

to identify numbers *1–10*

to pronounce /b/ and /y/

Key Vocabulary

- **balloon, birthday, cake, candle, children, hat, party**
- **how old**
- **are**
- **singing**
- **you**
- **happy, is**

WARM UP

1. **X** Review the TPR commands from the previous units. Act out opening a box, drinking, and singing. Call out a series of commands and have the students do them. For more information on TPR, see page ix.

2. Bring in photographs or magazine pictures of children ranging in age from one year old to eight years old. Let the class guess how old each child is by saying, "He's (two) years old."

You may want to tape the pictures to the board and write each child's (guessed) age under the picture. Ask the students, "How old is she/he?" "He's/She's (six) years old."

3. Introduce the word *birthday* and invite the students to talk about their birthdays.

4. Display the Poster for Unit 7.

PRESENTATION

Using the Page

ACTIVITY 1

Point. Listen. Sing together.

1. Focus attention on the picture. Point to the different objects related to the birthday party and identify them. Point out that the children in the picture are singing.

2. Review the words *cat* and *dog* by pointing to the picture and asking, "What animal is this?"

3. 🎵 🔊 Play the audio or sing the song several times for the students to repeat. To practice pronunciation, focus on /b/ in *birthday* and /y/ in *you*.

4. Find out who in the class has the next birthday. Sing the song again, substituting that student's name for Carmen.

5. 🎵 Focus attention on Homer and Hanna. Play the audio or read their conversation for the students to repeat.

6. Have the students work in pairs asking and answering, "How old are you?" "I'm (seven) years old."

Reaching All Students

Vocabulary Expansion Focus attention on the Picture Dictionary on pages 62–63. Have the students point to the birthday objects and foods as you say the words for them to repeat (*cake, present, balloons, ice cream, hamburger, hot dog, milk, pizza*).

Workbook

Page 53, Activity 1: How old are you? Draw candles on the cake. Have each student draw the number of candles on the cake that corresponds to his or her age. You may want to have the students color the cake and candles. Ask, "What color is your cake?" The students could answer, "It's (pink)."

Page 53, Activity 2: Write your answer. Read the question. Point to several students and ask, "How old are you?" Help the students write their correct age on the line provided. Have the students display their cakes to the class and say how old they are, "I'm (seven) years old."

Objectives

to name the days of the week
to talk about things one has
to use the simple present tense of *have*
to identify actions

Key Vocabulary

- cake, kite, present
- Sunday, Monday, Tuesday, Wednesday, Thursday, Friday, Saturday
- day, week
- have, opening

PRESENTATION

Warm Up

1. Bring in and display different kinds of calendars: wall calendars, desk calendars, calendars with a page for each day.

2. Help the students name the days of the week, repeating after you, as you point to each one on a calendar. Ask, "What day is today?" They should answer, "It's (Friday)."

3. ▮ Put a toy in a box and wrap the box with a sheet of paper and a ribbon. Act out opening the present (undoing the ribbon and taking off the wrapping) as you say, "I'm opening a present." Have the class act out the activity as you say it.

Using the Page

ACTIVITY 2

Look. Listen. Say.

1. ▮ Have the students look at the picture. Make sure they understand that it shows the days in a week. Point to the words for the days of the week and play the audio or say the words for the students to repeat.

2. ▮ Point to the birthday cake on the calendar. Ask the students what they think is happening. Play the audio or read the conversation several times for the students to repeat.

ACTIVITY 3

Listen. Read. Say.

1. ▮ Focus attention on the pictures. Ask the students what they think is happening. (*A boy is opening presents. Maybe it's his birthday.*)

2. ▮ Play the audio or read the conversation several times for the students to repeat.

3. Point to the other presents and ask individuals to identify them (*horse, cat*).

Reaching All Students

▮ **Bar Graph** Make a bar graph on the board showing the students' ages. Write numbers across the top and names down the left. Have each student tell his or her age and fill in the correct number of spaces on the graph.

▮ **Carmen's Birthday** Have the students look at the picture on page 62 and listen as you tell them about Carmen's birthday. "Today is Carmen's birthday. It's Thursday. She's seven years old. There is a birthday cake. There are balloons. There are party hats. Happy birthday, Carmen!" Then check understanding by asking questions such as "Is Carmen seven years old? What day is her birthday? How many (balloons) are there? What color is Carmen's hat?"

Days of the Week As often as possible, ask the students, "What day is it today?" The students should answer, "Today is (Monday)."

Workbook

Page 54, Activity 3: Write the days in order. Have the students write the days of the week in the correct order.

Page 55, Activity 4: Draw. Color. Cut. Ask the students what they do or want to do each day. Help them decide on one activity for each day of the week. Ask them to draw and color an appropriate picture above each day of the week. Then have them cut out the cards. You may want them to paste the cards on cardboard. Have the students put the cards in order.

2. Look. Listen. Say.

3. Listen. Read. Say.

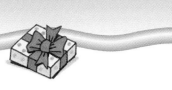 

4. Point. Say. Number.

1
———

———

———  ———

5. Listen. Point. Answer.

UNIT 7 • My Birthday

Objectives

to talk about parties
to identify foods
to identify actions
to use the present progressive tense
to sequence
to make associations

Key Vocabulary

- cake, hamburger, hot dog, ice cream, milk, pizza
- birthday, present
- please
- want
- eating, opening, saying "Good-bye," saying "Hello," singing

PRESENTATION

Warm Up

1. Have the students sing the song on page 62.

2. Review the actions the students learned in Units 5 and 6. *(eating, jumping)*

3. Display play food or pictures of the key food vocabulary or use Picture Cards to introduce those words. You may want to write the name for the food on the board as you present it. Ask the students to give you different food items, "David, give me the (hot dog)."

Using the Page

ACTIVITY 4

Point. Say. Number.

1. Ask the students to say what the people in each picture are doing.

2. Focus attention on the pictures. Point to each picture as you say the action, "They're eating cake and ice cream. They're saying 'Good-bye.' They're singing. He's opening presents. She's saying 'Hello.'"

3. 💡 Point out the 1 next to the first picture. *(She's saying "Hello.")* Have the students number the rest of the pictures in order (2–5) according to what they think happens at a birthday party. Encourage discussion, if all the students do not agree.
PROBABLE ANSWERS: 2. They're singing.
3. They're eating cake and ice cream. 4. He's opening presents. 5. They're saying "Good-bye."

ACTIVITY 5

Listen. Point. Answer.

1. 🎧 Focus attention on the picture. Point to the different food items and identify them or play the audio. Have the students point to the food items and repeat the words.

2. Have the students identify each kind of food by asking, "What is it?" They should answer, "It's (ice cream)."

3. 🎧 Play the audio or read the conversation several times for the students to repeat. Emphasize the word *please*.

Reaching All Students

📋 **Vocabulary Check** Have the students review the words for birthday objects and foods in the Picture Dictionary on pages 64–65.

Calendars Display a yearly calendar in the class. Cut out small birthday cakes and distribute one to each student. Have the students write their names on the cakes and tape them to the calendar on their birthdays. You may want to sing "Happy Birthday" on each person's birthday. For the students who have birthdays when school is not in session, you might celebrate six months from their real birthdays. If you have many students in your class, you might have one Happy Birthday Day each month.

💡 **Comparing Birthday Celebrations**
Discuss ways the students celebrate their birthdays. Do they celebrate their birthdays with parties? Do they do different activities than those shown at the U.S. birthday party in Activity 4? Have the students make posters that show what they do to celebrate their birthdays.

Objectives
to identify foods
to talk about things one wants
to use the simple present tense of *want*
to name the days of the week
to pronounce /g/, and /θ/

Key Vocabulary
- cake, hamburger, hot dog, ice cream, pizza
- Sunday, Monday, Tuesday, Wednesday, Thursday, Friday, Saturday
- want

PRACTICE

Warm Up
Write the word *cake* on the board and help the students spell the word. Lead a "cake cheer" by reading the chant and having the students yell out the letters.
Give me a C! *C*
Give me an A! *A*
Give me a K! *K*
Give me an E! *E*
What does it spell? *Cake!*

Using the Page
ACTIVITY 6
Listen and circle the foods.

1. Have the students identify all the food items in the pictures by asking, "What is it?" They should answer, "It's a (hot dog)."

2. Model the sample exercise. Have the students point to the first two pictures as you play the audio or read aloud the sentences, "I want milk. Circle the milk." Point out the circled answer.

3. Play the audio or read the audioscript aloud two or three times. Have the students circle the answers. Then check the students' work.
   AUDIOSCRIPT: 1. I want ice cream. 2. I want a hamburger. 3. I want pizza. 4. I want a hot dog.

ACTIVITY 7
Listen. Say. Do the actions.

1. Help the students make finger puppets like those pictured.

2. Play the audio or read the poem aloud for the students to repeat. As you recite the poem, do the actions. Start with all your fingers curled in a fist. Then as you say each day of the week, raise the corresponding finger. To practice pronunciation, focus on /g/ in *go* and /θ/ in *think*.

3. Have the students recite the poem and do the finger actions several times.

4. Focus the students' attention on Hanna. Read what she is saying. Ask the students to respond. Do this on a daily basis.

Reaching All Students
School Week If your school week is different from that described in the book, you may want to discuss the differences with the students. Ask, "What days do you go to school?"

Workbook Expansion Have the clerk and the shoppers in Workbook Activity 5 ask and answer questions. "What do you have?" (*I have a red hot dog.*)

Workbook
Page 57, Activity 5: Color. Cut. Play store.
Have the students color the food and cut it out. Put the students into small groups. Assign one student in each group to be the store clerk. The others are shoppers. Have the students give all their food to the store clerk who puts the food on a table. The shoppers and clerk take turns saying what they have and what they want. "I have (pink) cake." "I want (white) cake, please."

Language Activities Section, page 99
ANSWERS: 1. saying 2. singing 3. opening 4. eating

6. Listen and circle the foods.

I want  .

1. I want  .

2. I want a  .

3. I want   .

4. I want a  .

7. Listen. Say. Do the actions.

What day is it today?

Monday, and Tuesday, and Wednesday,
Thursday, and Friday, too.
These are the days we go to school.
I think it's fun, don't you?

8. Listen and draw a line.

Sunday

Monday

Tuesday

Wednesday

Thursday

Friday

Saturday

9. Play the guessing game.

1.

2.

3.

4.

5.

6.

I have a hamburger, milk, and cake.

It's number 4.

Objectives

to name the days of the week
to identify foods
to use the simple present tense of *have, want*

Key Vocabulary

• cake, hamburger, hot dog, ice cream, milk, pizza
• Sunday, Monday, Tuesday, Wednesday, Thursday, Friday, Saturday

PRACTICE

Using the Page

ACTIVITY 8

Listen and draw a line.

1. ⊘ Have the students identify all the food items in the pictures by asking, "What is it?" They should answer, "It's a (hamburger)."

2. 🎧 Model the sample exercise. Have the students point to the word *Sunday* and the pictures of milk and cake as you play the audio or read aloud, "Today is Sunday. I want milk and cake." Point out the answer lines.

3. 🎧 Play the audio or read the audioscript aloud two or three times. Have the students draw a line from the day of the week to the food or foods they hear.

AUDIOSCRIPT: 1. Today is Tuesday. I want pizza and milk. 2. Today is Thursday. I want a hot dog. 3. Today is Friday. I want a hamburger. 4. Today is Saturday. I want pizza and ice cream.
Then ask the students what they want from the pictures on the other days of the week.

Reaching All Students

Present Wish List Ask the students to pretend they can have whatever present they want. Have them say what they want. "I want a (bike)." Supply them with any vocabulary they need to express their desires.

APPLICATION

ACTIVITY 9

Play the guessing game.

1. 🎧 Focus attention on Homer and Hanna. Play the audio or read their conversation for the students to repeat.

2. 🎧 Model the language for the game by playing the audio or reading the audioscript. Pause after each sentence to allow the students to answer (answers in parentheses). Then let the students play the game in pairs. Encourage them to say their sentences in a different order.
AUDIOSCRIPT: 1. I have a hamburger, milk, and pizza. *(It's number three.)* 2. I have a hamburger, a hot dog, and milk. *(It's number two.)* 3. I have a hot dog, milk, and ice cream. *(It's number six.)* 4. I have a hamburger, a hot dog, and ice cream. *(It's number one.)* 5. I have a hot dog, milk, and cake. *(It's number five.)*

Reaching All Students

Birthday Cards Have the students make birthday cards for one another. Show the students how to fold a sheet of paper in half and draw a "birthday present" inside. Help them think of things the birthday child will really like. When they are finished, invite the class to sit in a circle with the birthday child in the middle. Each student can hand his or her "present" to the birthday child and say, "Happy Birthday." The birthday child should open the present, name it, and say whatever he or she can about it. "It's a red kite! Thank you. Ramón."

Workbook

Language Activities Section, page 100
ANSWERS: 1. want 2. have 3. want 4. have 5. have 6. want

Story Summary

Saturday is Ana's birthday. She doesn't know that her friends and family are giving her a surprise party.

Key Unit Vocabulary

are, balloon, birthday, cake, happy, hat, ice cream, party, Saturday

Word Bank

friends, surprise

BEFORE READING

WARM UP

Display pictures or Picture Cards of cakes, candles, and presents. Ask the students to point to something to eat at a birthday party. Say the word *cake* and have the students say it. Repeat the activity with something they bring to a birthday party and something on a birthday cake. Each time, say the word and ask the students to repeat the word.

PUT TOGETHER THE LITTLE BOOK

After the students remove pages 67–68 from their books, they can fold the pages in half to make the Little Book, *Ana's Birthday Party.*

PREVIEW THE LITTLE BOOK

1. After the students have assembled the books, encourage them to name objects they see in the pictures. Ask them what kind of party the people are having.

2. Read the title aloud and preview the pictures with the students. Let them tell what they see in each illustration. Encourage them to use words such as *hats, balloons, ice cream,* and *cake.* Ask the students to predict what the story is about.

SHARE NEW WORDS

Write the Word Bank words on the board and ask the students if they know any of the words. Then model saying each word and have the students repeat after you. Use each word in a sentence and encourage the students to make up sentences using these words.

DURING READING

READING THE LITTLE BOOK

The students should listen quietly to the story as you read it aloud or play the audio. Encourage them to ask questions and discuss the story on a second reading.

GUIDED READING

Read the story aloud. Point to the words as you read, and the students follow along. Make sure they use the pictures to help them understand what is happening in the text.

TEACHER TIPS

On a rereading, pause before you say words such as *hats, balloon, ice cream,* and *cake;* point to the picture and have the students supply the missing word.

REREADING

Review the students' predictions and compare them with what actually happens in the story. Quickly go over the story. You may assess the students' comprehension with questions such as these:

Page 1 *What day is it?*
Page 2 *What are the hats and balloons for?*
Page 3 *Who is here?*
Page 4 *Is Ana surprised? How can you tell?*

As necessary, point to objects and people in the illustrations to help the students answer the comprehension questions.

Ana's Birthday Party

by Mario Herrera

Today is Saturday.
It's Ana's birthday.

1

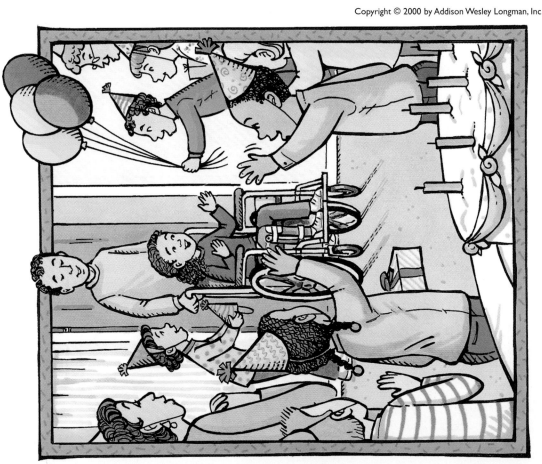

Surprise!
Happy Birthday, Ana!

4

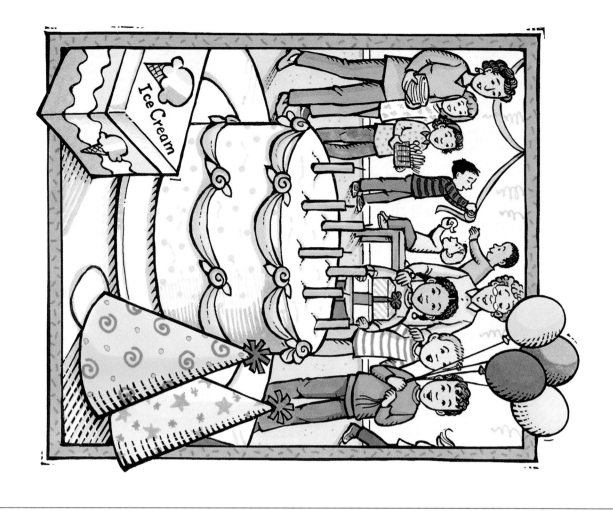

The hats and balloons are ready.
The ice cream and cake are ready.

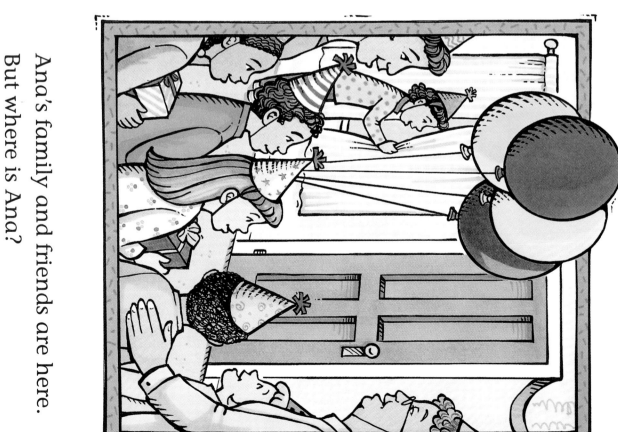

Ana's family and friends are here.
But where is Ana?

Activities for Developing Language

PREDICTING

Reread the book one page at a time. Ask the students what they predicted would happen after each page. Ask them what clues helped them make that prediction.

CONTEXT CLUES

Invite the students to open their Little Books to page 2. Say the word *cake* aloud. Ask them to find *cake* in the story and draw a circle around the word. Then ask them to look at the picture on page 2. If they find a cake in the picture, they should draw a line from the circled word to the cake in the picture. Repeat the activity with *hats, balloons,* and *ice cream.*

RETELLING THE STORY

Ask the students to use the pictures to help them retell the story to a partner.

BIRTHDAYS WE ENJOY

Invite the students to draw a picture of a birthday party. It could be their own or someone else's party. Encourage them to include details such as decorations, food, and so on. The students might want to share their drawings with their classmates.

PARTY TPR

Ask questions about birthday party activites: "What do you eat at a birthday party?" Say the word *cake* with the students. Invite them to use TPR to show making a cake. Some other actions to show include blowing up a balloon, blowing out candles, and putting on a party hat.

WRITE ABOUT IT!

Ask the students to write or dictate a party invitation to Ana's birthday party. Help them to include the time, date, and place. Suggest that they decorate the card so friends and family will want to come. Invite them to draw a picture for each new word for their own Picture Dictionary.

GRAMMAR CONNECTION: TYPES OF SENTENCES

Write the sentences from the Little Book on sentence strips. Ask the students to sort the sentences into sentences that tell something, those that ask something, and those that show feelings. Have them notice how each type of sentence has a particular type of end punctuation.

WORKBOOK

Little Book Comprehension, page 101.

BULLETIN BOARD IDEAS

You may wish to have the students hang their pictures of birthdays on a bulletin board display entitled *Birthdays.*

FAMILY CONNECTION

Invite the students to take their Little Books home and read them to their friends and family members.

Objectives

to identify the numbers *1–10*
to talk about parties
to use illustrations

Key Vocabulary

- **birthday, party**
- **have, want**
- **fish**

APPLICATION

Using the Project Page

Play the fishing game.

1. Have the students look at the pictures. Explain that this is a popular game that children often play at birthday parties in the United States. Help the students understand what is happening.

2. Help the students cut out different-colored fish from construction paper. Have them write a number from 1 to 10 on each. Then hand out paper clips and have the students put one paper clip on each fish.

3. Help the students make fishing poles by tying a piece of string to the end of a pencil. On the other end, have them tie a large open paper clip.

4. Put the students into groups and have them combine their fish on the floor. Then hand out the fishing poles. Have the students "catch" fish by hooking the large opened paper clip to the paper clips on the fish. As he or she "catches" a fish, have the other students ask, "What do you have?" He or she should answer, "I have a (blue fish). It's number (nine)." The student who catches the most fish and identifies them correctly wins.

Reaching All Students

Birthday Poem Play the audio or read the following poem aloud several times for the students to repeat. Have them do simple hand actions as they recite.

Ten Little Candles
Ten little candles on a chocolate cake.
Wh! Wh! Now there are eight.
Eight little candles on candlesticks.
Wh! Wh! Now there are six.
Six little candles and not one more.
Wh! Wh! Now there are four.
Four little candles—red, white and blue.
Wh! Wh! Now there are two.
Two little candles standing in the sun.
Wh! Wh! Now there are none!

Go Fish Have the students get their alphabet cards from their class folders. Put the students into small groups. The students in a group should combine and mix up their cards. One person deals out the cards to the players as well as to the "fish pile." The goal of the game is to make pairs of cards. The players look at their cards and put down all their pairs. Then the person on the left of the dealer asks someone in the group for a card he or she wants to match, "Do you have a (jacket)?" If that person has it, he or she must give it up. If that person doesn't have the requested card, he or she says, "Go fish," and the first person takes a card from the "fish pile." Then it is the next person's turn. The play continues until someone matches all his or her cards. The person with the most pairs wins.

Four Square Have the students divide two sheets of paper into four numbered sections. Then ask them to draw a food, animal, or birthday object of their choice, one in each square, on one of the sheets of paper. Put the students into pairs and have them ask each other what they drew. "What do you have for number one?" "I have a (worm)." They draw the corresponding picture on the second sheet of paper. When they are finished, have the students compare the two sets of papers.

Family Celebrations Have the students bring in objects, stories, or pictures from family celebrations. Have them share how they celebrate family events with the rest of the class.

PROJECT

Play the fishing game.

Make the fish and say what you have.

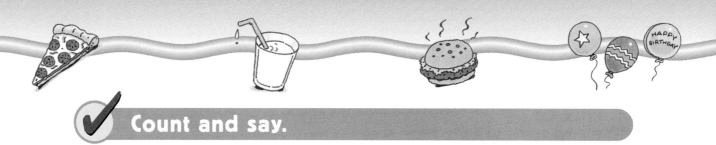

✓ Count and say.

Tell what it is and how many.

UNIT 7 • My Birthday

Objectives
to identify foods
to identify the numbers *0–10*
to count

Key Vocabulary
- cake, hamburger, hot dog, ice cream, milk, pizza
- balloon, candle, hat, kite, present
- birthday
- happy

ASSESSMENT

Warm Up
Review the words for birthday objects and key vocabulary foods by showing pictures for the students to describe. Encourage the students to say sentences such as "These are red balloons."

Using the Page
Count and say.

1. Read what Hanna is saying several times for the students to repeat. Get playing pieces and coins for the students to play with. A playing piece can be any small object such as an eraser, bottle cap, paper clip, or a piece of paper.

2. Have the students play in pairs or groups of three. Decide which sides of the coins will be worth one point and which will be worth two. The students take turns tossing the coins and moving their playing pieces two, three, or four spaces on the board. When they land, they must identify what the picture on the board is and how many of the object is shown, "It's seven birthday candles." If they answer incorrectly, they go back to where they were before their turn. The other players determine if the answers are correct. The first person to finish wins.

3. ☑ As the students play the game, walk around the room and observe how individual students are using the key vocabulary words. Check for objectives (1) the identification of birthday objects and foods and (2) the use of the number words for 1–10. Record your observations on the Student Oral Assessment Checklist on page xxi.

Reaching All Students

☑ **Picture Dictionary** Have the students identify the pictures on pages 70–71.

☑ **Who Has What?** Give each student a classroom object, play food, stuffed animals, and so on. Ask individuals to tell you what they have, "What do you have? " Prompt the students to answer, "I have a (fish)."

🔷 **Calendars** Have the students make their own calendars for a week. Encourage them to label the days of the week and draw an activity for each day. Have volunteers share their calendars with the class and tell what they are doing each day. Demonstrate how to cross off each day at the end of the day.

Birthday Game Wrap familiar objects or put them in bags. Have the students sit in a circle. Play some music and have the students pass a "present" around the circle. When the music stops, the student holding the present must open it and identify it. Continue with other objects.

Workbook
Page 59, Activity 6: Read and match. Have the students draw lines from each word to the correct picture.
ANSWERS: 1. bunch of balloons 2. bowl of ice cream 3. boy drinking glass of milk 4. girls singing 5. boy holding present 6. girl opening box

Objectives

to use the simple present tense of *have, want*
to identify foods
to name the days of the week

Key Vocabulary

- cake, hamburger, hot dog, ice cream, milk, pizza
- Sunday, Monday, Tuesday, Wednesday, Thursday, Friday, Saturday
- have, want

ASSESSMENT

Using the Page

Listen and circle the foods.

1. Have the students identify all the food items in the pictures.

2. 🎧 Play the audio or read the audioscript aloud. Have the students circle the words they hear.
   AUDIOSCRIPT: 1. I want a hamburger. 2. I have pizza. 3. I want milk. 4. I have a hot dog. 5. I want cake.

I can.

1. Read the statement for number 1 aloud to the students. Ask individuals, groups, or the whole class to name the foods. Have them circle the pictures for the words they can say.

2. Read the statement for number 2 aloud to the students. Ask individuals, groups, or the whole class to say the days of the week in order. Have them circle the pictures for the words they can say. Quickly note oral production in these activities on the Student Oral Assessment Checklist on page xxi.

Reaching All Students

Grab Bag Place objects such as classroom objects, play food, and toy animals in a bag or box. Let each student close his or her eyes, reach into the bag, select an item, and guess what it is without looking at it. Ask the student what he or she has, "What do you have?" "I have a (pencil)."

Simon Says Practice the commands, including eat, drink, open (your books), close (your books), by explaining that the students must do as you say only when the command starts with "Simon says." If you do not say "Simon says," they must not do anything. If anyone follows a direction not preceded by "Simon says," he or she is out of the game. The last student to be following the instructions wins the game.

Birthday Posters Ask each student to make a poster showing things he or she wants. They can draw pictures, cut them out of old magazines, or bring photographs from home. Display each student's poster. The student can use the poster to tell the class about what he or she wants for his or her birthday by saying, "I want a (kite)." You may need to help with new vocabulary.

Unit Mural Elicit all the words and expressions the students remember from this unit. Write them on mural or poster paper. Have the students illustrate the vocabulary. Use this to review vocabulary in subsequent classes.

Unit 7 Test See page xxxvii.

Workbook

🎧 ✓ **Page 60, Listen and circle.** Have the students identify all the food items and actions in the pictures. Play the audio or read the audioscript aloud two or three times for the students to complete the activity. Check to see that the students have circled the correct pictures.
AUDIOSCRIPT: 1. I want ice cream. 2. I have a balloon. 3. I want a hot dog. 4. I have a present. 5. I'm saying good-bye. 6. I'm drinking. 7. I'm singing.

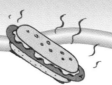

 Listen and circle the foods.

1. I want a   .

2. I have   .

3. I want  .

4. I have a   .

5. I want   .

 I can.

1. I can say foods.

2. I can say the days of the week.

SUNDAY	MONDAY	TUESDAY	WEDNESDAY	THURSDAY	FRIDAY	SATURDAY

8 My Toys

Communication Objectives

to identify and describe toys
to identify locations
to talk about things one wants
to identify the numbers *11–20*
to follow directions
to request and thank using *please*
and *thank you*
to identify colors

Language Objectives

to distinguish among the prepositions *in,*
on, and *under*
to use adjectives before nouns
to use the simple present tense of *want*
to pronounce /t/, /s/, and /b/

Learning Strategies and Thinking Skills

to apply prior knowledge
to understand sequence
to synthesize information
to use illustrations

Content Connections

Language Arts: to write conversations,
to make shopping lists
Literature: to recite poems
Mathematics: to add and subtract; to use
money; to sequence numbers; and to
measure distances
Social Studies: to act out buying and selling;
to make and read charts and graphs

Materials

New Parade 1 Student Book, pages 72–81
New Parade 1 Workbook, pages 61–68;
102–104
New Parade 1 Audio: Tape/CD
New Parade 1 Video and Video Guide
New Parade 1 Posters

Toys, catalogs, box, pencil, crayons or
markers, scissors, glue, paper, miniature
cars, 20 marbles, classroom objects, tape,
construction paper, paper clip, pictures of
toys, bags, boxes
Optional Materials: New Parade Picture
Cards—airplane, ball, bike, boat, car,
dolls, kite, skate; index cards, drawing
paper, poster paper; *Little Celebrations—*
Max's Box by Kristen Avery, and *Zithers*
by Marcia Vaughan

Key Vocabulary

- ball, bike, block, boat, car, doll, kite,
marble, plane, skate, toy, toy box
- eleven, twelve, thirteen, fourteen, fifteen,
sixteen, seventeen, eighteen, nineteen,
twenty
- please, thank you
- I'm, it's
- want
- moving
- what, what color, what's, where, where's
- in, on, under

Picture Dictionary

kite   soccer ball   basketball   boat   car
bike   block

Setting Up the Classroom

In advance, tell the students to bring one favorite toy to class for Warm Up 2, page T72. Prepare TPR commands with prepositions for Warm Up 3 on page T72. Be sure to read through the material before starting the unit, particularly the instructions for Activity 9, which requires some construction and items from home. Read the Little Book, *The Toy Shop* and think about what parts of the story you might act out for the students.

Using the Video and the Video Guide

Show the video to prepare for the unit. This will preview the language the students will learn about toys. Use the Video Guide to suggest where to stop and start the video. Plan to use the video often. You may want to show it at the beginning of each week during the unit. Encourage the students to interact with the video by answering the questions, singing, and doing the actions along with the children in the video.

Julia shows and names the toys in Sam's toy box. Ana and Sam play with marbles, talking about the colors and counting them (up to twenty). Ana asks Sam for a marble. "Do you want it?" "Yes, please. I want it." "Thank you!" They play with other toys, too (a bike, skates), sharing and saying, "Thank you."

Family Connections

Toward the end of the unit, ask the students to have one family member draw his or her favorite doll, toy, car, ball, kite, or bike. Then encourage the students to teach the family member the word for this toy.

Bulletin Board Ideas

On chart paper, copy the poem "The Toy Store" on page 74 and place it in the center of the bulletin board. Then encourage the students to draw pictures of toys, cut them out, and place them on the bulletin board.

Little Book: The Toy Shop

Summary: A shopkeeper challenges a boy and girl to count the number of toys they see while exploring the toy shop.

8 My Toys

1. Listen. Point. Say.

Objectives

to identify and describe toys
to identify colors
to talk about things one wants
to use the simple present tense of *want*
to use adjectives before nouns

Key Vocabulary

- **ball, bike, block, boat, car, doll, kite, marble, toy**
- **want**
- **what**

WARM UP

1. Display a group of toys from the key vocabulary list on a table. Ask the students if they know the names of any of the toys. Pick up each one and say its name. Then ask the students the names in random order. Ask, "What's this?" "It's a (ball)."

2. Have the students bring their favorite toys to class and talk about them.

3. 🕱 For practice with prepositions, say, "Put your hands on your desk. Put your hands under your desk. Put your hands in your pockets." See page ix for more information.

4. 🕱 Have the students take turns standing or sitting on, in, or under objects and furnishings in the classroom. Each student asks, "Where am I?" The other students answer, "He's/she's (under the table)."

5. Display the Poster for Unit 8.

PRESENTATION

Using the Page
ACTIVITY 1
Listen. Point. Say.

1. Show pictures of toys in catalogs or use Picture Cards. Elicit the names of toys the students know. Then point to each toy and say, "This is a (ball)."

2. 🖉 Focus attention on the catalog pictured on the page. Play the audio or read the conversation aloud several times for the students to repeat.

3. ⊘ Provide the students with catalogs containing pictures of toys. Read what Hanna is saying. Then have the students work in pairs to tell each other what they want from the catalogs. Have volunteers report to the class what their partners want. Check to see that the students place the adjectives (color or size) before the noun (toy).

Reaching All Students

Vocabulary Expansion Focus attention on the Picture Dictionary on pages 72–73. Have the students point to the toys as you say the words for them to repeat (*kite, soccer ball, basketball, boat, kite, boat, car, bike*). Then have the students say what color each toy is.

◁⫙▷ **Writing** Have the students work individually or in pairs to write the additional conversations they create from Activity 1.

Workbook

🖉 **Page 61, Activity 1: Cut. Listen and glue.** Have the students identify and cut out the toys along the bottom of the page. Then play the audio or read the audioscript several times. The students match the correct toy to each picture. Make sure to give the students enough time to glue down their pictures. Then have the students describe the pictures by saying, "He has the blocks. She has the (white and black) ball."
AUDIOSCRIPT: 1. I want the blocks, please. 2. I want the ball, please. 3. I want the doll, please. 4. I want the kite, please.

Objectives

to identify toys
to identify locations
to distinguish among the prepositions *in, on,* and *under*
to identify the numbers *11–20*
to understand sequence
to pronounce /t/

Key Vocabulary

• ball, block, car, kite, marble, toy, toy box
• eleven, twelve, thirteen, fourteen, fifteen, sixteen, seventeen, eighteen, nineteen, twenty
• in, on, under
• where

PRESENTATION

Warm Up

Put a box on the table and place a toy car *on, under,* and *in* it as you describe each location, "The car is on the box. The car is under the box. The car is in the box." Continue with other objects and locations.

Using the Page
ACTIVITY 2
Listen. Say. Do the actions.

1. Play the audio or read the poem about the toy box aloud several times for the students to repeat. As you recite the poem, do the actions illustrated in the book. To practice pronunciation, focus on /t/ in *toys.*

2. Have the students read and recite the poem. Help them make the hand actions. Repeat until the students can recite the poem and do the actions. Use this poem when you are putting away any toys in the classroom.

ACTIVITY 3
Listen. Point. Say.

1. Have the students identify the toys.

2. Focus attention on the location of the toys. Have the students point to each toy in the picture and identify the location of each.

3. Play the audio or read Hanna and Homer's conversation several times for the students to repeat.

4. Play the audio or read the audioscript aloud several times for the students to complete the activity.

AUDIOSCRIPT: 1. Where's the kite? 2. Where's the ball? 3. Where's the teddy bear?
ANSWERS: 1. It's in the box. 2. It's in the box. 3. It's in the box.

5. Have the students work in pairs to ask and answer questions about where the toys are.

ACTIVITY 4
Listen. Point. Say.

1. Play the audio or read the numerals in order several times for the students to repeat.

2. Say the numerals in mixed up order and have the students point to the numbers.

Reaching All Students

Following Directions Play Simon Says using action vocabulary the students have learned. Remind the students to do the action only when you say "Simon says" first. For example, (Simon says): *stand, sit, put,* and *move* different parts of their bodies.

Workbook

Page 63, Activity 2: Count and write the number. Have the students count the objects in each set and write the correct number on each line. Then have the students present their pages and say what the items are.

Language Activities Section, page 102
ANSWERS: 1. under 2. in 3. on 4. on 5. in 6. under

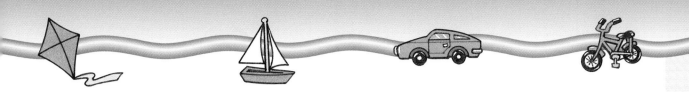

2. Listen. Say. Do the actions.

My toys are in my toy box.

I take them out to play.

And when I've finished playing,

I put them all away.

3. Listen. Point. Say.

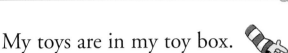

Where is the kite?

It's in the box.

4. Listen. Point. Say.

11
eleven

12
twelve

13
thirteen

14
fourteen

15
fifteen

16
sixteen

17
seventeen

18
eighteen

19
nineteen

20
twenty

5. Listen. Read. Circle.

	13	**(15)**	19
1.	16	20	11
2.	**14**	19	12
3.	18	17	20

6. Listen and say together.

The Toy Store

I see balls and bats and cars.
I see boats and planes.
I see wagons, ropes, and dolls.
I see ships and trains.

I see games and tops and trucks.
I see bears and bikes.
I see swings and slides and skates.
I see drums and kites.

Of all the toys I can see,
I want one for me!

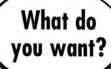

What do you want?

UNIT 8 • My Toys

Objectives
to identify the numbers *11-20*
to identify toys
to pronounce /s/ and /b/
to apply prior knowledge

Key Vocabulary
- ball, block, car, kite, plane, skate, toy
- eleven, twelve, thirteen, fourteen, fifteen, sixteen, seventeen, eighteen, nineteen, twenty
- want

PRACTICE

Warm Up

1. Get 20 marbles. Have the students count the marbles from 1–20 several times in order.

2. Have volunteers read the rows of numbers aloud in Activity 5 until all are identified.

3. 🔆 Focus attention on the picture at the bottom of the page. Ask the students to name as many kinds of toys as they can.

Using the Page
ACTIVITY 5
Listen. Read. Circle.

1. 🎧 Model the sample. Have the students point to the first row of numbers as you play the audio or say, "Circle the number fifteen." Point out the answer circle.

2. 🎧 Play the audio or read the audioscript aloud several times for the students to complete the activity. Have them circle the numerals they hear.
AUDIOSCRIPT: 1. Circle the number twenty. 2. Circle the number fourteen. 3. Circle the number seventeen.
ANSWERS: 1. The number 20 is circled.
2. The number 14 is circled.
3. The number 17 is circled.

ACTIVITY 6
Listen and say together.

1. Show toys or pictures of toys, such as *bat, plane, drum,* and *skate,* to introduce or review the words for toys in the poem.

2. 🎧 Point to the toys on the page as you play the audio or read the poem for the students to repeat as a class, in groups, or individually. To

practice pronunciation, focus on /s/ in *see* and /b/ in *box.*

3. Read what Hanna is asking. Have the students say which toy they want.

4. Help the students use their fingers to count the toys named in the poem *(twenty).*

Reaching All Students

☑ **Vocabulary Check** Have the students review the words for toys in the Picture Dictionary on pages 74–75.

🔄 **Numerical Order** Write from *one* to *twenty* on cards. Give one card to each student. Let the students work together to put the numbers in order. Then have them line up and count off their numbers.

🔄 **Labeling** Have the students label all the toys in the picture in Activity 6 by writing the correct name next to each picture.

Workbook

Page 64, Activity 3: Draw a line from one to two to three, and so on. Point to the page and say, "What's this? I don't know." Point to the dots and say, "Dots." Point to the numbers and say, "Numbers." The students join the numbers in order.

Page 64, Activity 4: Write your answer. When the students have finished joining the dots, ask, "What is it?" The students should answer, "It's a bike." Help them write *bike* on the line provided. You may want the students to color their pictures and show their pictures to the class. Ask, "Is it (red)?" Encourage the students to answer, "Yes" or "No."

Objectives

to identify and describe toys
to talk about things one wants
to request and thank
to identify colors
to use adjectives before nouns

Key Vocabulary

• ball, block, boat, car, doll, kite, marble
• want
• in, on, under
• please, thank you

PRACTICE

Warm Up

Have the students sing "Old MacDonald Has a Farm" on page 52, substituting numbers, ". . . And on his farm he has (11 cows, 12 ducks). . . ."

Using the Page

ACTIVITY 7

Look. Listen. Play store.

1. Focus attention on the pictures. Make sure the students understand they are going to act out buying things.

2. Set up a table with toys. Have the students make money or coupons that say "1 toy."

3. Play the audio or read the conversation for the students to repeat.

4. Have the students come to the "store" and ask for different items. Have them use the conversation as a model. Encourage them to say the adjective before the noun when describing what they want. Also, have them say, "please" and "thank you."

ACTIVITY 8

Listen. Read. Circle.

1. Model the sample exercise. Have the students point to the first two pictures as you play the audio or read the sentences, "The marbles are on the chair. Circle the chair with the yellow marbles." Point out the answer.

2. Play the audio or read the text several times for the students to follow along in their books. Have the students circle the picture that matches the text.
ANSWERS: 1. The black and white toy dog is circled. 2. The orange cars are circled. 3. The green ball is circled.

Reaching All Students

Money Instead of coupons, you may want to make play money for the students to use in Activity 7. Put a price tag on each item. Model the conversation, "How much are (the blue marbles)?" "They're (two dollars)." "Here's (two dollars)." "Thank you." "You're welcome." You might want to tell the students they can only spend a certain amount of money. Challenge them to see who can buy the most items. Have them tell what they bought.

Workbook

Page 65, Activity 5: Listen and color. Have the students color one of the toys in the speech balloon above each child's head. Play the audioscript several times for the students to complete the activity.
AUDIOSCRIPT: 1. He wants a car. Color the car green. 2. She wants blocks. Color the blocks yellow. 3. She wants marbles. Color the marbles red, orange, and blue. 4. He wants the ball. Color the ball black and white.

Page 66, Activity 6: Find the toys in each picture. Help the students describe the position of the toys in each picture. Then help them choose the correct word and draw a circle around it. Have the students describe their answers for the class.
ANSWERS: 1. The dolls are *in* the box. 2. The dolls are *on* the chair. 3. The kite is *on* the table. 4. The kite is *under* the table. 5. The cars are *under* the chair. 6. The cars are *on* the chair.

Language Activities Section, page 103
ANSWERS: 1. green 2. red 3. orange 4. blue

7. Look. Listen. Play store.

What do you want?

Here are the blue marbles.

I want the blue marbles, please.

Thank you.

8. Listen. Read. Circle.

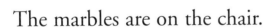

The marbles are on the chair.

1. The dog is in the box.

2. The cars are under the chair.

3. The ball is on the table.

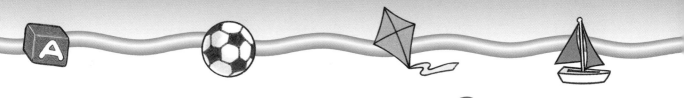

9. Play the Ruler Races game.

Count the squares and say.

10. Cut. Listen. Paste.

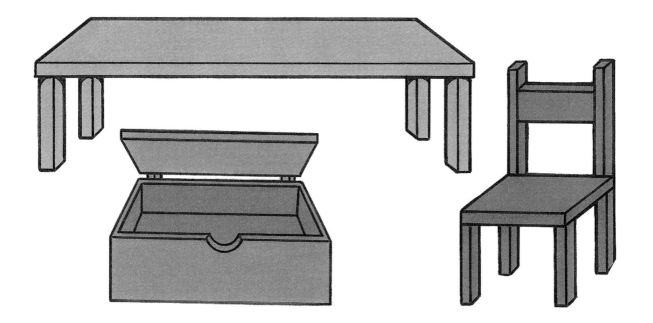

Objectives

to identify and describe toys

to identify locations

to distinguish among the prepositions *in, on,* and *under*

to use illustrations

Key Vocabulary

- car
- what color
- in, on, under
- I'm, it's
- moving

APPLICATION

Using the Page

ACTIVITY 9

Play the Ruler Races game.

1. Bring to class miniature car toys or ask the students to bring one from home. Set up the classroom so that there is a starting line and a finish line marked in tape on the floor.

2. Divide the class into groups of three or four. Have each group cut out the ruler on page 109. Each group will also need a game spinner. These can easily be made from sturdy paper. Draw a circle and divide it into (six) sections. Cut out an arrow. Attach the arrow to the center of the circle with a clip.

3. Focus attention on the pictures in the book. Set up a finish line. Explain how the game works. The cars are lined up on the floor. A player spins the spinner and then uses the ruler to measure that many squares from the front of his or her car. Then the car is placed at the end of the distance. Players take turns spinning and moving their cars. The first person to cross the finish line wins. You may want the winners of each group to compete in a tournament. You may want to draw the tournament flow chart on the chalkboard to illustrate the results.

4. 🎧 Play the audio or read the conversation several times for the students to repeat.

5. As the students are playing the game, encourage them to say what is happening by describing the car that is moving and how many units it is being moved, "My (car) is (orange). I'm moving (two) squares."

ACTIVITY 10

Cut. Listen. Paste.

1. Have the students cut out the toys on page 109.

2. 🎧 Play the audio or read the audioscript for the students to complete the activity. AUDIOSCRIPT: 1. Put the blue boat *on* the table. 2. Put the yellow car *under* the table. 3. Put the red bike *in* the box. 4. Put the orange ball *under* the chair. 5. Put the green doll *on* the chair. 6. Put the pink blocks *in* the box. 7. Put the blue bike *on* the table. 8. Put the orange marbles *under* the table. 9. Put the purple car *on* the chair. 10. Put the doll with the yellow dress *on* the table.

3. ☑ Help the students paste the items *in, on,* or *under* the furniture. Check to see if they have glued the cutouts in the correct places.

Reaching All Students

🔲 **Measuring** Have the students work individually, in pairs, or in groups to use their rulers to measure other things in the classroom. Have them name the objects and their measurements.

🔲 **Shopping Lists** Have the students work in pairs or groups to write shopping lists of things they want.

Hide the Object Ask one student to leave the room while you and the rest of the class hide a toy. Call the student back and prompt him or her to ask questions using prepositions of place to try to find the object, "Is it under the table? Is it on the chair?" When the student locates the toy, he or she gets to hide a toy for the next student.

Story Summary

A shopkeeper challenges a boy and girl to count the number of toys they see while exploring the toy shop.

Key Unit Vocabulary

block, doll, fifteen, in, on, toy, twenty

Word Bank

shop

BEFORE READING

WARM UP

Display a group of toys on a table or shelf. Say the name of each toy and ask the students to repeat the name with you. Ask them to choose the toy they like best and point to it as you keep score on the board. Add the scores and ask the students to say what toy their classmates like best.

PUT TOGETHER THE LITTLE BOOK

Have the students remove pages 77–78 from their books and fold the pages in half to make the Little Book, *The Toy Shop*.

PREVIEW THE LITTLE BOOK

1. Ask the students to look at the pictures as they unfold their books. Encourage them to name the toys they see in the pictures. Ask them where they think this story takes place.

2. Read the title aloud and point to the pictures with the students. Encourage them to tell what they see happening on each page. Ask, "What toys do you see? Who is talking on this page?" Ask the students to predict what they think the characters are saying.

SHARE NEW WORDS

Write the Word Bank word *shop* on the board. Then say the word aloud and have the students repeat it after you. Point to illustrations in the story to help explain the meaning of *shop*.

DURING READING

READING THE LITTLE BOOK

Invite the students to listen to the story as you read it aloud or play the audio as they follow along in their books. Tell the students they can ask questions and discuss the story on a second reading.

GUIDED READING

Reread the story aloud, tracking the print as you read. Encourage the students to join in when they can.

TEACHER TIPS

On a rereading, pause before you say the last word in each sentence. Encourage the students to use predictable text or context clues to help them supply the word.

REREADING

Discuss the students' predictions with them and compare to the outcome of the story. Quickly review what happens in the story. You may assess their comprehension with questions such as these:

Page 1 *Where is this story?*
Page 2 *Where are the blocks?*
Page 3 *How many dolls are on the shelf?*
Page 4 *What does the shopkeeper ask the children?*

Use the illustrations in the story to help the students answer the comprehension questions.

The Toy Shop

by Mario Herrera

There are many toys
in a toy shop.

1

How many toys
do you see?

Many! Many! Many!
We see many toys in the toy shop!

4

Fifteen! Fifteen! Fifteen!
I see fifteen blocks on the table!

Twenty! Twenty! Twenty!
I see twenty dolls on the shelf!

AFTER READING

Activities for Developing Language

CLASSIFYING

Ask the students to look at the toys in the story and classify them into different categories such as things to play make-believe with and things for building.

SEQUENCING

Draw three boxes and label them 1, 2, 3. Invite volunteers to draw three events in the order they happen in the story.

ACTING OUT THE STORY

Assign the parts of shopkeeper and two children to three students and invite them to role play the story. Encourage them to use the text to help them remember what to say.

COUNTING UP TO TWENTY

Invite the students to count from one to twenty. Model the numbers and ask the students to repeat the words as they count.

WRITE ABOUT IT!

Provide the students with a toy catalog or magazines with pictures of toys. Ask the students to cut out one picture or draw a picture of one toy they would like to have. Encourage them to write or dictate why they would like to have it. Invite the students to draw a picture for each new word for their own Picture Dictionary.

GRAMMAR CONNECTION: PRONOUN *I*

Write the sentence *I see fifteen blocks on the table.* Point out that the pronoun *I* is always a capital letter. Ask the students when they use the word *I* in a sentence. Then have them use *I* in a sentence to tell about their favorite toy.

WORKBOOK

Little Book Comprehension, page 104.

BULLETIN BOARD IDEAS

You may wish to have the students display their pictures of favorite toys on a bulletin board display entitled *Our Favorite Toys.*

FAMILY CONNECTION

Invite the students to take their Little Books home and share them with their friends and family members.

UNIT 8 • My Toys

Objectives
to identify and describe toys
to identify locations
to distinguish among the prepositions *in, on,* and *under*
to follow directions

Key Vocabulary
- ball, bike, boat, doll, kite, plane, skate
- what's, where's
- in, on, under

APPLICATION

Using the Project Page

Play the Hide the Toy game.

1. Gather a variety of classroom objects, toys, and picture cards of other vocabulary items. Make sure there are bags, boxes, and so on around the room. You may want to preteach words such as *shelf, cabinet,* as is relevant to your own classroom.

2. Focus the students' attention on the pictures. Explain that they are going to play a game. You are going to "hide" objects in the room, and they are to describe where they are.

3. 🎧 Play the audio or read the conversation for the students to repeat.

4. Ask the students to put their heads on their desks, hidden in their arms. Hide the objects in, on, and under other things in the classroom.

5. Ask the students where different items are and have them describe the location. When possible, have them use color or size to describe the objects. Ask, "Where's the (red block)?" "The (red block) is *on* the (desk)." You may want to divide the class into two teams. Ask members of each team where an object is. The first to answer correctly scores a point for his or her team. The team with the most points wins.

Ask. Make a graph. Color.

1. 🎧 Play the audio or read Homer and Hanna's conversation several times for the students to repeat. Make sure that the students understand that *favorite* means the thing you like the best.

2. Have the students interview one another to find out what their favorite toys are. Have the students fill in the names of two other favorite toys on their graphs. You may want to provide the students with a class list to aid them in their surveys.

3. As a class, compile the results of the survey on the board. Then help the class fill in the graphs in their books to illustrate the results.

Reaching All Students

Show and Tell Have the students bring in one of their favorite toys from home. Have them display the toy and describe it to the class. Depending on the ability of your students, you can adjust the complexity of the description. They can tell the toy's color and size, when and where they got the toy, how long they have had the toy, and so on.

Twenty Questions Put an assortment of classroom objects and toys or pictures of toys on a table. Divide the students into groups of three or four. Give one student in each group one of the objects from the table, making sure that the other students don't see what it is. The students in the groups ask *yes/no* questions to guess what the student has, "Do you have a (ball)?" The student with the object can only say *yes* or *no*. The group that guesses with the fewest questions wins. Have the students take turns being the one to answer the questions.

Workbook

Page 67, Activity 7: Read and look. Have the students read each sentence and draw a line to the correct picture. Have the students work in pairs to check their answers.

PROJECT

Play the Hide the Toy game.

Ask. Make a graph. Color.

What's your favorite toy?

A ball.

Favorite Toys										
	1	2	3	4	5	6	7	8	9	10
ball										
bike										
boat										
doll										
kite										
plane										
skates										

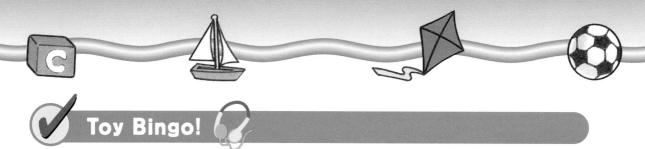

Toy Bingo!

Draw 4 toys. Then listen.

The red ball is under the chair.

Objectives

to identify and describe toys
to identify locations
to distinguish among the prepositions *in, on,*
and *under*
to identify colors

Key Vocabulary

• ball, bike, block, boat, car, doll, kite, marble,
 plane, toy
• in, on, under

ASSESSMENT

Warm Up

1. Have the students say the chant on page 74.

2. Remind the students that they played Body
Bingo in Unit 3 and Animal Bingo in Unit 6.
Have them look at the bingo boards on pages
30 and 60. To review the rules, ask them what
they yell as soon as they complete a row across
or up and down, after listening and covering
each picture. *(Bingo!)*

3. Have the students take turns describing the
pictures in each row, "It's an (orange ball). It's
on the chair." Continue until all the pictures
have been identified.

Using the Page

Toy Bingo

1. The students draw pictures of a red ball on a
bed, a blue ball sticking out from under
a bed, a pink block on a chair, and a yellow
plane on a table in any of the four empty
squares.

2. Have the students cut or tear 16 pieces of
paper large enough to cover a square on the
Bingo card. They may use small coins or
stones if they prefer.

3. Play the audio or read the audioscript
aloud. Have the students cover the correct
pictures with a piece of paper.
AUDIOSCRIPT: 1. The red hat is on the chair.
2. The yellow kite is under the table. 3. The
red ball is under the chair. 4. The blue ball is
under the bed. 5. The green car is in the box.
6. The purple block is in the box. 7. The
orange marbles are on the table. 8. The red
ball is on the bed. 9. The orange ball is on the
chair. 10. The blue car is under the chair.
11. The pink doll is in the box. 12. The pink

block is on the chair. 13. The green kite is
on the chair. 14. The yellow plane is on
the table. 15. The red bike is on the table.
16. The green boat is on the table.

4. Read what Hanna is saying to Homer
several times for the students to repeat. After a
student has filled a row, have him or her
describe each picture in the Bingo row. They
should describe the object and where it is, for
example, "The green boat is on the table."
Record your observations on the Student Oral
Assessment Checklist on page xxi.

5. You may want to extend the activity by
creating your own scripts or by asking
individuals to call out the descriptions.

Reaching All Students

Linked Response Give each student a Picture
Card or an object. Ask a student what she or he
has. That student answers and then asks the next
student the question. "Teresa, what do you have?"
"I have a (doll). Luis, what do you have?"

Identifying Numbers When the students
can say the names of the numbers *11–20,* write
one number on the board at a time and say,
"What number is this? Jump this many times.
Show me this many fingers."

Drawing and Grouping Distribute a
sheet of drawing paper to each student. Tell them
to draw a group of 15 toy cars on the front of the
paper, and a group of 16 blocks on the back.
Instruct them to circle a group of ten objects in
each drawing. Then have them write the number
15 on the front of their papers and the number
16 on the back. Have the students describe the
toys in their groupings.

Objectives

to identify and describe toys
to identify locations
to identify the numbers *11–20*
to synthesize information

Key Vocabulary

• ball, block, boat, car, marble
• eleven, twelve, thirteen, fourteen, fifteen, sixteen, seventeen, eighteen, nineteen, twenty
• in, on, under

ASSESSMENT

Warm Up

Display a group of toys. Have the students count the number of toys and name them.

Using the Page

Listen. Read. Circle.

1. Focus attention on the pictures. Ask the students to describe the toys and their locations, for example, "The red blocks are in the box."

2. Play the audio or read the text several times for the students to follow along in their books. Have the students circle the picture that matches the text.
   ANSWERS: 1. The red blocks are circled.
   2. The orange marbles are circled. 3. The red boat is circled.

I can.

1. Read the statement for number 1 aloud to the students. Ask individuals, groups, or the whole class to identify the toys *(car, boat)*. Have them circle the pictures for the words they can say.

2. Read the statement for number 2 aloud to the students. Ask individuals, groups, or the whole class to say where the toys are located. Have them circle the pictures for the prepositions they can say *(on, under, in)*.

3. Read the statement for number 3 aloud to the students. Ask individuals, groups, or the whole class to identify the numbers. Have them circle the numbers they can say. Note oral production in these activities on the Student Oral Assessment Checklist on page xxi.

Reaching All Students

Vocabulary Check Point to the toys in the Picture Dictionary on pages 80–81. Have the students identify each toy.

Addition/Subtraction Problems Have the students work in pairs. Supply each pair with twenty rods or any other small item. Write addition equations on the board. Have one person in each pair count the number of rods for the first number in the equation and say, "I have (seven rods)." Have the partner count the rods for the second number in the equation and say, "I have (six rods)." Have both partners count the total. *(thirteen)* Ask, "What's the answer?" Do the same for subtraction equations.

Number Dictations Say a series of numbers from 0–20 in mixed-up order and have the students write the numbers they hear on a sheet of paper.

Unit Mural Elicit all the words and expressions the students remember from this unit. Write them on mural or poster paper. Have the students illustrate the vocabulary. Use this to review vocabulary in subsequent classes.

Unit 8 Test See page xxxviii.

Workbook

Page 68, Listen. Read. Circle. Play the audio or read the text several times for the students to follow along in their books. Have the students circle the picture that matches the text.

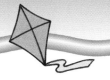

Listen. Read. Circle.

1. The blocks are in the box.

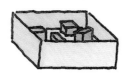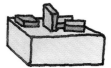

2. The marbles are under the chair.

3. The boat is on the table.

I can.

1. I can talk about toys.

2. I can say where things are.

3. I can say numbers.

Having Fun!

Communication Skills

to identify activities
to describe how people feel
to say what one wants
to use polite requests
to introduce oneself
to give personal information

Language Objectives

to distinguish between *this/that*, *these/those*
to ask and answer questions
to use the present progressive tense
to use the simple present tense of *be*
to distinguish among the prepositions *in*, *on*, and *under*
to pronounce /š/, /h/, /ŋ/, /y/

Learning Strategies and Thinking Skills

to apply prior knowledge
to follow directions
to make associations
to make connections
to use illustrations

Content Connections

Art: to make collages; to draw pictures; to make a puppet and puppet theater
Music: to sing songs
Social Studies: to survey; to act out buying and selling; to use simple coordinates

Materials

New Parade 1 Student Book, pages 82–91
New Parade 1 Workbook, pages 69–78; 105–107
New Parade 1 Audio: Tape/CD
New Parade 1 Video and Video Guide
New Parade 1 Posters
Classroom objects; toys; scissors; paper; crayons or markers; straws or craft sticks; glue; poster paper; action pictures

Optional Materials: New Parade Picture Cards—playground, kick, kite, bike, jump, eat, run; old magazines; *Little Celebrations—Dancing Dinosaurs* by Maurice Devin, *Tee-Ball* by Barry Gordon, *My Friends* by Marcia Vaughan, and *Sharing Danny's Dad* by Angela Shelf Medearis

Key Vocabulary

• ball, bike, car, jump rope, kite, puppet, skate
• name, brother, sister
• how many, how old, what's
• is, clap, have, want
• catching, dancing, doing, eating, flying a kite, jumping, jumping rope, kicking, reading, riding a bike, running, singing, skating, sleeping, swimming, throwing, watching TV, wearing
• please, thank you, Turn on the lights. You're welcome.
• I'm, he's, she's
• not
• your
• that, these, this, those
• happy, sad
• in, on, under

Picture Dictionary

jumping flying throwing riding skating swimming running kicking

Setting Up the Classroom

Make sure you go through the material before starting the unit so that you can plan each day's lesson and gather together the supplies you will need. Take out the Homer and Hanna puppets that the the students made in Unit 1. For reviews and warm ups you will need the pictures of animals and people that you used in earlier units. Read the Little Book, *Playing Is Fun!* and think about any sentences you might want the students to recite.

Using the Video and the Video Guide

Use the video at the beginning of the unit to introduce the students to the language they will learn in the unit. The students may not understand everything at first. Help them use the context to get an idea of what is happening. You should show the video again, especially at the beginning of each week. The students will understand more each time they view it and learn the words and patterns in the unit. The Video Guide will suggest places to stop and start the video. Encourage the students to interact with the video by answering the questions, singing, and doing the actions along with the children in the video.

In the park, children are playing as Julia narrates their actions, "She's jumping rope. He's riding a bike." A boy rides his bike while we hear the song "Is He Skating?" Sam and Ana talk about their feelings, "I'm happy!" "I'm sad." Ana offers Sam different things to try to make him happy. "Do you want my ball? Do you want my kite?" Later, Ana and Sam look at each other from different parts of the park and try to guess what the other is doing, "What's she doing?" "Is she sleeping? No, she's not. She's eating!" Sam asks Ana for some cookies, and she shares them. They are both happy.

Family Connections

Encourage the students to talk with their family and friends about what fun activities they like to do and then report the results back to the class.

Bulletin Board Ideas

On a slip of paper, write the title *Having Fun!* and place it at the top of the bulletin board. Then on a large sheet of paper, make a chart with three columns with the headings *At Home, At School,* and *At the Beach.* Beside each heading, draw a simple picture of an object associated with each place. For example, you might want to draw a simple house beside the words *At Home.* Then have the students draw or find pictures of people doing their favorite activities in each place. Use the bulletin board to elicit sentences such as "He's playing in the sand." and "She's swimming."

Little Book: Playing Is Fun!

Summary: Children at the playground have fun as they ride bikes, jump ropes, kick balls, play catch, and fly kites on a sunny day.

9 Having Fun!

1. Listen. Sing together.

If you're happy and you know it, clap your hands.
If you're happy and you know it, clap your hands.
If you're happy and you know it,
Then your face will surely show it.
If you're happy and you know it, clap your hands.

2. Let's show and tell.

This is my kite.

That's my jump rope.

These are my skates.

Those are my cars.

Objectives

to describe how people feel
to distinguish between *this/that* and *these/those*
to pronounce /š/ and /h/

Key Vocabulary

• car, jump rope, kite, skate
• clap
• happy, sad
• that, these, this, those

WARM UP

1. Introduce or review the word *clap* by clapping your hands for the students.

2. 🎧 Play the audio or say the following chant and demonstrate the actions. Then have the students repeat the words and do the actions with you.
Stand up *(clap, clap)*; sit down *(clap, clap)*
And show me one! *(hold up 1 finger)*
Look up *(clap, clap)*; look down *(clap, clap)*
And show me two! *(hold up 2 fingers)*
Reach up *(clap, clap)*; reach down *(clap, clap)*;
And show me three! *(hold up 3 fingers)*
Jump up *(clap, clap)*; jump down *(clap, clap)*
And show me four! *(hold up 4 fingers)*

Point up *(clap, clap)*; point down *(clap, clap)*
And show me five! *(hold up 5 fingers)*

3. Introduce the words *happy* and *sad* by using facial expressions. Have the students make happy and sad faces the way mime artists do. Hold your hands together high above your face. Make a happy face. Say, "I'm happy." Then, move your hands slowly down over your face and change your smile into a frown as your hands drop below your face. Say, "I'm sad." Bring them up again to change your sad face back into a happy face.

4. Display the Poster for Unit 9.

PRESENTATION

Using the Page

ACTIVITY 1

Listen. Sing together.

1. 🎧 📻 Play the audio or sing the song several times as you clap. Have the students sing and clap. To practice pronunciation, focus on /h/ in *happy* and /š/ in *show*.

2. Help the class decide on other feelings and actions that can be substituted in the song such as *mad/stomp your feet* and *sad/sit and cry*. Provide vocabulary as needed.

ACTIVITY 2

Let's show and tell.

1. Hold a book in your hands and say, "This is my book." Then do the same with two books and say, "These are my books." Point to a book on a student's desk and say, "That is (Sara's) book." Point to several books on a student's desk and say, "Those are (Juan's) books."

2. Focus attention on the pictures. Read each sentence for the students to repeat.

3. Have the students talk about other classroom objects to practice *this* or *that*, *these* or *those* in the proper situations.

Reaching All Students

☑ **Acting** Have the students work in pairs. Observe as one acts out feelings while the other describes them, for example, "You're happy."

Workbook

Page 69, Activity 1: Read and circle the answer.
Have the students look at the pictures, read the sentences, and circle the correct picture.
ANSWERS: 1. This is my bike. 2. These are my skates. 3. That is my jump rope. 4. This is my ball.

Language Activities Section, page 105
ANSWERS: 1. this 2. these 3. this 4. those 5. these 6. that

Objectives

to identify activities
to apply prior knowledge
to use illustrations

Key Vocabulary

- ball, kite
- catching, dancing, doing, eating, flying a kite, jumping rope, kicking, singing, skating, throwing

PRESENTATION

Warm Up

1. ⊙ Build background by focusing on the animal movements the students learned in Unit 6. Invite the students to take turns showing the class how animals move. Then have the students say the action words that describe how that animal is moving, for example, "The (frog) is (jumping)."

2. ⊀ As a follow-up, you might use the movements described to play Simon Says, for example, "Simon says, jump like a frog."

Using the Page

ACTIVITY 3

Listen. Read. Say.

1. ♫ Focus attention on the picture. Point to each child in the picture and play the audio or read what he or she is doing several times for the students to point and repeat.

2. Ask individuals to point to each of the children in the picture and say what he or she is doing.

3. ♫ Play the audio or read Homer and Hanna's conversation for the students to repeat. Have them point to Alex in the picture.

4. Say an action (*He's kicking a ball.*) and have the students point to and describe the child doing that action in the picture, "It's that boy. He's wearing a white shirt and blue pants."

5. ⊘ Have the students look at the picture. Ask, "What's (she) doing?" "(She's) (jumping rope)."

Reaching All Students

Vocabulary Expansion Focus attention on the Picture Dictionary on pages 82–83. Find out if any of the students know the names of any of the actions. Have the students point to each picture and repeat the word or phrase.

◀◼▶ **Action Collages** Have the students work in groups. Give each group an action. Have the students cut out pictures from old magazines of people doing their action and arrange the pictures in a collage. Display the collages in the room and have each group describe the people and what they are doing. Refer to the collages throughout the unit to reinforce the vocabulary.

◀◼▶ **Drawing Pictures** Have the students draw pictures of the members of their family having fun. Encourage individuals to talk about their pictures, describing the people and telling what they are doing. "This is Ben. He is running. That is Alice. She's wearing a red jacket. She's jumping rope."

Information Gap Have the students work in pairs. Student A should look at the picture for Activity 3, while Student B should have his or her book closed. Student A should secretly point to one of the people pictured and say, "It's a (boy)." Student B should guess the action by saying, "Is he (dancing)?" Student A should answer "No, he's not" until Student B guesses correctly. Have the students take turns guessing.

Workbook

♫ **Page 70, Activity 2: Listen and draw.**
Play the audio or read the audioscript several times for the students to complete the activity. Circulate around the room to check the students' work.
AUDIOSCRIPT: 1. She's riding a bike. 2. He's kicking a ball. 3. She's jumping rope. 4. He's singing a song. 5. She's skating.

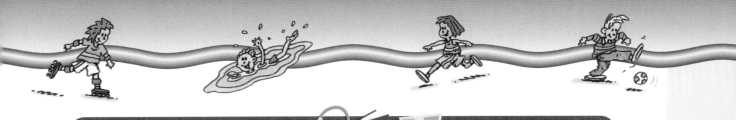

4. Listen. Sing together.

Is he skating?
Is he skating?
No, he's not.
No, he's not.
Is he riding his bike?
Is he riding his bike?
Yes, he is.
Yes, he is.

5. Listen. Circle the answer.

Yes, he is.
No, he's not.

1.

Yes, she is.
No, she's not.

2.

Yes, he is.
No, he's not.

3.

Yes, she is.
No, she's not.

Objectives

to identify activities
to use the present progressive tense
to pronounce /ŋ/ and /y/
to use the simple present tense of *be*

Key Vocabulary

- bike, ball
- jumping rope, kicking, riding a bike, running, skating, throwing
- is, not
- he's, she's

PRACTICE

Warm Up

Play the audio or read the poem for the students to repeat. Have them act out the words.

What are you doing?
I'm walking in place.
What are you doing?
I'm running a race.

What are you doing?
I'm eating a hot dog.
What are you doing?
I'm jumping like a frog.

What are you doing?
I'm going to sleep.
Shhh. Be quiet,
And don't make a peep.

Using the Page
ACTIVITY 4

Listen. Sing together.

1. Focus attention on the picture. Ask, "What is the boy doing?" *(riding his bike)*

2. Play the audio or sing the song to the students (tune of "Frère Jacques") for them to repeat. To practice pronunciation, focus on /ŋ/ in *skating* and /y/ in *Yes*.

3. Help the students decide on additional actions that can be substituted in the song.

ACTIVITY 5

Listen. Circle the answer.

1. Model the sample exercise. Focus attention on the first picture. Ask, "Is he running?" Have the students read the circled answer "Yes, he is."

2. Play the audio or read the questions. Have the students circle the answers. For the negative answers, have the students tell what the people in the pictures are doing.
AUDIOSCRIPT: 1. Is she riding a bike? 2. Is he throwing the ball? 3. Is she jumping rope?
ANSWERS: 1. No, she's not. She's skating. 2. No, he's not. He's kicking a ball. 3. Yes, she is.

Reaching All Students

Vocabulary Check Have the students review the words for the actions in the Picture Dictionary on pages 84–85.

Workbook

Pages 71 and 73, Activity 3: Read. Color. Cut. Make a book. Read aloud each page of the book with the students. Have them color the pictures, cut out the pages, and put them together in order. Next play the audio or read the audioscript several times for the students to repeat.

Black bug, black bug
What do you see?
I see a red dog looking at me.

Red dog, red dog
What do you see?
I see a blue bird singing to me.

Blue bird, blue bird
What do you see?
I see an orange horse running for me.

Orange horse, orange horse
What do you see?
I see a green frog jumping to me.

and so on.

UNIT 9 • Having Fun!

Objectives

to say what one wants
to use polite requests
to identify activities
to use the present progressive tense

Key Vocabulary

- want
- running, skating
- please, thank you, you're welcome
- that, these, this, those

PRACTICE

Warm Up

1. Put classroom objects or toys on a table and use either the Homer or Hanna puppet from Unit 1. Ask the puppet, "What do you want?" The puppet can answer, "I want a (truck)." You should hand the puppet the truck. Demonstrate this dialogue several times. When the students are familiar with the question and the response, ask individuals, "What do you want?" Have each student say what he or she wants and take an item.

2. To introduce or review polite responses, demonstrate the following dialogue using the Hanna puppet.
Teacher: What do you want?
Hanna: I want a (doll), please.
Teacher: Here's the doll.
Hanna: Thank you.
Teacher: You're welcome.

3. As often as possible, ask the students questions about what they are doing that they can answer in the negative. "Are you reading? Are you dancing?" Encourage them to answer by saying, "No, I'm not."

Using the Page

ACTIVITY 6

Ask and answer.

1. 🎧 Focus attention on the pictures. Play the audio or read the conversations several times for the students to repeat.

2. Have pairs of students take turns practicing *this, that, these, those* using the conversation as a guide.

3. 🎧 Focus attention on Homer and Hanna. Ask, "What is Hanna doing?" (*She's giving Homer a hot dog.*) Play the audio or read the

conversation several times for the students to repeat. Encourage the students to use these polite responses whenever it is suitable in the classroom.

ACTIVITY 7

Guess the action.

1. 🎧 Focus attention on the pictures. Play the audio or read the conversation aloud several times for the students to repeat. Make sure the students understand that they are going to play a guessing game.

2. Start the game by pantomiming an action the students know. Ask the class, "What am I doing?" Encourage the students to guess. Have them use the conversation as a model. Have the student who correctly guesses, lead the game and pantomime another action.

Reaching All Students

🔁 **Play Store** Put a variety of objects on two tables. Ask the students to come to one table and say what they want. If they point to an item on the table that is close, they must use *this* or *these*. If they point to an item on the other table, they must use *that* or *those*. Have them use the conversations in Activity 6 as a model. To expand this activity, you may want the students to use play money they make to "buy" the items. They can practice counting the money and making change.

Acting It Out Do an activity similar to Activity 7, but instead of acting out one action, act out several in a row. Have the students identify each action. As the students get accustomed to this activity, add to the number of actions acted out.

8. Ask a friend. Write.

1. What's your name? _____

2. How old are you? _____

3. How many brothers do you have? _____

4. How many sisters do you have? _____

9. Listen and act out.

UNIT 9 • Having Fun!

Objectives

to ask and answer questions
to introduce oneself
to give personal information
to make connections
to make associations

Key Vocabulary

• name
• brother, sister
• how many, how old, what's
• have
• I'm
• your
• Turn on the lights.

APPLICATION

Using the Page
ACTIVITY 8
Ask a friend. Write.

1. Divide the students into pairs.

2. 🎧 Play the audio or read Homer and Hanna's conversation several times for the students to repeat. Make sure they understand they are going to ask their partners the questions and write their partner's answers on the lines provided. Give the students enough time to ask and write the answers.

3. You may want to have the students ask and answer additional questions. For example, they might ask, "How many dogs do you have? How many cats do you have? How many fish do you have? How many birds do you have?"

ACTIVITY 9
Listen and act out.

1. 🎧 Focus attention on the three pictures. Play the audio or read the conversation aloud to the students.

2. 💡 Divide the class into pairs. Have the students make up dialogues based on the results of their survey in Activity 8. After the pairs have practiced their dialogues, you may want some pairs to act out their dialogues.

Reaching All Students

Writing Scripts Have the students work in groups. Ask each group to choose a fairy tale or fable and write scripts for the story they choose. Help them make puppets and act out their plays for the class.

Vocabulary Review Explain to the students what an *opposite* is by showing pictures that illustrate some opposites they know such as *black/white*. When they understand what an opposite is, divide the class into two teams. Say a word to the first members from each team. The first one to correctly give the opposite word wins a point for his or her team. The team with the most points wins. Some opposites from the words they have learned during the year are: *long/short, big/little, boy/girl, man/woman, brother/sister, mother/father, hello/good-bye,* and *stand/sit*.

Poems and Songs Review any or all of the poems and songs the students have enjoyed throughout the year.

Follow Directions Give common classroom commands such as *Turn on the lights*. As the students do the actions, have classmates ask, "What are you doing?" Provide help as needed for responses.

Workbook

Page 75, Activity 4: How many are in your family? Count. Have the students count the family members and pets in their families. Encourage them to add other items to their graphs that they are interested in counting and comparing. Then have them color the corresponding blocks in the graph. Have the students show their graphs to the class and describe the results, "I have (three) sisters."

Language Activities Section, page 106
ANSWERS: 1. reading 2. flying 3. watching 4. riding 5. kicking 6. eating

Story Summary

Children at the playground have fun as they ride bikes, jump ropes, kick balls, play catch, and fly kites on a sunny day.

Key Unit Vocabulary

ball, flying kites, jumping rope, kicking, riding bikes

Word Bank

sun, fun

BEFORE READING

WARM UP

Ask the students what they like to do on the playground to have fun. List their responses on the board. Then invite the students to act out each activity as you point to it on the board.

PUT TOGETHER THE LITTLE BOOK

Ask the students to remove pages 87–88 from their books and fold the pages in half to make the Little Book, *Playing Is Fun!*

PREVIEW THE LITTLE BOOK

1. After the students have assembled the books, invite them to look at the pictures. Ask them to tell where the story takes place. Display a picture or Picture Card of a playground.

2. Read the title aloud and point to the pictures with the students. Discuss what they see happening on each page. Ask, "What are the children doing?" Suggest that the students predict what the book is about.

SHARE NEW WORDS

Write the Word Bank words *sun* and *fun* on the board. Then say each word aloud and have the students repeat it after you. Display pictures of the sun. Ask what color the sun is and what shape it is.

DURING READING

READING THE LITTLE BOOK

The students can listen to the story as you play the audio or read it aloud. Some may wish to follow the text as the story is read. Tell the students they can ask questions and discuss the story after they hear it read aloud.

GUIDED READING

Guide the students to look at the pictures before you read. Then read the story aloud, tracking the print as you go. Encourage the students to track the print as they read along.

TEACHER TIPS

On a rereading, pause before you say the nouns in each sentence. The students can use the pictures to help them supply the word.

REREADING

Remind the students of their predictions and compare them with what actually happened in the story. Quickly review what happens in the story. You may assess their comprehension with questions such as these:

Page 1 *Where are the children?*
Page 2 *What are the children playing?*
Page 3 *What are they flying?*
Page 4 *Are the children happy or sad at the playground?*

Use the illustrations in the story and ask the students' to recall their own experiences to help them answer the comprehension questions.

Playing Is Fun!

by Mario Herrera

Many children are
at the playground.
They're riding bikes.
They're jumping rope.

Many children are playing
at the playground.
They're all having fun!

4

They're kicking balls.
They're playing catch.

They're flying kites
in the sun.

Activities for Developing Language

VISUALIZING

Ask the students to look at the illustrations and choose one child who is playing. Suggest they pretend to be that child and tell what the child is doing, including what the child sees and what objects he or she is touching.

SUMMARIZING

Reread the last page of the story. Then ask the students to tell what the story is about. *(Many children have fun playing at the playground.)*

ACT IT OUT

Display pictures or Picture Cards of flying a kite, riding a bike, jumping rope, kicking balls. Write these actions on slips of paper and put them in a box. Have four students choose one slip of paper each and, in turn, act out the action written on the slip. Encourage the rest of the class to guess the action.

MATH

Ask the students to list the ways the children in the story have fun. You may want to have them vote on their favorite way to have fun. Record the results in a bar graph and have the students tell which activity gets the most and least votes.

WRITE ABOUT IT!

Invite the students to draw a picture of what they like to do best at the playground. Then have them write or dictate a sentence about it. Invite the students to draw a picture for each new word for their own Picture Dictionary.

GRAMMAR CONNECTION: VERB *ARE*

Write on the board the sentence *Children are playing.* Then substitute *Jan and Mike* for *Children.* Repeat, using *You* and *They.* Explain that all these words are used in sentences with *are.*

WORKBOOK

Little Book Comprehension, page 107.

BULLETIN BOARD IDEAS

Using mural paper, you may wish to have the students draw and display a mural of what they like to do on the playground. Title the mural *Our Class at Play.* Children may continue to add to the mural as the unit progresses.

FAMILY CONNECTION

Invite the students to take their Little Books home and share them with their friends and family members.

Objectives

to say what one wants
to use polite requests
to use the present progressive tense
to make a puppet and puppet theater

Key Vocabulary

- puppet
- I'm
- catching, dancing, doing, eating, flying a kite, jumping, jumping rope, kicking, reading, riding a bike, running, singing, skating, sleeping, swimming, throwing, watching TV, wearing

APPLICATION

Warm Up

Have the students get out the Homer and Hanna puppets they made in Unit 1. Have them use the puppets to act out simple conversations. For example, "What do you have?" "I have a (ball)." "What do you want?" "I want that (kite), please." "Here's the (kite)." "Thank you." "You're welcome."

Using the Project Page

Make a puppet.

1. Focus attention on the pictures. Make sure the students understand that they are going to make a puppet of themselves.

2. Provide scissors, colored markers, and paper with which the students can make puppets.

3. Have the students draw themselves. Have them color the clothes to match the ones they are wearing. Have them cut out their figures. Help them glue a long straw or stick to the backs of their figures.

4. When the puppets are completed, encourage the students to introduce their puppets, tell who each puppet is, and tell what each is wearing and doing. "Hello. This is Carlos. He's wearing an orange shirt and blue pants. He is sleeping."

Make a puppet theater.

1. Supply the students with long pieces of paper on which to draw or paint.

2. Focus attention on the picture. Point out that the students have drawn a classroom. Encourage the students to draw a picture in front of which they will put on a mini-play using their puppets. Let them use their imaginations, for example, the scene could be a classroom, a home, a playground, or an imaginary place.

Reaching All Students

Let's Pretend Ask the students to pretend that they are at the playground or at a party. Have them pantomime an activity they would be doing in the pretend place. Ask the rest of the class to guess what they are doing.

Conversation Plays Look through the book and choose favorite or difficult conversations for the students to act out in a play using their puppets, for example, playing store, talking about clothes, family members, or animals. Divide the students into groups and have each group create its own dialogue. Have them practice their scripts several times and then have each group present its play to the class.

PROJECT

Make a puppet.

1.

2.

3.

Make a puppet theater.

Let's play! 🎧

Listen and find the picture.

What's in D4?

It's a girl. She's jumping rope.

UNIT 9 • Having Fun!

Objectives
to identify activities
to distinguish among the prepositions *in, on,* and *under*
to use the present progressive tense
to apply prior knowledge
to use simple coordinates

Key Vocabulary
- dancing, eating, flying a kite, jumping rope, reading, riding a bike, running, singing, sleeping, swimming, watching TV
- in, on, under

ASSESSMENT

Warm Up

☑ Review key vocabulary words by showing pictures or Picture Cards of people and animals doing different actions for the students to identify. Check to see how many words the students can say.

Using the Page
Let's play!

1. 💡 Draw a grid on the board like the one in the book but without pictures. Point to the numerals across the top of the grid and the letters down the left-hand side of the grid. Remind the students that they used a similar grid in Unit 5. Ask volunteers to point to different boxes, for example, "Point to *B2.*"

2. Focus attention on the grid in the book. Have the students practice putting their fingers on a letter and a number and then moving their fingers together. Have them identify the box, "It's (*B3*)."

3. 🎧 Focus attention on Homer and Hanna. Play the audio or read their conversation several times for the students to repeat. Have the students point to *D4.* Ask, "What's in *D4?*" Have the students answer, "It's a girl. She's jumping rope."

4. Call out coordinates and ask individuals to say what is pictured there. For the pictures of the actions, say, "Look at *A1.* What's the boy doing?" The students should look and answer, "He's sleeping." Or say, "Look at *C1.* Where's the doll?" (*It's in the box.*)

5. You may want to divide the class into two teams. Take turns calling out coordinates and having alternating team members identify the pictures. Teams get one point for each correct identification. The team with the most points wins.

6. ☑ As the students give their answers, check for objectives: (1) the identification of actions and (2) the correct use of the prepositions *in, on,* and *under.* Record your observations on the Student Oral Assessment Checklist on page xxi.

Reaching All Students

☑ **Vocabulary Check** Point to the actions in the Picture Dictionary on pages 90–91. Have the students identify what each person is doing.

☑ **Scrambled Words** Write the key vocabulary words with their letters in mixed up order on the board. (You may want to include vocabulary from other units.) Have the students work individually, in pairs, or in groups to unscramble the words. You may want to make the activity into a race and see who first unscrambles the words correctly. Another option is to divide the class into two teams and have members on each team try to unscramble the words. The first person to successfully unscramble a word scores a point for his or her team. The team with the most points wins.

☑ **Looking Back** During the last few weeks of school, the students may enjoy looking back through their books and talking about previously used pages to find out how much more they can say now about each picture. You may want to do some of the favorite activities from the previous units.

Objectives

to identify activities
to describe how people feel
to use the present progressive tense

Key Vocabulary

- dancing, flying a kite, jumping, jumping rope, reading, riding a bike, running, skating, throwing
- is, not
- he's, she's

ASSESSMENT

Using the Page

Listen. Circle the answer.

1. 🎧 Have students look at the pictures and listen as you play the audio or read the questions. The students circle the correct answers.
   AUDIOSCRIPT: 1. Is she jumping? 2. Is he riding his bike? 3. Is she throwing a ball? 4. Is he flying a kite?
   ANSWERS: 1. Yes, she is. 2. Yes, he is. 3. No, she's not. She's reading. 4. No, he's not. He's skating.

2. Have the students identify the action in each picture. Use the Student Oral Assessment Checklist on page xxi to record each student's oral presentation.

I can.

1. Read the statement for number 1 aloud to the students. Ask individuals, groups, or the whole class to identify the actions (*kicking a ball, jumping rope, running*). Have them circle the pictures for the words they can say.

2. Read the statement for number 2 aloud to the students. Ask, "Is the face happy?" (*Yes.*) Encourage the students to talk using the words they have learned during the school year. Note oral production in these activities on the Student Oral Assessment Checklist on page xxi.

Reaching All Students

Unit Mural Elicit all the words and expressions the students remember from this unit. Write them on mural or poster paper. Have the students illustrate the vocabulary. Use this to review vocabulary in subsequent classes.

Unit 9 Test See page xxxix.

Workbook

🎧 📝 **Page 76, Listen. Circle the answer.** Play the audio or read the questions several times. Have the students circle the correct answers.
AUDIOSCRIPT: 1. Is she drinking milk? 2. Is he dancing? 3. Is he running? 4. Is she jumping rope? 5. Is she riding a bike? 6. Is she dancing? 7. Is he throwing a ball?
ANSWERS: 1. No, she's not. 2. No, he's not. 3. Yes, he is. 4. No, she's not. 5. Yes, she is. 6. No, she's not. 7. Yes, he is.

The following Workbook pages are a practice test for Units 7–9. Check the answers. You may want to review areas with which they had difficulty before they take the test on pages xliv-xlv.

🎧 📝 **Page 77, Listen and circle.** Play the audio or read the script several times for the students to complete the activity.
AUDIOSCRIPT: 1. Circle the cake. 2. Circle the milk. 3. Circle the kite. 4. Circle the doll on the chair. 5. Circle the boat. 6. Circle the number thirteen. 7. Circle the hot dog.

📝 **Page 78, Read and match.** Have the students draw lines from each word to the correct corresponding picture.
ANSWERS: 1. girl drinking 2. boy singing 3. girl jumping rope 4. boy skating 5. girl riding a bike 6. boy kicking a ball 7. girl running

📝 **Page 78, Say what each boy and girl is doing.** Have the students look at the pictures in the activity above and tell what the boys and girls are doing, for example, "The girl is running."

✓ Listen. Circle the answer. 🎧

1.   Yes, she is.
                                     No, she's not.

2.   Yes, he is.
                                     No, he's not.

3.   Yes, she is.
                                     No, she's not.

4.   Yes, he is.
                                     No, he's not.

✓ I can.

1. I can say actions.

2. I can speak English.

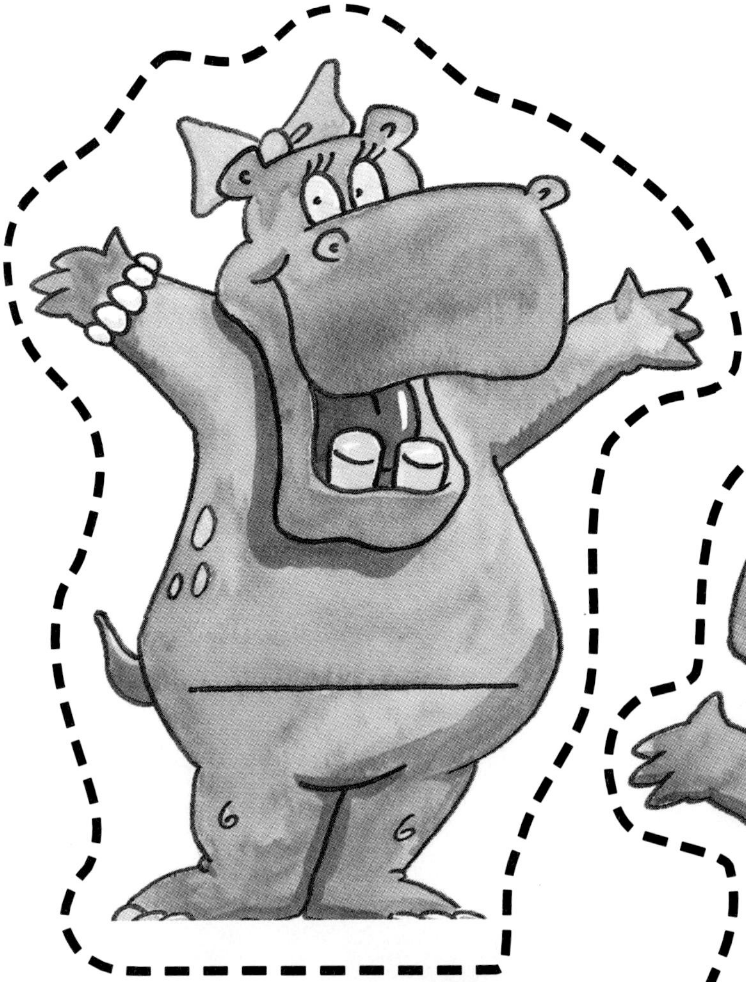

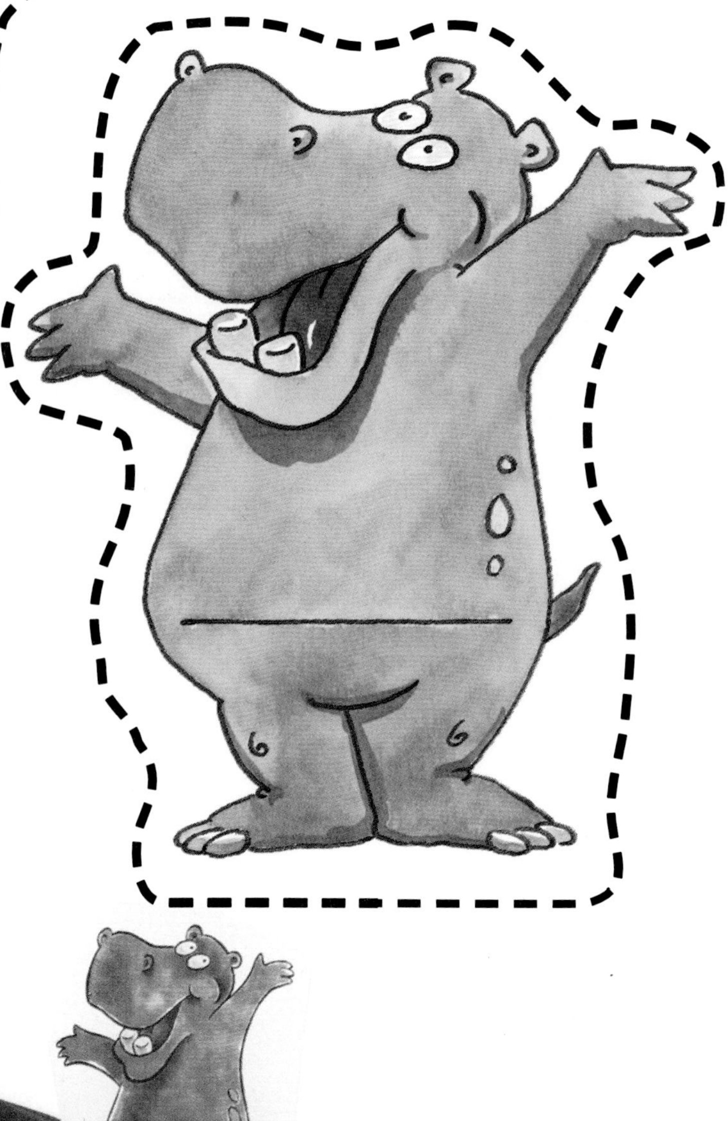

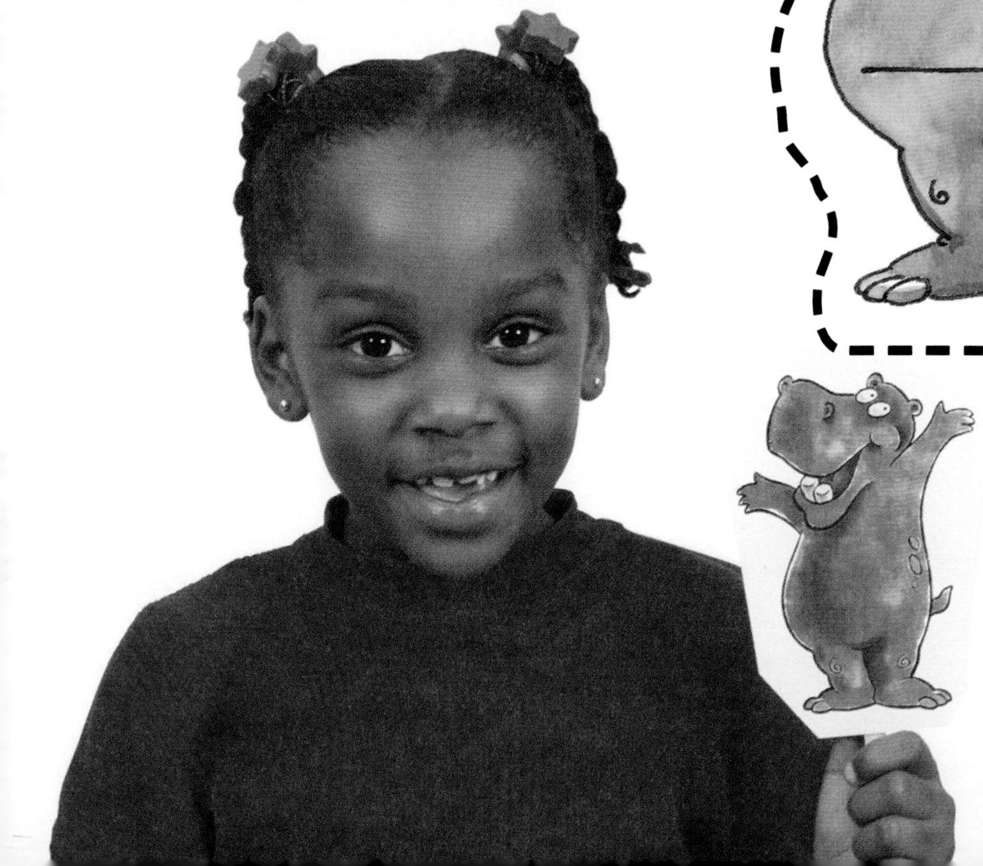

2

ALPHABET

A a   B b

C c   D d   E e

F f   G g   H h

2

Ii

Jj

Kk

Ll

Mm

Nn

Oo

Pp

Qq

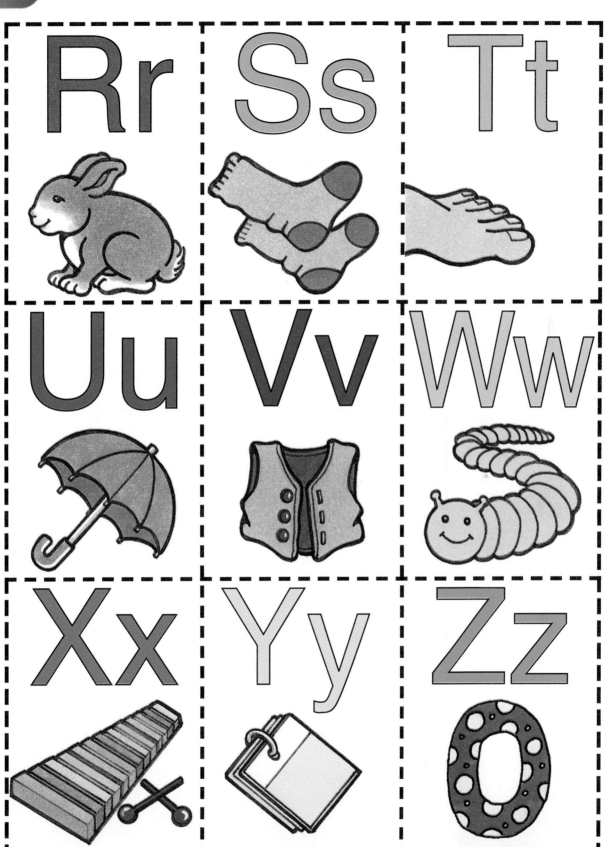

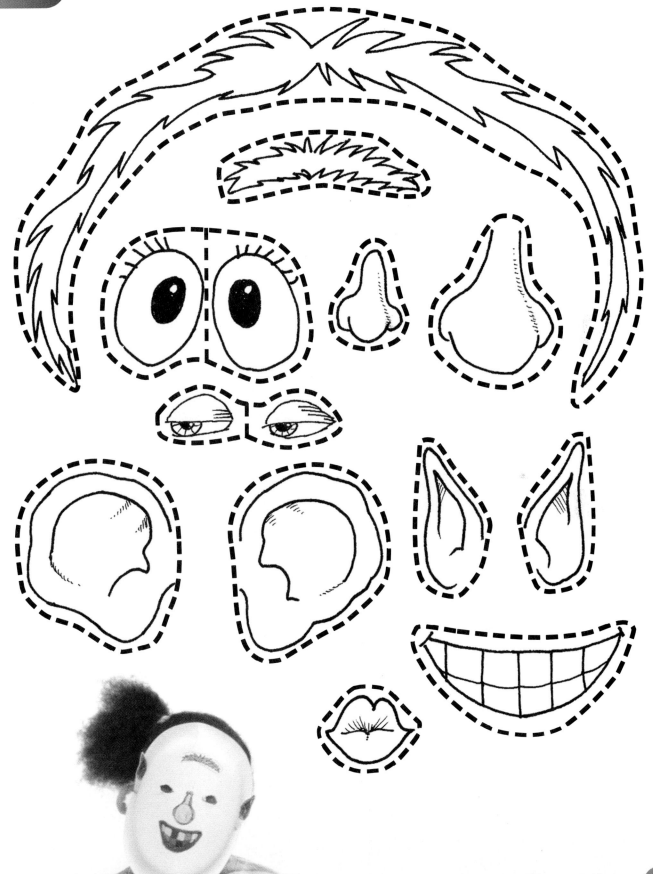

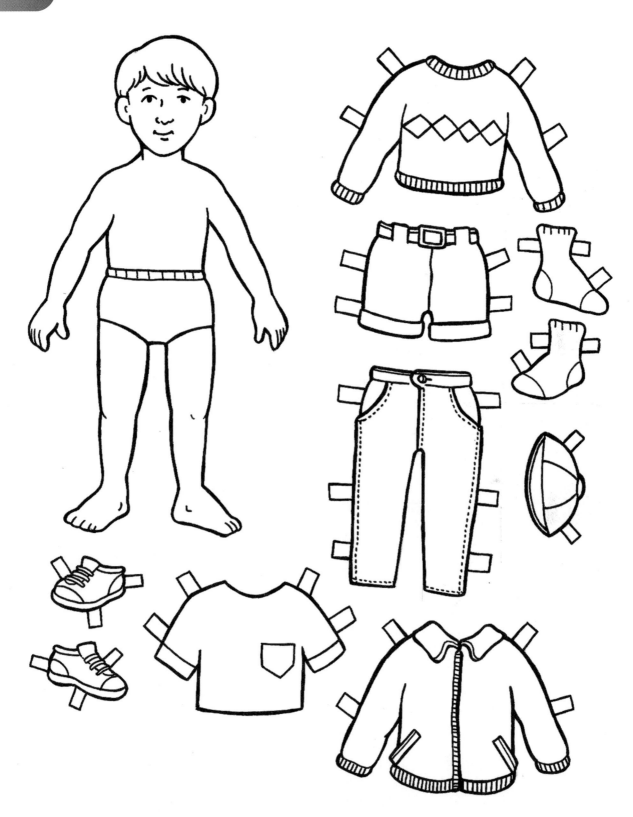

The International Phonetic Alphabet

IPA Symbols

Consonants

/b/	**b**a**b**y, clu**b**
/d/	**d**own, to**d**ay, sa**d**
/f/	**f**un, pre**f**er, lau**gh**
/g/	**g**ood, be**g**in, do**g**
/h/	**h**ome, be**h**ind
/k/	**k**ey, cho**c**olate, bla**ck**
/l/	**l**ate, po**l**ice, mai**l**
/m/	**m**ay, wo**m**an, swi**m**
/n/	**n**o, opi**n**ion
/ŋ/	a**ng**ry, lo**ng**
/p/	**p**a**p**er, ma**p**
/r/	**r**ain, pa**r**ent, doo**r**
/s/	**s**alt, medi**c**ine, bu**s**
/š/	**s**ugar, spe**ci**al, fi**sh**
/t/	**t**ea, ma**t**erial, da**t**e
/θ/	**th**ing, heal**th**y, ba**th**
/ð/	**th**is, mo**th**er, ba**th**e
/v/	**v**ery, tra**v**el, o**f**
/w/	**w**ay, any**o**ne
/y/	**y**es, on**i**on
/z/	**z**oo, cou**s**in, alway**s**
/ž/	mea**s**ure, gara**g**e
/č/	**ch**eck, pic**t**ure, wa**tch**
/ǰ/	**j**ob, refri**g**erator, oran**g**e

Vowels

/ɑ/	**o**n, h**o**t, f**a**ther
/æ/	**a**nd, c**a**sh
/ɛ/	**e**gg, s**ay**s, l**ea**ther
/ɪ/	**i**n, b**i**g
/ɔ/	**o**ff, d**augh**ter, dr**aw**
/e/	**A**pril, tr**ai**n, s**ay**
/i/	**e**ven, sp**ea**k, tr**ee**
/o/	**o**pen, cl**o**se, sh**o**w
/u/	b**oo**t, d**o**, thr**ough**
/ʌ/	**o**f, y**ou**ng, s**u**n
/ʊ/	p**u**t, c**oo**k, w**ou**ld
/ə/	**a**bout, penc**i**l, lem**o**n
/ɚ/	moth**er**, Sat**ur**day, doct**or**
/ɝ/	**ear**th, b**ur**n, h**er**

Diphthongs

/ɑɪ/	**i**ce, st**y**le, l**ie**
/ɑu/	**ou**t, d**ow**n, h**ow**
/ɔɪ/	**oi**l, n**oi**se, b**oy**

The English Alphabet

Here is the pronunciation of the letters of the English alphabet, written in International Phonetic Alphabet Symbols.

a	/e/
b	/bi/
c	/si/
d	/di/
e	/i/
f	/ɛf/
g	/ǰi/
h	/eč/
i	/ɑɪ/
j	/ǰe/
k	/ke/
l	/ɛl/
m	/ɛm/
n	/ɛn/
o	/o/
p	/pi/
q	/kyu/
r	/ɑr/
s	/ɛs/
t	/ti/
u	/yu/
v	/vi/
w	/ˈdʌbəlˌyu/
x	/ɛks/
y	/wɑɪ/
z	/zi/

Vocabulary

Numbers indicate units in *New Parade* Book 1.

a 1
am 1
are 3, 4, 5, 7
arm 3

baby 2
ball 8, 9
balloon 7
bathroom 5
bathtub 5
bed 5
bedroom 5
big 3, 6
bike 8, 9
bird 6
birthday 7
black 4
block 8
blue 1
boat 8
body 3
book 1
book bag 1
bookcase 5
boy 2
brother 2, 9
brown 3
bug 6

cake 7
candle 7
car 8, 9
cat 6
catching 9
chair 1, 5
children 7
circle 1, 5
clap 9
closet 5

clothes 4
clown 3
color 1, 3
Come here. 2
cooking 5
cow 6
crawling 6

dancing 9
day 7
desk 1
dining room 5
do 2, 5
dog 6
doing 5, 6, 9
doll 8
dress 4
duck 6

ear 3
eating 5, 6, 7, 9
eight 1
eighteen 8
eleven 8
eye 3

face 3
family 2
father 2
fifteen 8
finger 3
fish 6, 7
five 1
flying 6
flying a kite 9
Fold the (shirt). 4
foot (feet) 3
four 1
fourteen 8

Friday 7
frog 6

Get the book. 1
girl 2
Go to (your desk). 2
good morning 1
good-bye 1, 2
green 1

hair 3
hamburger 7
hand 3
Hang up the (dress). 4
happy 7, 9
hat 4, 7
have 2, 3, 7, 9
he 4
he's 2, 5, 9
head 3
hello 1, 2
her 3
hippopotamus 6
his 3
horse 6
hot dog 7
house 5
how many 2, 3, 5, 9
how old 7, 9

I'm 1, 2, 8, 9
ice cream 7
in 5, 8, 9
is 1, 2, 4, 5, 6, 7, 9
it 1, 4
it's 1, 6, 8

jacket 4
jump 2

jump rope 9
jumping 6, 9
jumping rope 9

kicking 9
kitchen 5
kite 7, 8, 9
knee 3

lamp 5
leg 3
little 3, 6
living room 5
long 3

man 2
marble 8
marker 1
milk 7
Monday 7
monster 3
mother 2
mouth 3
move 3
moving 8
my 2

name 1, 9
nine 1
nineteen 8
no 1
nose 3
not 9

on 8, 9
one 1
Open/Close your book. 1
opening 7
orange 3

pants 4
party 7
pencil 1
pick up 3
pink 4
pizza 7
plane 8
playing 5
please 7, 8, 9
Point to (the chair). 2
present 7
puppet 9
purple 3
Put on your (hat). 4
Put the (shirt) away. 4
put 5
put down 3

Raise your hand. 1
reading 5, 9
rectangle 5
red 1
riding a bike 9
running 6, 9

sad 9
Saturday 7
say 6
saying "Good-bye" 7
saying "Hello" 7
see 2, 5, 6
seven 1
seventeen 8
she 4
she's 2, 5, 9
shirt 4
shoe 4
short 3
shoulder 3

Show me (the book). 2
singing 7, 9
sister 2, 9
Sit. 2
Sit down. 1
six 1
sixteen 8
skate 8, 9
skating 9
skirt 4
sleeping 5, 6, 9
sock 4
sofa 5
square 5
Stand up. 1
stove 5
Sunday 7
sweater 4
swimming 6, 9

table 1, 5
Take off your (shoes). 4
teacher 1
ten 1
thank you 8, 9
that 9
the 1
these 4, 9
they 3
they're 3, 5, 6
thirteen 8
this 1, 2, 4, 9
those 9
three 1
throwing 9
thumb 3
Thursday 7
toe 3
touch 3

toy 8
toy box 8
triangle 5
Tuesday 7
Turn on the lights. 9
TV 5
twelve 8
twenty 8
two 1

under 8, 9

walk 2
want 7, 8, 9
watching TV 5, 9
wearing 4, 9
Wednesday 7
week 7
what 1, 4, 5, 6, 8
what color 1, 3, 4, 8
what's 1, 4, 5, 8, 9
where 5, 8
where's 8
white 4
who 5
who's this 2
woman 2
worm 6

yellow 3
yes 1
you 2, 7
you're welcome 9
your 1, 9

zero 2

Index

Numbers indicate units in *New Parade* Book 1.

Scope and Sequence for Starter

Unit	Title	Theme	Communication Objectives
1	My Class	school	to introduce oneself and exchange greetings; to identify classroom objects; to identify the colors *red* and *yellow;* to identify circles and numbers *1–3*
2	My Home	family members and rooms in a house	to greet and take leave; to identify family members and rooms in a house; to identify the colors *blue* and *green;* to identify squares, circles, and the numbers *1–4*
3	My Body	parts of the body	to identify parts of the body; to identify feelings and the sizes *big* and *little;* to identify the colors *black* and *brown;* to identify triangles and the numbers *1–5*
4	My Clothes	clothing	to identify clothing items; to describe the weather; to use polite expressions; to identify the colors *orange* and *purple;* to identify rectangles
5	My Toys	toys	to identify toys; to make polite requests; to use polite expressions; to identify the colors *pink* and *white;* to identify shapes and the numbers *1–7*
6	Helpers	community helpers and their vehicles	to identify community helpers and vehicles; to use polite expressions; to identify the numbers *1–9*
7	The Playground	playground equipment and activities	to identify playground equipment; to identify actions; to say what one is doing; to identify the numbers *1–10*
8	Animals	pets and zoo animals	to identify pets and zoo animals; to identify animal actions and sounds; to make polite requests
9	Party Food	parties and food	to identify food and party items; to express likes and dislikes; to make polite requests; to identify colors, shapes, and the numbers *1–10*

Scope and Sequence for Starter

Language Objectives	Learning Strategies/ Thinking Skills	Content Connections
to understand commands; to understand questions with *is*	to classify; to follow directions; to listen to language models; to manipulate objects; to use visual cues; to use charts and songs, mime and gestures	Art; Literature/Language Arts; Math; Music
to understand commands; to understand questions with *is*; to use *this is* in sentences; to understand plural nouns and the prepositions *in* and *on*	to classify; to follow directions; to listen to language models; to use mime and gesture; to use visual cues	Art; Literature/Language Arts; Math; Music
to understand commands; to answer questions with *What* and *How many*; to use adjectives; to understand the prepositions *is, on,* and *under*	to classify; to follow directions; to listen to language models; to manipulate objects; to use mime and gesture; to use visual cues	Art; Literature/Language Arts; Math; Music
to understand commands; to understand questions with *is* and *are*; to use plural nouns; to use *this is* and *these are* in sentences	to classify; to follow directions; to listen to language models; to make asociations; to manipulate objects; to use visual cues	Art; Literature/Language Arts; Math; Music
to understand commands; to use plural nouns; to use *this is* and *these are* in sentences; to use negation with *be*	to classify; to follow directions; to listen to language models; to manipulate objects; to use prior knowledge; to use visual cues	Art; Literature/Language Arts; Math; Social Studies
to understand commands; to understand questions with *What, Who,* and *How many*; to understand the prepositions *in, off, on,* and *out of*	to classify; to follow directions; to listen to language models; to make associations; to manipulate objects; to use visual cues; to place new words in context	Art; Literature/Language Arts; Math; Music; Social Studies
to understand commands; to understand questions with *What* and *How many*; to use the present progressive tense; to understand the prepositions *into, out of, up,* and *down*	to follow directions; to listen to language models; to manipulate objects; to use mime and gesture; to use prior knowledge; to use visual cues	Art; Literature/Language Arts; Math; Music
to understand commands; to answer questions with *What* and *Which*; to use adjectives; to use the present progressive tense; to understand the prepositions *behind* and *in front of*	to classify; to follow directions; to listen to language models; to use mime and gesture; to use prior knowledge; to use visual cues	Art; Literature/Language Arts; Math; Music
to understand commands; to answer questions with *What*; to use the present progressive tense; to understand the preposition *beside*	to classify; to follow directions; to listen to language models; to manipulate objects; to sequence; to use mime and gesture; to use prior knowledge; to use visual cues	Art; Literature/Language Arts; Math; Music; Social Studies

Scope and Sequence 1

Unit	Title	Theme	Communication Objectives
1	My Class	school	to introduce oneself and exchange greetings; to identify colors, numbers, and classroom objects
2	My Family	family members	to talk about one's family; to say the letters of the alphabet
3	My Body	parts of the body	to identify and describe parts of the body; to identify colors; to differentiate between *big* and *little, long* and *short*
4	My Clothes	clothing	to say what one is wearing; to name one's favorite colors and clothing; to identify colors; to follow directions
5	My House	rooms and furniture	to identify rooms and furniture; to identify actions, shapes, and locations; to identify family members
6	Animals	animals	to identify and describe animals; to identify animal actions
7	My Birthday	parties	to say one's age; to name the days of the week; to talk about parties and food; to talk about what one has and wants
8	My Toys	toys	to identify and describe toys; to talk about things one wants; to identify numbers and colors
9	Having Fun	outdoor activities	to identify activities; to say what one is doing and what one wants; to describe how people feel

Language Objectives	Learning Strategies/ Thinking Skills	Content Connections
to use the simple present tense of *be*; to answer *yes/no* questions; to answer questions with *what* and *what color*	to classify; to understand sequence; to make associations	Art; Math; Music
to use the simple present tense of *be*, *see*, and *have*; to use *he* and *she*; to use plural nouns; to answer questions: *Who's this?* and *How many?*	to classify; to make associations; to sequence	Art; Literature/Language Arts; Math; Music; Social Studies
to use plural nouns; to use *his* and *her*; to use predicate adjectives;	to relate part to whole; to compare and contrast; to classify	Art; Music; Science; Social Studies
to use prenominal adjectives; to use the present progressive tense; to use plural nouns; to understand *this/that*	to classify; to sequence	Art; Math; Music; Social Studies
to use the preposition *in*; to use prenominal adjectives; to use the simple present and the present progressive tenses; to answer questions with *what, where,* and *how many*	to classify; to use prior knowledge; to relate part to whole; to compare and contrast	Art; Literature; Math; Social Studies
to use the simple present and the present progressive tenses; to use prenominal adjectives; to use plural nouns	to classify; to sequence; to make associations; to use prior knowledge; to make comparisons *(big/little)*	Art; Literature; Music; Science; Social Studies
to use the simple present and the present progressive tenses; to answer *how old* questions	to sequence; to make associations	Art; Literature; Math; Music; Social Studies
to use the prepositions *in, on,* and *under*; to use prenominal adjectives; to use the simple present tense of *want*	to use prior knowledge; to understand sequence; to synthesize information; to use illustrations	Literature/Language Arts; Math; Social Studies
to use the present progressive tense; to use *this/that, these/those*; to use prenominal adjectives; to use the prepositions *in, on,* and *under*	to use prior knowledge; to make associations; to follow directions; to make connections; to use illustrations	Art; Music; Social Studies

Scope and Sequence 2

Unit	Title	Theme	Communication Objectives
1	This Is My Class	school	to introduce oneself and exchange greetings; to count; to talk about classroom activities
2	On the Playground	outdoor activities	to count by tens; to identify playground objects and actions; to identify location
3	This Is Our House	home and family	to talk about one's family and home; to describe locations; to identify rooms and objects in a house
4	My Community	buildings and places	to name buildings in a community; to describe locations; to answer and make up riddles
5	Workers	workers and vehicles	to associate community workers, vehicles, and places; to name the days of the week; to describe locations; to generate questions
6	My Day	daily routines	to describe daily routines; to tell time and time of day; to name actions; to identify articles of clothing
7	Food	food and drink	to name foods and drinks; to express likes and dislikes; to offer and order food; to use polite expressions
8	At the Zoo	animals and actions	to identify and describe animals; to tell what actions animals can and cannot do; to answer questions with affirmative and negative statements; to name parts of animal bodies
9	Celebrations	months and parties	to name the months; to tell how one celebrates; to discuss the frequency of actions; to plan a celebration

Language Objectives	Learning Strategies/ Thinking Skills	Content Connections
to use the simple present and the present progressive tenses; to use *my* and *your*	to use prior knowledge; to classify; to compare and contrast; to identify details; to solve problems; to sequence; to use illustrations	Art; Literature/Language Arts; Math; Music; Science
to use the present progressive tense; to use *there is* and *there are;* to use prepositions of place	to alphabetize; to compare and contrast; to cooperate with peers; to make connections to real life; to note details in illustrations; to preview and predict; to reread and revise writing; to use rhyme; to use text features; to visualize; to write and follow directions	Art; Language Arts; Math; Music; Physical Education; Science; Social Studies
to use *there is/isn't* and *there are/aren't;* to use *our;* to use prepositions of place	to classify; to compare and contrast; to identify details; to make connections to real life; to generalize; to self-assess; to sequence; to use prior knowledge; to visualize	Art; Literature/Language Arts; Math; Music; Social Studies
to use prepositions of place; to use the simple present tense of *be*	to compare and contrast; to draw conclusions; to make connections to real life; to reason deductively; to use music and rhyme; to visualize	Art; Literature/Language Arts; Math; Music; Social Studies
to answer questions with *what, when, where,* and *who;* to understand *does* in questions; to use the simple present tense; to use prepositions of place; to use *to be*	to classify; to compare and contrast; to compose a story plot; to cooperate with peers; to draw conclusions; to make connections to prior learning; to make connections to real life; to reread for details and self-assessment; to set a purpose for reading	Art; Drama; Literature/Language Arts; Math; Music; Social Studies
to use the simple present tense	to use prior knowledge; to classify; to compare and contrast; to cooperate with peers; to draw conclusions; to identify with characters; to note details; to sequence	Art; Literature/Language Arts; Math; Music; Science; Social Studies
to use *a, an,* and *some;* to use the simple present tense in questions and replies	to compare and contrast; to classify; to use prior knowledge; to cooperate with peers; to reason deductively; to recall by visualizing; to skim and scan	Art; Health; Literature/Language Arts; Math; Music; Science; Social Studies
to use *can/can't, does/doesn't;* to use the possessive adjectives *its* and *their;* to use *has/have*	to classify; to compare and contrast; to identify details; to identify realism and fantasy; to use prior knowledge; to draw conclusions; to predict by using key words; to visualize	Art; Health; Literature/Language Arts; Music; Science; Social Studies
to use the frequency adverbs *always* and *never;* to use the simple present tense	to compare and contrast; to cooperate with peers; to graph information; to memorize for future reference; to predict; to reason deductively; to reflect and self-assess; to sequence; to use prior knowledge; to use illustrations	Literature/Language Arts; Math; Physical Education; Science; Social Studies

Unit	Title	Theme	Communication Objectives
1	My Activities	daily activities	to identify the sequence of activities; to tell about daily activities; to tell time; to tell when one does activities; to use classroom language
2	Family Activities	family	to identify occupations; to describe family member's occupations; to name people with whom one does activities; to tell frequency; to suggest or invite
3	City and Country	places to live	to identify things and activities in the country and the city; to identify farm animals and city pets; to express preferences; to tell where one lives and what one has to do
4	Animal Homes	animals and habitats	to tell where animals live; to identify geographical features; to tell what animals can and can't do; to describe animals and habitats; to tell about one's abilities; to make up riddles and answer them
5	The Weather	weather and clothes	to identify seasons; to associate clothing and activities with weather conditions and seasons; to tell about today's weather; to tell about yesterday's weather; to describe habitats and climates
6	The Five Senses	the senses	to identify parts of the body; to identify the five senses; to tell how things look, feel, sound, smell, and taste; to talk about today and yesterday; to name the verbs of the senses
7	The Foods I Eat	meals and food	to express likes and dislikes; to tell what one eats at specific meals; to make, accept, and reject polite offers; to identify quantities and kinds of foods
8	Health Habits	healthful habits	to describe healthful habits; to tell what one ate and drank; to tell frequency of habits; to tell time; to write a letter
9	TV and Movies	entertainment	to describe a TV show or movie; to identify types of TV shows; to express and explain likes and dislikes; to tell a story; to tell what one watched on TV; to read and talk about a TV schedule; to read and write a movie review

Language Objectives	Learning Strategies/ Thinking Skills	Content Connections
to use the simple present tense; to use *before* and *after;* to ask and answer questions with *what, what time,* and *how many*	to compare and contrast; to listen for detail; to use prior knowledge; to sequence; to use charts; to organize information	Art; Literature/Language Arts; Math; Music
to use the simple present tense; to use frequency adverbs; to ask and answer questions with *he/she;* to answer *Who . . . with?* questions	to make associations; to become aware of how one learns; to classify; to listen for detail; to use charts; to use prior knowledge; to use selective attention during listening	Art; Literature/Language Arts; Social Studies
to use the simple present tense; to use adverbs of frequency; to use *there is/there are* and *have to/has to;* to use possessive nouns	to compare and contrast; to listen for detail; to summarize; to use charts; to use prior knowledge	Art; Music; Science
to use the simple present tense; to use *can* and *can't;* to use negative and affirmative short answers	to use prior knowledge; to use visual cues; to use charts; to classify; to compare and contrast; to use a Venn diagram; to use selective attention during listening	Art; Language Arts; Music; Science
to use the simple present tense; to use the simple past of *be;* to use the present progressive tense	to make associations; to use charts; to classify; to compare and contrast; to use prior knowledge; to use selective attention during listening; to listen for detail	Art; Literature; Music; Science; Social Studies
to use the simple present tense; to use the present progressive tense; to use the simple past tense of *be* and *go;* to use linking verbs with predicate adjectives	to associate; to classify; to listen for detail; to predict; to use prior knowledge	Art; Literature; Science
to use *would you like;* to use *some* and *any;* to use frequency words	to compare and contrast; to classify; to preview; to use prior knowledge; to use selective attention during listening; to listen for detail	Art; Literature/Language Arts; Music; Social Studies
to use affirmative and negative imperatives; to use the past tense forms *ate* and *drank;* to use *did* in *yes/no* questions; to use *did/didn't* in short answers	to brainstorm; to classify; to compare and contrast; to preview; to listen for detail; to draw conclusions	Art; Health; Literature/Language Arts; Math; Music
to use the simple past tense; to ask and answer *yes/no* questions; to use the simple present tense	to use prior knowledge; to compare and contrast; to classify; to make a chart to represent information; to use selective attention while listening	Art; Literature/Language Arts; Music

Scope and Sequence 4

Unit	Title	Theme	Communication Objectives
1	All About Us	oneself and one's family	to describe oneself and others; to describe emotions and feelings; to make comparisons; to name parts of the body
2	Last Weekend	daily and weekend activities	to talk about what one did in the past; to talk about common weekend and daily activities; to tell time
3	Let's Eat!	food	to order food from a menu; to express wants and preferences; to read and write recipes; to understand U.S. money
4	Your Health	health and safety	to talk about illnesses, accidents, and safety; to give advice; to talk about what one should and shouldn't do to stay healthy; to discuss consequences of actions
5	Dinosaurs	extinct and endangered animals	to describe and compare dinosaurs and endangered animals; to describe events in the past; to discuss reasons for events; to talk about habitats and characteristics of animals
6	Then and Now	life in the past	to discuss events and life in the past; to discuss inventions and how they changed our lives; to identify and explain anachronisms; to compare the past and the present
7	Days and Dates	holidays and future plans	to discuss future plans; to read about and discuss holidays; to name days and months and use a calendar
8	It's Fun!	hobbies and sports	to talk about hobbies and sports; to express opinions; to describe activities using adjectives of attitude; to tell what happened in the past; to listen to and understand sports news
9	Show Time!	puppet shows	to discuss and write stage directions and dialogue; to put on a puppet show; to use vocabulary related to plays

Language Objectives	Learning Strategies/ Thinking Skills	Content Connections
to use adjectives to describe people and emotions; to use clauses with *when* and *than;* to use comparatives ending in *-er*	to compare measurements; to use music and rhyme; to sequence; to solve problems	Art; Literature/Language Arts; Math; Music
to use the past tense of irregular verbs; to use *before* and *after;* to form the past tense from base verbs; to use the simple present tense	to order events in sequence; to use music and rhyme; to tell about events from different viewpoints; to solve riddles	Art; Literature/Language Arts
to use *any* and *some;* to use *would like;* to use count and noncount nouns to use *let's* in suggestions	to classify; to use song and rhyme	Literature/Language Arts; Math
to use *should* and *shouldn't;* to use reflexive pronouns; to use regular past verbs	to use rhyme and chant; to make generalizations	Art; Health; Literature/Language Arts
to use the past tense of regular verbs; to use comparatives ending in *-er;* to use *why* and *because;* to use the adjective *ago*	to compare and contrast; to categorize; to recognize cause and effect; to make inferences; to use music and rhyme; to use context to aid memory	Art; Literature/Language Arts; Math; Science; Social Studies
to use the past tense of regular and irregular verbs; to use the past tense in the negative; to ask and answer *wh-* and *yes/no* questions in the past	to compare and contrast different historical periods; to put events in chronological order; to use rhyme; to place new words in context to aid memory	Literature/Language Arts; Science; Social Studies
to use *going* to indicate the future; to use ordinal numbers; to use *wh-* questions in the future tense	to sequence; to use rhyme; to place new words in context to aid memory; to make inferences; to make predictions	Literature/Language Arts; Math; Social Studies
to use superlative adjectives; to use adjectives of attitude such as *boring;* to use *like to;* to use the past tense	to use rhyme; to place new words into context to aid memory; to express opinions; to rank; to make comparisons; to draw conclusions; to solve logic problems	Literature/Language Arts; Math and Logic
to use the past tense; to make and respond to offers with *would like* and *let's*	to summarize; to order events in a story; to synthesize information by outlining; to order tasks; to identify author's purpose; to identify characters, action, and plot; to make inferences	Art; Literature/Language Arts

Unit	Title	Theme	Communication Objectives
1	My Family's Story	family events	to describe one's family; to discuss important family events; to understand a family tree; to discuss names for family relationships; to talk about physical characteristics and occupations
2	My Time	daily schedules	to talk about chores and schedules; to give reasons; to state likes and dislikes; to write a schedule
3	In the U.S.A.	geography	to learn about places in the U. S.; to talk about places and transportation; to use compass directions; to discuss travel plans; to locate places on a map
4	Shopping	shopping for clothes	to talk about and describe clothing; to ask for and give directions; to discuss clothing and prices; to discuss preferences; to understand print ads
5	What a Trip!	vacations	to talk about vacations; to say what one did and what one was doing; to talk and write about the weather; to tell narrative stories
6	Communication	ways of communicating	to learn ways to communicate; to learn names of different languages; to learn the parts of a magazine/newspaper; to conduct an interview; to produce a newspaper or a magazine
7	Just Imagine!	inventions	to talk about inventions; to speculate about what things might be; to describe what things are made of; to use creative thinking; to read about inventors and inventions
8	A Small World	discoveries and inventions around the world	to discuss contributions from different people and countries; to talk about where and why products were made; to read informational articles; to learn names of countries and related adjectives
9	It's TV Time	TV show	to discuss personal preferences about TV shows; to take part in an interview; to prepare and put on TV shows; to use words related to TV

Scope and Sequence 5

Language Objectives	Learning Strategies/ Thinking Skills	Content Connections
to use comparative and superlative adjectives; to use adjectives that describe people; to use possessive nouns; to understand past tense verb forms	to figure out riddles; to use graphic organizers; to visualize; to draw conclusions	Art; Literature/Language Arts; Math
to use the simple present tense; to use *going to* to indicate the future; to read large numbers; to use *spend* + gerund	to use graphic organizers; to classify; to evaluate; to create and figure out riddles	Literature/Language Arts; Math; Music
to use comparatives and superlatives with *most* and *-est;* to use *going to* to indicate the future; to use possessive pronouns	to make up and answer riddles; to evaluate and compare; to make lists of superlatives for study; to use prior knowledge; to use the library	Art; Math; Music; Social Studies
to use comparatives and superlatives with *more* and *most*	to use music and rhythm; to read maps; to compare items; to analyze the language of advertising; to make vocabulary flashcards; to draw conclusions	Art; Consumer Awareness; Math; Social Studies
to use the past and the past progressive tenses; to use comparatives with *worse* and *worst;* to use superlatives	to use a calendar; to make charts; to keep a diary; to analyze data; to use prior knowledge	Art; Literature/Language Arts; Music; Science
to use the future tense with *will/won't;* to write and ask *wh-* questions	to classify; to understand main ideas; to follow a sequence of events	Art; Literature/Language Arts; Math; Music; Social Studies
to use *might* and *may;* to use infinitives of purpose; to use *made of*	to solve puzzles; to think creatively; to brainstorm; to compare objects	Music; Science; Social Studies
to use the past tense; to use passive constructions; to use speculative language; to use adjectives of origin	to make inferences; to use music and rhyme; to solve a puzzle; to answer *true/false* questions	Art; Music; Social Studies
to use *would rather;* to generate information questions; to use present, past, and future tenses; to use the language for making suggestions: *let's*	to compare preferences; to use songs and chants to practice vocabulary; to listen for information	Art; Literature/Language Arts; Math; Music; Social Studies

Scope and Sequence 6

Unit	Title	Theme	Communication Objectives
1	Famous People	biographies	to discuss favorite performers and famous people; to talk about events in the past; to ask and answer questions; to complete timelines
2	My Story	personal experiences	to talk about personal experiences; to read and write friendly letters; to conduct a survey; to fill in a personal questionnaire
3	Jobs	careers	to discuss career aptitudes and requirements; to interview someone
4	The Future	the future	to make predictions; to talk and write about the future; to conduct an opinion poll; to say a poem; to plan and put on a radio show
5	The Planets	planets and outer space	to learn facts about the planets; to make comparisons; to read and write about imaginary trips to another planet
6	Adventures	adventure stories	to discuss leisure time activities and adventure stories; to tell what one would or wouldn't like to do; to narrate past events
7	Records	games and contests	to discuss games, contests, and records; to ask and answer information questions; to organize a classroom "Olympics"
8	Symbols	nonverbal communication	to discuss signs and symbols; to make suggestions; to give and follow directions; to read and write a poem
9	On Stage	talents and entertainment	to discuss personal talents and entertainment; to state opinions; to read and write reviews; to conduct a survey; to plan and put on a talent show; to follow directions; to tell and appreciate jokes

Language Objectives	Learning Strategies/ Thinking Skills	Content Connections
to use regular and irregular past tense; to use appropriate form questions	to use music and rhythm; to understand chronological order; to skim for information; to sequence events in a time line; to conduct research; to guess a person's identity from clues	Art; Drama; Literature/Language Arts; Music; Social Studies
to use past participles; to use the present perfect	to brainstorm; to figure out meaning from context; to identify main ideas; to conduct a survey; to make charts and graphs; to make predictions; to skim for specific information; to use pictures to determine meaning	Drama; Literature/Language Arts; Music; Social Studies
to use gerunds; to use present conditionals (*if* clauses)	to use word parts to figure out meaning; to get meaning from context; to organize information; to explain something to others	Art; Literature/Language Arts; Social Studies
to use the future tense with *will;* to use *may, might, could*	to use pictures to make predictions; to make vocabulary flashcards; to use drawings and diagrams; to understand cause and effect	Art; Literature/Language Arts; Math; Science; Social Studies
to use comparative and superlative forms of adjectives; to use contrary-to-fact conditionals (*if* + past tense + *would* + verb); to form questions	to read and interpret graphs and diagrams; to make comparisons	Art; Literature/Language Arts; Math; Music; Science
to use *if* clauses and modals; to use the past tense	to figure out meaning from context; to summarize a story; to identify main ideas; to use graphic organizers	Geography; Literature/Language Arts
to use superlative forms; to use *most/fewest* + nouns; to form information questions	to skim; to use headings to locate information; to categorize; to gather information for reports	Geography; Literature/Language Arts; Math; Music
to use *might, could,* and *must* to express probability; to understand and write directions; to use color idioms	to give and interpret nonverbal messages; to figure out meaning from context; to use illustrations	Art; Literature/Language Arts; Math; Social Studies
to use the language of opinion; to understand directions; to use *good at* + gerund	to use music and rhyme; to understand and use synonyms and antonyms; to order tasks, to classify; to listen for details	Art; Drama; Literature/Language Arts; Music

You may want to begin each week with a showing of the *New Parade* video for the unit.

	1 session a week of 40 to 60 minutes	2 sessions a week of 40 to 50 minutes	2 sessions a week of 50 to 60 minutes
Week 1	Video Focus, Part A **Warm up and Presentation** Two pages per session	Video Focus, Part A **Warm up and Presentation** One page per session	Video Focus, Part A **Warm up and Presentation** One page per session Corresponding Workbook pages at end of each session
Week 2	Video Focus, Parts B & C **Practice** Two pages per session	Video Focus, Parts B & C **Practice** One page per session	Video Focus, Parts B & C **Practice** One page per session Corresponding Workbook pages
Week 3	Video Focus, Part D **Application and Reading** Two pages per session + Little Book	Video Focus, Part D **Application and Reading** One page per session + Little Book	Video Focus, Part D **Application and Reading** Little Book in last 20 minutes of second session and corresponding Workbook pages
Week 4	Video Focus, Part E **Assessment** Two pages per session	Video Focus, Part E **Assessment** One page per session	Video Focus, Part E **Assessment** One page per session Corresponding Workbook pages at end of each session

Time Guidelines

	3 sessions a week of 40 to 60 minutes	4 sessions a week of 40 to 50 minutes	5 sessions a week of 40 to 60 minutes
Week 1	Video Focus, Part A **Warm up and Presentation** One page per session Corresponding Workbook pages on third session	Video Focus, Part A **Warm up and Presentation** One page per session Corresponding Workbook pages on third session Fourth session for oral or written practice	Video Focus, Part A **Warm up and Presentation** First session, first unit page Second session, Reaching All Students and Workbook page Third session, second unit page Fourth session, Reaching All Students and Workbook page Fifth session for oral and written practice
Week 2	Video Focus, Parts B & C **Practice** One page per session Corresponding Workbook pages on third session	Video Focus, Parts B & C **Practice** One page per session. Corresponding Workbook pages on third session Fourth session for oral and written practice	Video Focus, Parts B & C **Practice** First session, third unit page Second session, Practice and Workbook page Third session, fourth unit page Fourth session, Practice and Workbook page Fifth session for oral and written practice
Week 3	Video Focus, Part D **Application and Reading** One page on first and third sessions Little Book and corresponding Workbook pages on second session	Video Focus, Part D **Application and Reading** One page on first and third sessions Little Book on second session Fourth session for Project and Little Book follow up	Video Focus, Part D **Application and Reading** First session, fifth unit page Second session, Practice and Workbook page Third session, Little Book Fourth session, Project Fifth session, Project and Little Book follow up
Week 4	Video Focus, Part E **Assessment** One page per session Corresponding Workbook pages on third session	Video Focus, Part E **Assessment** One page per session Corresponding Workbook pages on third session Fourth session for Journal	Video Focus, Part E **Assessment** First session, ninth unit page Second session, Practice and Workbook page Third session, tenth unit page Fourth session, Practice and Workbook page Fifth session for Journal

Notes